T0385460

THE

PUBLICATIONS

OF THE

SURTEES SOCIETY

VOL. CLXXXV

THE

PUBLICATIONS

OF THE

SURTEES SOCIETY

ESTABLISHED IN THE YEAR

M.DCCC.XXXIV

VOL. CLXXXV

FOR THE YEAR M.CM.LXXII

At a COUNCIL MEETING of the SURTEES SOCIETY, held in Durham Castle on December 13th, 1971, the Dean of Durham in the chair, it was ORDERED—

"That the second volume of Dr. D. A. Kirby's edition of Durham Parliamentary Surveys should be printed as a volume of the Society's publications."

W. A. L. SEAMAN,
Secretary.

29th August, 1972.

PARLIAMENTARY SURVEYS

OF THE

BISHOPRIC OF DURHAM

VOLUME II

EDITED BY

Dr. DAVID A. KIRBY

PRINTED FOR THE SOCIETY BY
NORTHUMBERLAND PRESS LIMITED
GATESHEAD
1972

CONTENTS

PREFACE

This volume continues the series of surveys taken of the lands and property of the See of Durham by order of the Commonwealth Parliament prior to the sale of ecclesiastical temporalities. Volume I contained surveys of property in the Darlington Ward of county Durham, and this present includes the remainder of the surviving surveys, covering the Chester, Easington and Stockton Wards. Readers are referred to the first volume for a general introduction to the surveys, and to the land they recount.

SURVEY OF THE MANOR OF CHESTER LE STREET

Manerium de
Chester in Le Streete
cum incibus
Membris apertinen

A perfect and exact Survey of the aforesaid Mannor of Chester in Le Street with the appertenances and of the said several townships of Chester in the Streete East Bolden West Bolden Whiteborne Cleadon and Ryton had made and taken as well by we John Duncalfe gent. John Husband gent. and Christopher Mickleton gent. in the Month of April in the year of our Lord 1647 By virtue of a Commission to us and others directed bearing date the nine and twentieth day of March 1647 made from the Trustees in the said Commission named authorised with others by two several Ordinances of Parliament for the Archbishops and Bishops lands throughout the whole kingdom, as also by the presentment of the several Juries hereafter named by we sworn to enquire upon several articles given to them in Charge The tenor and effect of which Survey and presentment as well by we and of the said Jury hereafter followeth vzt.

The Jury's verdict of Chester in the Streete taken the 6th May 1647.

1. Imprimis to the first Article we have nothing to present within 6 miles of Durham or Newcastle and 7 miles from the sea.

2. Item to the second we present concerning the demeasne lands of Chester in a schedule here annexed 3, 4, 5. It. to the third we have not anything to present nor to the fourth nor fifth.

3. Item. A Common of pasture belonging to Chester Mannor vzt. with Plawsworth Walridge Edmunbyers, Nettleswerth Pelton Tribley Whitehall Twisell and Orpeth with other towns and villages adjacent thereunto but the certain number of acres we are not certain, and as for Improvement the Bishop cannot improve without the consent of Freeholders Tennants and Copyholders

6. Item to the sixth there is £5 per annum per forth of one fishing upon the water of Weare holden by the Lord Lumley by lease from the Bishop of Durham We present that the mannor is divided from the Lands of Lord Lumley and others by the River of Wear, and that the fishing of the said River belongs partly to the Bishop vzt. the one half thereof or that side that washeth the Bishop's lands and the said fishing belonging to the Bishop is letten by lease for diverse years to come to the said Lord Lumley at the rent of £5 per annum. but what the fishing is yearly worth above the rent reserved they know not.

7. Item one water corn mill now in the tenure or occupation of Mrs. Elizabeth Millatt for the tenure of three lives yet being for anything we know There names are Thomas King, Tymothy King and Alice King yearly rent £8. 8s. od. more worth £4.

8. Item the tennants ought not to grind at the mill

9. Item not anything to present for or freehold Item a slate or stone quarry near Plawsworth The Bishop's waste of which the late Bishop nor any of his predecessors have made no profitt nor likely to do as we concieve.

10. Item not anything to present but 10s. per annum forth of Roger field in the possession of one George Clarke.

11. Item not anything to present.

12. The copyholders are all of Record and those which were not found the copies are hereunto annexed in a schedule.

13. Item the Jury are certain.

14. Item nothing to present.

15. Item no other but such as is formerly set down in a schedule hereunto annexed of the demeasne lands.

16. Item we have not any but such as are perfected in one schedule hereunto annexed.

17. Item not anything to present.

18. There is not any.

19. We know not what profit the Lord hath of all.

20.21. We know not any.

22.23. There is not any.

24. There is no woods.

25. Item we do not know.

26. We do not know.

For coalmines belonging to the Bishop of Durham.

Urpeth colliery for a lease of three years at the rent of £2. 13s. 4d. per annum William Thornton and the immediate tennant A lease of Blackburne Colliery for three lives yet in being vzt. Sir Francis Liddell Mr. James Clavering Henrie Morley the immediate tennant Mr. John Claverin Mr. Raiphe Cole and Sir John Marley £20 per annum.

Ladenfield field 16s. in the occupation of Baronet Liddell and Baronet Blaxton.

Outrents freerents per the Bishop Colliery in Chester being letten to Sir Henrie Vayne and others by lease Plawsworth Colliery by Lease to Edward Parkinson and Mrs. Jane Hutcheson.

The names of the Jurors	Railph Haswell
Raiph Suerties senior	Leonard Rutter
William Pearson	Robert Robinson
John Watson	Richard Somerside
Robert Darling	Robert Marley
Stephen Wheldon	Robert Fletcher
John Robinson	William Snaith
Lawrence Fletcher	Richard Fletcher
Roger Watson	John Tewer

Chester le Street Leaseholds

Robert Smith assigned to George Clarke and Richard Hedworth 6 October 16 Jac. 26 April 19 Car. The moytie of all those lands meadows and pastures in Chester by the name of one Cavill of land and then or late in the tenure and occupation of the said Robert Smith, which said premisses are part and parcel of the tenements called the 12 Cavills of land. For the lives of Robert Smith the younger then 10, Francis Snayth then 5 and Ellinor Snaith then 12 years (who is since dead).

Rent £1. os. od. And also paying one bushell of wheat Duresme measure at Martinmas or 8s. in lieu thereof at the choice of the Bishop.

And also doing and performing such customes duties and services as have been accustomed formerly providing for the King and Bishop one draught of oxen upon two days warning with cart and carriage as formerly accustomed.

RICHARD HEDWORTH Esq.

4 May 13 Car. All those lands meadows and pastures in Chester by the name of one Cavill of land lately demised unto the said Richard Hedworth and now in the occupacon of him or his assigns.

For the lives of John Fletcher aged 24 (since dead) Thomas Middleton then 30 son of Anthony Middleton of Whickham and of Robert Featherston then aged 21 son of John Featherston of Chester.

Rent £1. os. od. And also paying one bushell of wheat Duresme measure at Martinmas or 8s. in lieu thereof at the choice of the Bishop And also doing and performing such customs duties and services as have been accustomed formerly providing for the King and Bishop one draught of oxen upon 2 days warning with cart or carriage as formerly accustomed
assigned to

JOHN FLETCHER

15 June 13 Car. All those lands meadows and pastures (parcel of the Cavill of land aforesaid) that is to say in the high northfield, the northmost of the long Rigg lying upon the shott called Raynebower, the 2 westmost Riggs lying upon the Shotts extending to Lamburne letch and one Rigg on Bedon Flatt shotts in the meadow maines and great dale lying in the midst of the fields there with a small rigg or butt adjoining to the southend whereof one daile in the bancke at Stone Cross Stile one dale extending down to the water-side lying next to John Browne one butt lying near to the damns end and one rigg end extending from the old Dykestead to the waterside in the crooke, long rigg lying near the waterside one Short Rigg lying on the middle Shott one single Rigg in the high end adjoining on Porters headland one dale in the Thornes at the waterside the western part on the dale of the high end next to Leanard Rutter and the eastmost half of a dale adjoining to William Marley and pasture gate and oateage in the pasture maines and other the grounds aforesaid belonging to half a Cable (which said lands were put forth to the said John Fletcher for the full moytie of the Cavill aforesaid).

Mable Fletcher widdow relict of John Fletcher is now possessed of these aforesaid lands.

GEORGE CLARKE, gentleman, holds by grant from Edward Robert, Elizabeth his wife and Richard Somerside
6 October 16 Jac. By demise from Leonard Somerside.
4 April 13 Jac. to George Clarke.
23 March 14 Chas. One cavill of land then or late in the tenure of and occupation of Leonard Somerside

For the lives of Thomas Somerside, 30, Robert Somerside 14, son of the said Leonard Somerside.

Rent £1. os. od. And also paying one bushell of wheat Duresme measure at Martinmas or 8s. in lieu thereof at the choice of the Bishop.

And also doing and performing such customs duties and services as have been accustomed formerly providing for the King and Bishop one draught of oxen upon 2 days warning with cart and carriage as formerly accustomed.

ROBERT SNAITH assigned to George Clarke 6 October 16 Jac. 16 March 1 Car. One cavill of land (vzt) the upper part of one Rigg of arrable in the north field of Chester containing half an acre or thereabouts lying on the west side of Leonard Ashells land there and extending northwards to Benwell Flatt one broad rigg of the same field lying the hither side of Longburne Letch upon the east side of Mr. John Hedworth's land there, one long Rigg in the same field lying in a place called the Raynebower on the southside of William Marley's land there, one dale of meadow in the uppermost sheeth in the Meadow Maynes aforesaid of Chester, lying on the southside of Will Harrison's land there, one rigg lying in the same sheth on the southside of Robert Sympson's land there a long Rigg extending with the low end thereof to the waterside towards the east and with the other end near unto Foulebrigg on the west lying on the southside of John Brownes land there One great dale of meadow lying north and south in the midst of the meadow maines aforesaid and adjoining upon the eastside of Mr. John Hedworth's land there and another dale in the same field extending down to the waterside lying on the southside of Mr. Rich Hedworth's land there and likewise 4 pasture gates and one half in the pasture maines of Chester in the summer time and two horsegates in the same pasture in the winter time (which said lands are set forth to the said George Clarke for a full moytie of all the arable ground and meadow grounds and pasture gates belonging to the cavill of land aforesaid).

Rent £1. os. od. And also paying one bushell of wheat Duresme measure at Martinmas or 8s. in lieu thereof at the choice of the Bishop.

And also doing and performing such customs duties and services as have been accustomed formerly providing for the King and Bishop one draught of oxen upon 2 days warning with cart and carriage as formerly accustomed.

CHARLES FLETCHER and GEORGE CLARKE from Charles Porter, Charles Fletcher and Agnes Askell.

6 October 16 Jac. One cavill of land late in the tenure and occupation of Charles Porter, Charles Fletcher and Agnes Askell.

For the lives of Charles Porter then 16 son of the said Charles Porter (since dead) Lawrence Fletcher then 17 son of Charles Fletcher and Leonard Askell son of the said Agnes Askell (since dead).

Rent £1. os. od. And also paying one bushell of wheat Duresme measure at Martinmas or 8s. in lieu thereof at the choice of the Bishop.

And also doing and performing such customs duties and services as have been accustomed formerly providing for the King and Bishop one draught of oxen upon 2 days warning with cart and carriage as formerly accustomed.

Which said lease being to the use of the said Ann Askell as to the one moytie of the said premisses the said Ann died and her estate and interest after her death did fall and come to her eldest son Leo Askell And the said Leo being siezed and possessed thereof by Indenture Date 13 December 22 Jac. did grant and assigne all his Estate and Interest therein unto Richard Clarke of Chester aforesaid which by Richard Clarke's assignment bearing date 14 March 2 Car. did grant and assign all his Estate and interest therein unto George Clarke of Chester aforesaid gentleman who is now tennant thereof his heirs and assigns for and during the lives aforesaid.

ROBERT AYTON of Herrington

5 March 15 Car. One cavill of land late in the tenure or occupation of Thomas Smith

For the lives of Robert Ayton son of the said Robert Ayton then 8 and of John Ayton son of the said Robert Ayton then aged 2 and of George Clarke son of George Clarke of Chester then 12.

Rent £1. os. od. And also paying one bushell of wheat Duresme measure at Martinmas or 8s. in lieu thereof at the choice of the Bishop.

And also doing and performing such customs duties and services as have been accustomed formerly providing for the King and Bishop one draught of oxen upon 2 days warning with cart and carriage as formerly accustomed.

LAWRENCE FLETCHER
14 August 3 Car. Half a cavill of land.

For the lives of Agnes Simpson wife, Robert Simpson now aged 48, George Simpson then aged 14, (since dead), and Ann Simpson then 12 years.

Rent £1. 0s. 0d. And also paying one bushell of wheat Duresme measure at Martinmas or 8s. in lieu thereof at the choice of the Bishop.

And also doing and performing such customs duties and services as have been accustomed formerly providing for the King and Bishop one draught of oxen upon 2 days warning with cart and carriage as formerly accustomed.

RALPH MORLEY son of William Morley
30 June 10 Car. The moytie of one cavill of land.

For the lives of Elizabeth daughter of the said William Marley then 3 years William son of William Marley of Hedley Hall then 14 years and Leonard Somersyde of Chester yeoman.

Rent £1. 0s. 0d. And also paying one bushell of wheat Duresme measure at Martinmas or 8s. in lieu thereof at the choice of the Bishop.

And also doing and performing such customs duties and services as have been accustomed formerly providing for the King and Bishop one draught of oxen upon 2 days warning with cart and carriage as formerly accustomed.

PHILLIPP CHILTON
15 October 19 Jac. One cavill of land.

For the lives of said Phillipp then 10, Isabell Harrison wife of John Harrison now aged 80 years and Alice Chilton sister of Phillipp Chilton then aged 13.

Rent £1. 0s. 0d. And also paying one bushell of wheat Duresme measure at Martinmas or 8s. in lieu thereof at the choice of the Bishop.

And also doing and performing such customs duties and services as have been accustomed formerly providing for the King and Bishop one draught of oxen upon 2 days warning with cart and carriage as formerly accustomed. And within 3 years then next ensuing bring in to the said Bishop or his successors a true survey containing the quantities of all the ground belonging to the said premisses with the abutting and boundering of every part and parcel thereof And shall once within the space of every 10 years during the said term renew the said survey.

GUY BAYNBRIGG late of Chester and **JOHN FLETCHER** same, yeoman both deceased
27 September 21 Jac.
to
RALPH HASWELL of Chester
15 December 18 Car. One cavill of land which were in the tenure or occupation of the said Guy Baynbrigg And the 4th part of the said cavill was in the tenure and occupation of the said John Fletcher.

For the lives of William Snaith then 12, Ann Snaith then 8, children of Robert Snaith and Robert Fletcher then 10, son of the said John Fletcher.

Rent £1. 0s. 0d. And also paying one bushell of wheat Duresme measure at Martinmas or 8s. in lieu thereof at the choice of the Bishop.

And also doing and performing such customes duties and services as have been accustomed formerly providing for the King and Bishop one draught of oxen upon 2 days warning with cart and carriage as formerly accustomed.

Guy Baynbrigg being dead the said ¾ of the aforesaid cavill came to the possession of Elizabeth Baynbrigg widdow mother of the said Guy as sole Administratrix which the said Elizabeth being thereof possessed dyed after whose death the said 3 parts came to the possession of Arthur Baynbrigg being sole Executor of the last will and testament of the said Elizabeth which said Arthur in consideration of £19. 5s. 0d. did bargan, sell and sett over unto Ralph Haswell of Chester, aforesaid, Blacksmith the said 3 parts of the cavill of land during the said tenure. With a promise that if £91. 5s. 0d. and £2. 13s. 0d. for interest were paid at the house of Ralph Haswell in Chester by the said Arthur Baynbrigg his heirs and executors or Administrators at May day thence next after then it would be lawfull to re-enter otherwise not.

JOHN BROWNE
30 June 10 Car. The full moytie of one cavill of land.

For the lives of Peter Darling then 12 son of Robert Darling of Plawsworth yeoman, Thomas Haswell son of Ralph Haswell of Chester then 5, and Agnes Moreburne aged 2 daughter of Thomas Moreburne of Chester yeoman

Rent £1. os. od. And also paying one bushell of wheat Duresme measure at Martinmas or 8s. in lieu thereof of the choice of the Bishop.

And also doing and performing such customs duties and services as have been accustomed formerly providing for the King and Bishop one draught of oxen upon 2 days warning with cart and carriage as formerly accustomed.

KATH PORTER
20 July 13 Car. to
JOHN WATSON deceased and LAWRENCE FLETCHER
17 March 13 Car. One cavill of land late demised to Charles Porter the younger like in the occupation of the said now in the tenure of Roger Watson Flatcher.

For the lives of Elz. Porter then 6, Jane Porter then 4, and of Ann Porter then 2 daughters of the said Katherine Porter.

Rent £1. os. od. And also paying one bushell of wheat Duresme measure at Martinmas or 8s. in lieu thereof of the choice of the Bishop.

And also doing and performing such customs duties and services as have been accustomed formerly providing for the King and Bishop one draught of oxen upon 2 days warning with cart and carriage as formerly accustomed.

ROGER WATSON son and heir of John Watson.
8 September 19 Jac. Half a cavill of land
For the lives of George Watson then 11, said Roger Watson then 8, and Thomas Watson then 2, natural children of the said John Watson.

Rent £1. os. od. And also paying one bushell of wheat Duresme measure at Martinmas or 8s. in lieu thereof of the choice of the Bishop.

And also doing and performing such customs duties and services as have been accustomed formerly providing for the King and Bishop one draught of oxen upon 2 days warning with cart and carriage as formerly accustomed.

LEONARD RUTTER assignee of John Rutter
6 September 16 Jac. One cavill of land late in the tenure of the said
Leonard Rutter

For the lives of John Rutter aged 2, George Rutter aged 8 weeks
sons of Leonard Rutter of Chester.

Rent £1. os. od. And also paying one bushell of wheat Duresme
measure at Martinmas or 8s. in lieu thereof of the choice of the
Bishop.

And also doing and performing such customs duties and services
as have been accustomed formerly providing for the King and
Bishop one draught of oxen upon 2 days warning with cart and
carriage as formerly accustomed.

Memorandum
That a cavill consisteth of arable land meadow and pasture vzt. 9
rood of arable land at 5s. per acre in toto 11s. 3d. of meadow 3 acres
10s. per acre 30s. of pasture 6 gates 12s. per gate Toto £3. 6s. od.
The whole sum is £5. 13s. 3d.

The whole rent of the 12 cavills paid yearly at Martinmas and
Penticost unto the Exchequer of Durham amounts to £16. 16s. od.
The improvement besides the rent of the lands at £51. 16s. 4d.

RICHARD HEDWORTH assignee of William Morley on 6 May
9 Car.
28 June 15 Car. Two parcells of ground called by the names of the
Ewres and Flowers parcel of the demesne lands of Chester late in
the occupation of the said William Morley and Thomas Simpson.

For the lives of Ralph Morley then 6, Ann Morley then 11, and
Jane Morley then 8, all children of the said William Morley.

Rent 13s. od.

Idem RICHARD
1 August 7 Car. A parcel of pasture ground lying near the Southburne late demised to John Hedworth.

For 21 years. Rent 9s. 8d.

Idem RICHARD
23 September 6 Car. One close being parcel of the Ures near Chester
lying near unto Kelseygate containing 3 acres late in the tenure

of Roger Simpson and now in the tenure of the said Robert Hedworth.

For 21 years. Rent 7s. 6d.

JOHN HEDWORTH
20 November 6 Car. to
WILLIAM MORLEY
10 October 10 Car. to
ROBERT CLUGH
28 June 15 Car. 1 parcel of pasture ground lying near the Southburne, 1 close containing 3 acres. And also 1 parcell of meadow ground being the one half of the Low Flowers which are parcel of the ground called the Eures near Chester le Streete then in the tenure or occupation of the said John Hedworth.

For 21 years. Rent 19s. 2d.

JOHN ROBINSON
16 February 6 Car. The one half of pasture ground commonly called Dunfford Ewers near Chester late in the tenure of Jane Athy, widdow and now in the occupation of him the said John Robinson.

For 21 years. Rent 9s. 8d.

CHARLES MARLEY son of Anthony Marley late of Chester by
demise of the last will and testament of Anthony Marley 29 September 6 Car.
9 May 1632. The 4th part of a parcel of ground commonly called Dunfforth Ewers near Chester then in the tenure of the said Anthony Marley.

For 21 years. Rent 4s. 10d.

RALPH HASWELL
23 September 3 Car. Half of the parcel of meadow ground lying near Chester (being parcel of the Low Flowers) now in the tenure of the said Ralph Haswell.

For 21 years. Rent 4s. 5d.

ALSE HADDOCK relict of William Haddock
13 February 6 Car. The half of one parcel of meadow ground near Chester in the Street being parcel of the Low Flowers late in the tenure of Thomas Hindmiers.

For 21 years. Rent 4s. od.

ELIZABETH PORTER assignee of Charles Porter the elder late of Chester deceased

23 September 6 Car. The fourth part of a parcel of ground commonly called Dunfforth Ewres.

For 21 years. Rent 4s. 1od.

Memorandum

That parcel of the demesne lands in Chester called Ewres and Flowers consist part of arable lands and some little inclosure being a moorish ground much overrun with thicks The rent of it to the Bishop is £4. 5s. 4d. The improvement above the rent £7. 0s. 8d. In toto £10. 6s.

ELIZABETH MILLOTT

21 September 17 Jac. Water corn mill in Chester with the damn tolne suite and suckane to the said mill belonging And also the Common Bakehouse of Chester late in the tenure of John King of the City of Durham Notarie Publique For the lives of Thomas King then 15, Timothy King then 12, and Alice King then aged 10 natural children of Thomas King of Chester.

Rent £8. 0s. od. 8s. od. (or a bushell of sound wheat).

Memorandum

The mill and bakehouse have formerly been demised by the lessee at £40 per annum The lessee abiding all hazards And this present year are let by the standing committee of this County at £32 The said Committee standing to repair the same The yearly rent to the Bishop is £8. 8s. od. The casualties considered we conceive the improvement to be £22. 12s. od. besides the present rent Second. That the improvement and the rent being added together the purchase will be £31.

HENRY LAMBTON son and heir of Sir William Lambton knight late deceased last survivor of Sir William Lambton. Sir William Wray and William Lambton

All that close or pasture ground called Bedon Flat late in the occupation of Thomas Millott and now in the possession of Henry Lambton Esq.

For the lives of Robert Millott of Whitehill Esq. deceased Elz. Millott then aged 10 and Jane Millott then aged 4.

Rent £2. 10s. 0d. and one fat calf at Penticost or 6s. 8d. Improvement 3s. 4d.

Chester le Street Copyholds

RICHARD HEDWORTH

12 July 17 Car. 5 acres, 1 rood and 20 perches of land in the westfield on the west side of Charles Porters lands and the lands of George Sallett on the east side the lands of Robert Fletcher on the south and the lands called Whittell on the north. And also 6 acres of land lying on the East part of the lands of Robert Robson and the lands of Robert Fletcher on the south and the lands of George Sallett on the west and common on the north as it is now divided.

By surrender of Ralph Thompson and Anne his wife. Fine 3s. 4d.

Idem and ROBERT SOMERSIDE

13 April 11 Car. The whole tenure late Anne Boromans and the pasture for one beast in Holmehill the half of another husband from the feast of the Invention of the Holy Crosse 1636 to the end terme of 21 years without any rent paying for the five first years and paying from thenceforth to the said William Younghusband £13. 0s. 0d. per annum only besides the Lord's farm and services therefore due.

By surrender of John Hedworth. Fine 4s. 0d.

Idem

4 May 13 Car. One acre of land called Whiniplech.

By surrender of John Hedworth. Fine 2d.

Idem

4 May 13 Car. One close called Barrass field.

By surrender of Thomas Mayne. Fine 6s. 8d.

Rents for these four copyholds 6s. 4½d.

GEORGE CLARKE, gent.

25 June 21 Jac. In right of Katherine his wife the whole tenure called Sanderfield the half of a husband land and one meadow

called Checker meadow one messuage and half of a husband land pasture for one beast in Holmehill the half of another husband land and pasture for 2 beasts in Holme Hill And also one close called Milner lands and also a close called Turne Moor containing 6 acres of land And also one cottage and one garden sometimes John Sanders.

By surrender of Richard Clarke, gent. Rent £2. 16s. 5½d. Fine 19s. 11d.

LEONARD SMITH
4 May 13 Car. Pasture for 6 beasts in Holme Hill
As heir to his father. Fine 2s. 0d.

Idem
One cottage (the copy not extant).
As heir to his father. Fine 2s. 0d.

Idem
dat ut supra. One husbandry land and one half as it is now divided in 2 closes (vzt. one close in the low northfield containing 31 acres of land and one rood more or less abutting upon Newbrigfield on the east side and the north loaning on the west Pelaw brooks and the straight loaning on the north side And one other close in the high northfield containing 15 acres of land 3 roods and 13 perches abutting on the north loaning on the east And the lord's lands on the west and the lands of Lawrence Foster on the north and the lands of William Marley and the Lord's land on the south together with pasture for 3 horses in the burne greene).

By surrender of Raiph Hedworth and Phillipp Hall. Fine 13s. 4d.
Rent for these three copyholds £1. 1s. 4½d.

RAIPHE MARLEY son and heir of William Marley
2 September 22 Car. 17 acres, 3 roods and 5 perches of land lying in Barrack as it is divided.
As heir to his father. Fine 6s. 0d.

Idem
dat ut supra. 10 acres of land lying in the north field parcel of a land containing 20 acres of land as it is divided.
As heir to his father. Fine 4s. 0d.

Idem

dat ut supra. 10 acres of lands (parcel of 20 acres lying in the north field adjacent upon the main land on the west and Leonard Smith on the north and Hall Close and Pelton Fell on the South.

As heir to his father. Fine 1s. 8d.

Idem

dat ut supra. Half of a tenure late Robert Humbles

As heir to his father. Fine 1s. 9d.

Idem

dat ut supra. Half of a cottage with a garden late in the occupation of Robert Porter (one house formerly granted to Anthony Marley parcel of the premisses excepted).

As heir to his father. Fine 1s. 6d.

Idem

dat ut supra. One parcel of land called Bracks containing 3 acres of land and 4 acres of land in Kelshetts (parcel of a husbandland).

Fine 6d.

Rent for these six copyholds 17s. 8½d.

ROBERT FLETCHER son of John Fletcher

23 April 13 Car. One house lying in Chester with a garden on the backside and 2 parts of one close called the Maynesworne Close containing 3 roods of land parcel of the third part of one tenure late Richard Awdes

By surrender of Robert Sanders and Anne his wife.

Rent 3s. 11½d. Fine 2s. 0d.

JOHN OWEN

16 May 19 Car. 1 cottage and 1 garden belonging late in the tenure and occupation of Lawrence Fletcher containing in length 40 yards and in breadth 14 yards.

By surrender of Lawrence Fletcher. Rent 1s. 0½d. Fine 4d.

CHARLES FLETCHER

11 June 15 Jac. 3 parts of one parcel of Exchequer land in 8 parts divided parcel of one parcel of Land Chequor.

By surrender of Robert Porter. Fine 2d.

Idem
16 May 13 Jac. The half of one cottage.
  By surrender of Michael Johnson. Fine 8d.

Idem
4 May 13 Car 3 acres of land in a close lying between the lands of
Michael Hall gent. on the south and Leonard Smythe on the north.
  Fine 1s. 0d.

Idem
dat ut supra. 5 acres of land lying in a close ut supra on the south
and north and pasturegate for 1 horse in burn green.
  By surrender of Raiph Hedworth and Michael Hall. Fine 1s. 3d.

Idem
dat ut supra. 3 acres of land and 3 roods lying ut supra
  By surrender of Raiph Hedworth and Michael Hall. Fine 1s. 8d.

Idem
dat ut supra. 5 acres of land lying ut supra
  By surrender of Raiph Hedworth and Michael Hall. Fine 1s. 8d.

Idem
20 April 39 Elz. One messuage
  By surrender of Elizabeth Hedworth widdow. Fine 1s. 0d.
  Rent for these seven copyholds 6s. 10d.

LAWRENCE FLETCHER
4 May 13 Car. 8 acres of land lying in a close adjacent to the lands
of Leonard Smyth on the south belonging to the town of Pelaw
on the north and the lands of Roger Haswell on the west called
Ellisopps Close and pasture for 1 horse in Burnegreene.
  By surrender of Ralph Hedworth and Phillip Hall. Fine 2s. 8d.

Idem
dat ut supra. 8 acres 6 perches of land lying in a close adjacent to
the lands of Leonard Smyth on the south belonging to the town of
Pelaw on the north and the lands of Roger Haswell on the west
and a close called Ellisopp on the east And also 4 acres 3 roods 14
perches of land adjacent upon the lands of Anne Halliday on the

south and the Fyne Dike on the north and without the garden on the east And the lands of Leonard Rutter on the west and pasture for the third part of one best gate and pasture for the eight part of one best gate in the burne greene.

By surrender of Ralph Hedworth and Phillip Hall. Fine 2s. 8d.

Idem

dat ut supra. 8 acres of land lying in a close adjacent to the lands of Leonard Smyth on the south lands belonging to the town of Pelaw on the North and the lands of Roger Haswell on the west and the Close called Ellisopps on the east.

By surrender of Ralph Hedworth and Phillip Hall. Fine 1s. 4d.

Idem

12 April 8 Car. One dwelling house with a garden late in the tenure of John Trumble parcel of one messuage and half of a fourth part of one land of husbandrie in 4 parts divided.

By surrender of Raiph Marley. Fine 1s. 6d.

Idem

25 October 13 Car. One cottage late Robert Young and a little garden to the said cottage belonging (excepting and reserving the west part of a garden late in the possession of George Hodshon) as it is now divided.

By surrender of George Clarke gent. Fine 6d.

Rent for these five copyholds 9s. 4½d.

RICHARD FLETCHER

20 April 6 Car. Half of one cottage.

As heir to his late father Marmaduke Fletcher. Fine 2s. 6d.

Idem

dat ut supra. One messuage.

As heir to his late father Marmaduke Fletcher. Fine 2s. od.

Idem

dat ut supra. Pasture for one beast in Holme Hill

As heir to his late father Marmaduke Fletcher. Fine 1d.

Idem

21 April 7 Car. Pasture for one beast in Holme Hill

By surrender of John Whelpden. Fine 2d.

Idem

dat ut supra. 3 acres of land and 36 perches lying at the end of the garden in west lonning of Charles Porters south and west and 13 acres of land 1 rood and 36 perches lying on the west of Robert Fletcher and the church lands and lands of George Clarke lying on the south and west parts and the lands of Roger Simpson on the west.

By surrender of Raiph Hedworth and Phillipp Hall. Fine 1s. 0d.

Idem

4 May 13 Car. 5 acres 2 roods and 35 perches in Kelshetts adjacent to the tenement of William Marley on the south and the lands of Leonard Rutter on the east and the lands of Leonard Rutter and Thomas Postgate on the north and the close of William Marley on the east.

By surrender of Ralph Hedworth and Phillip Hall. Fine 1s. 8d.

Idem

dat ut supra. 4 acres of land and 1 rood and 20 perches in the southfield south lonning on the east and the lands of George Clarke on the south and west and the lands of Roger Simpson on the north and pasture for one horse in the Burne Green.

By surrender of Ralph Hedworth and Phillipp Hall. Fine 1s. 4d.

Rent for these seven copyholds 8s. 10½d.

RAIPH HASWELL

16 October 4 Car. One parcel of land in Chester on the west part of the town containing in length 20 yards and in breadth 20 yards.

By surrender of Richard Haswell. Fine 8d.

Idem

14 May 12 Car. Of the Bishop's waste one parcel of land in Chester on the west of the town there containing in length 20 yards and in breadth 25 yards and of no increase.

Fine 1d.

Idem

9 October 13 Car. One close called Well Close lying in the New-

bridgefield gate 2 parts of one close called Plainsworne Close.
By surrender of Robert Fletcher. Fine 6d.

Idem
5 May 13 Car. 14 acres 17 perches on the High Northfield adjacent
to the lands of Roger Haswell on the East and the Mainlands on
the west and south and Benwell Flatt on the north and one half
pasturegate for one horse in the Burne Green.
By surrender of Raiph Hedworth and Phillipp Hall. Fine 4s. 8d.

Idem
26 June 21 Jac. The 15th part of Holme Hill.
By surrender of Thomas Andrew. Fine 2s. 0d.

Idem
31 March 22 Car. The half of one cottage with a garden late Henry
Stodderts.
By surrender of Charles Fletcher. Fine 1s. 0d.

Idem
31 March 22 Car. The half of one cottage late William Wrights
By surrender of Charles Fletcher. Fine 1s. 8d.
Rent for these seven copyholds 4s. 8½d.

LEONARD RUTTER
4 May 13 Car. 10 acres of land lying to the end of a garden extending itself eastwards to Ryhill and the Church lands lying on the
south side of Burne Brooke on the north part and the lands of
John Robson on the west And also 12 acres of land 3 roodes and
one perch in the Kelshetts lying upon the lands of Mr. Hedworth
on the north and the lands of Robert High and John Humble on
the east and the water of Wear on the south and the lands of William Marley and Leonard Smith on the east and pasture for one
horse on the Burne Greene.
By surrender of Raiph Hedworth and Phillip Hall. Rent 4s. 8d.
Fine 4s. 4d.

WILLIAM SNAITH son and heir of Robert Snaith deceased
2 November 22 Car. 1 acre of land 3 roods and 8 perches in the westfield lying to the garden late of the said Robert and 6 acres 1 rood

and 4 perches of land adjacent to the lands of Charles Porter on the east and the lands of Whitehill on the west north and south seven acres and 2 roods of lands adjacent upon the lands of John Watson on the south and the hedge of northfield on the west lands belonging to the Church on the north and east whereof 5 Riggs of the said 7 acres and 2 roods of land lying between the lands of the church and 5 acres and 1 rood lying in Bowden Crooke in the same field adjacent upon the footway leading to Lambton And also 1 acre 2 roods and 20 perches not divided And pasture for 1 house in the Burne Greene.

As heir to his father. Rent 4s. 8½d. Fine 11s. 0d.

RICHARD PEARSON
4 May 13 Car. One close containing 2 roods and 28 perches of land lying in the west field adjacent upon the lands of Leonard Rutter on the east Robert Fletcher on the south Richard Nicholson on the west and the Moor on the north.

By surrender of Phillipp Hall and Raiph Hedworth. Rent 1s. 1½d. Fine 6d.

ROBERT ROBINSON
4 May 13 Car. One close containing 4 acres of meadow 2 ridges and 28 perches lying in the westfield upon the lands of Leonard Rutter on the east Robert Fletcher on the south Richard Nicholson on the west and the Moor on the north.

By surrender of Raiph Hedworth and Phillipp Hall. Rent 1s. 5d. Fine 6½.

ROGER SIMPSON and Anne his wife
20 April 16 Car. Half of half a land of husbandry and the half of 2 acres of land in Kelshetts and the half of pasture for one beast in foggage (the half of pasture for one beast in the faughs excepted).

By surrender of James Lowes and Elizabeth his wife. Fine 1s. 4d.

Idem
4 May 13 Car. 1 parcel of land called Welburne Riding.

As heir to his father George. Fine 3d.

Idem
4 May 13 Car. 3 acres of land and 36 perches lying in the west field

at the end of his garden adjacent to the land of George Clarke on the north and Charles Porter on the west and south 5 acres and 2 roods lying upon the High Peece on the south Charles Porter's on the West on the west part and of John Hedworth and Richard Fletcher on the east and the half of one pasture for one house in Burne Greene.

By surrender of Raiph Hedworth and Phillipp Hall. Rent 1s. 0d.

Idem

dat ut supra. 8 acres of land in Kelshetts Welhill lying on the west part of the common street and upon the lands of Anne Gibson widdow on the north George Clarke on the west and Richard Fletcher on the south and the half of one pasture for a horse in the Burne Greene.

By surrender of Raiph Hedworth and Phillip Hall. Fine 2s. 4d.

ANNE the wife of Roger Simpson
5 May 1 Car. One parcel of land of the waste of the Lord containing in length 28 yards and in bredth 8 yards and one barn thereupon built lying on the east side of his tenement and of one garden lying on the south side of the house of length and breadth 4 yards of land.

As heir to her father Thomas Liddell. Fine 1d.

Idem: ROGER
4 May 13 Car. One parcel of land late of the waste of the Lord containing 4 acres of land lying on the south of one close of John Harrison of Waldridge one parcel of the said John on the west one close called Mordey on the East and the moor called Chester Moore of the waste of the Lord on the south.

As heir to his father. Fine 1s. 4d.
Rents for these six copyholds 6s. 5½.

JOHN CONYERS Baronett
29 November 19 Car. 1½ acres of land adjacent to the customary lands of Nettlesworth Greaneside and Morleyhead late Lord's waste.

By surrender of Sir John Claxton Knt. Fine 6d.

Idem
dat ut supra. All right state title tenure and demand which Sir John

Claxton had of and in one cottage called Morley Head and also one acre

By demise of Thomas Foster. Fine 1s. od.

Idem

29 November 10 Car. One cottage called Marleyheads and one acre of land.

By surrender of John Claxton Esq. Fine 1s. od.

Idem

dat ut supra. One parcel of land called Brakenhirst nigh Broome Close containing 4 acres of land and also one parcel of land containing 22 acres of land late of new increase containing 28 acres of land late of the Lord's waste a parcel whereof lying together between Morleyhead Greaneside and Nettlesworth and certain acres of land lying together betwixt husbands close deanelow Haynooke and Meadow Field other acres apud Nettlesworth sometimes included.

By surrender of John Claxton Esq. Fine 1s. 6d.

Idem

dat ut supra. All the Right State title tenure of life and demand which Sir John Claxton knt. had of one parcel of land called Brakenhirst nigh Broome close containing 4 acres of land And also one parcel of land containing 22 acres of land late of new increase lying on the west of Nettlesworth And also one other parcel of land late of new increase containing 28 acres late Lord's waste whereof parcel of the aforesaid acres of land lying together between Morleyhead Greeneside and Nettlesworth and certain other lands lying between Hudson's Close Smethy Dene low Haggnooke Meadowfield and other acres lying at Nettlesworth field long since inclosed.

By demise of Thomas Foster for and during the life of Sir John Claxton. Fine 1s. 6d.

Rent for these five copyholds 19s. od.

MARMADUKE HEDWORTH

14 March 15 Car. One cottage and one garden lying between the tenement of the said John on the east part and the tenement late Richard Atkinson and now Margarett Penn on the south.

By surrender of John Hedworth. Rent 6s. 8d. Fine 1s. 8d.

ANNE PUNSHON now heir of Thomas Punshon daughter and heir of Michael Chapman.
22 April 16 Jac. One tenement in Chester containing 22 ell in length and 52 in breadth.
As heir to her father. Rent 2d. Fine 6d.

GEORGE SALLETT
4 May 13 Car. One close containing 3 acres 3 roods and 10 perches of land lying on the part of Raiph Thompson on the west Richard Nicholson on the east Robert Fletcher on the south and Greene Delfe on the north.
By surrender of Raiph Hedworth and Phillip Hall. Rent 1s. 0½d. Fine 3s. 0d.

KATHERINE COLE late relict of Richard Cole
25 October 18 Car. Half of one cottage and parcel of a garden on the backside containing in length 9½ yards and in breadth to the east another corner 7 yards of land with freen entry and passage to a certain fountain or well to draw water in a garden late Robert Gibson's adjacent to the said parcel of garden.
As heir to her husband. Rent 6d. Fine 1s. 0d.

GEORGE FETHERSTON
13 April 11 Car. The north parcel of one cottage in length 8 yards and the north parcel of one garden on the backside containing in length 42 yards and in breadth 80 yards
As heir to his father Leonard Fetherston. Rent 4d. Fine 6d.

THOMAS HUNTER
4 October 19 Car. One house with a parcel of Garden on the backside containing in length 14 yards in breadth 5 yards of land parcel of one cottage and of one garden by demise from the feast of St. Hellen last past for 21 years.
Rent 1s. 0d. Fine 4d.

THOMAS MADDESON
20 October 2 Car. The half of one messuage and one garden lying between the tenement of Nicholas Nicholson on the south and

the tenement of Robert Foster on the north (6½ yards of land parcel of the premisses excepted).

By surrender of John Maddison his father. Rent 4d. Fine 1s. 4d.

ELIZABETH LAX WIDDOW

31 November 22 Car. The west half of one parcel of land called Wheatley containing 20 acres more or less late in the tenure of Robert Tempest together with the half of one messuage or house and other buildings thereupon built late in the occupation of Garrard Lax as it is lately divided between the said Garrard and Robert Heighington.

In widdowright. Rent 3s. 4d. Fine 1s. 8d.

ROBERT HEIGHINGTON

20 April 13 Car. Two halves of one parcel of land called Wheatley containing 20 acres of land late in the tenure of Robert Tempest.

By surrender of Gerrard Lax. Rent 3s. 4d. Fine 3s. 4d.

WILLIAM PORTER

25 October 18 Car. The half of one cottage with a garden lying to the house of Robert Dent on the south and the house of John Browne on the north.

By surrender of Robert Porter his brother. Rent 8d. Fine 4d.

JOHN CARLILE

24 May 12 Car. Of the Lord's waste one rood of moor or waste called Barras Loning adjacent to the lands of Anne Shaw on the east as it is now inclosed as a new increase.

Rent 2d. Fine 2d.

ROBERT CLUGH

4 May 13 Car. I acre of land adjacent to the land of Thomas Gibson on the north and the lands of Richard Taylor on the east and the lands of John Humble on the south and the lands of Leonard Rutter on the west.

By surrender of Raiph Hedworth and Phillip Hall. Fine 4d.

Idem

20 October 5 Car. One messuage with a garden on the backside.

By surrender of Martine Nicholson. Fine 6d.

Idem

25 October 18 Car. One close called Birds Close containing 1 acre of land.

By surrender of William Parson. Fine 4d.
Rent for these three copyholds 10d.

JANETT the wife of Richard Taylor
9 October 13 Car. One house containing in length 10 yards and one garden on the backside containing 10 yards in length and 3 in breadth.

By surrender of her husband. Rent 11¼d. Fine 1s. 4d.

ELIZABETH wife of Robert Ayton and Anne wife of Richard Harrison daughters and coheirs of Thomas Smith
One parcel of land called by the name of Simpson's Waste which Thomas Smith their father had.

By surrender of John Lodge. Fine 2s. 0d.

Eadem

The half of a close called Newfield which Isabell Smith by demise from John Meaburne 18 October 3 Car. had during her life and after her decease to the heirs apparent of Thomas and Isabell Smyth.

Fine 6s. 8d.
Rent for these two copyholds 3s. 8d.

GEORGE BROUGH, son and heir of Thomas Brough
19 October 11 Car. Two parts of one cottage with a garden in three parts divided.

Rent 1s. 1d. Fine 2d.

ROBERT HODSHON, brother and heir of George Hodshon
21 April 23 Car. Half of a cottage.

Fine 10d.

Idem

dat ut supra. 5 acres of land in Kelshetts.

Fine 1s. 0d.

Rent for these two copyholds 2s. 3¾ d.

HENRY SMATHWAITE son and heir of Henry Smaithwaite deceased

2 May 18 Car. On cottage.
Rent 4d. Fine 6d.

MARTINE NICHOLSON and Elizabeth his wife

20 October 2 Car. One parcel of land of Lord's waste built lying at the north end of Chester near Streetegate containing in length 15 elves and in breadth 14 yards
By surrender of John Johnson younger. Rent 4d. Fine 2d.

MARY HASTWELL widow

14 October 15 Car. One cottage.
By surrender of John Calverly gent. Fine 4d.

Eadem

dat ut supra. One tofte one croft which she had from her husband Phillipp Hastwell deceased.
In widdowright. Fine 6d.
Rent for these two copyholds 3s. 5½d.

THOMAS HASTWELL

2 May 16 Car. One messuage late Rowland Bills
By surrender of Ralph Hedworth. Fine 4d.

Idem

dat ut supra. Half of one messuage lying in Chester and the half of one husbandland to the same messuage belonging and pasture for one beast in the Holme Hill.
Fine 2.
Rent for these two copyholds 2s. 8d.

ROBERT DICKENSON son and heir of Thomas Dickenson deceased

21 April 23 Car. The 7th part of the whole tenure (with one house excepted and reserved adjoyning to the land of the aforesaid Thomas by the south and the land of Anne Gibson widdow on the west and the pasture maines on the north and east.

Fine 4d.

Idem

dat ut supra. Half of one cottage the half of one tenement with a garden in Chester.
Fine 2d.

Idem

dat ut supra. 2 acres 5 perches of land in Kelshetts as by the measure and bounds are divided.
Fine 8d.
Rent for these 3 copyholds 2s. 10½d.

WILLIAM DANISON son and heir of Richard Danison deceased 5 October 18 Car. One piece of a cottage lying by the south nigh the sea containing in length 19½ ells and in breadth from the fore part 15 ells.
Fine 6d.

Idem

dat ut supra. One close called Burne Greene Close containing half an acre of husband land.
Fine 4d.

Idem

dat ut supra. 1 acre 3 roods 20 perches and one other rood of land lying in a certain place called Jones Rone as with a hedge lately inclosed adjoining to the lands of John Browne on the north and west the south loaning on the east and the common on the south.
Fine 8d.
Rent for these three copyholds 10d.

STEPHEN WHELDON
4 May 13 Car. 3 acres of land lying in the horse close adjoining upon Pelton Field upon the west Bollam Flat upon the north and the lands of Richard Pearson on the west.
By surrender of Roger Pearson. Fine 8d.

Idem

dat ut supra. 3 acres of land in the Horse Close adjacent upon

Pelton Stellas on the south Roger Pearsons on the west Pelton Flatt on the north and the lands of Richard Pearson on the east.

Fine 1s. od.

Rent for these two copyholds 1s. 4¼d.

ROGER WATSON

16 May 19 Car. 6 acres of land lying in the southfield on the east part nigh the lands of Robert Oliver on the west the Kings Streete and the lands of Raiph Gibson on the north and south the lands of John Watson and one acre at the Garthesend on the east being George Clarke and on the north the lands of Ann Gibson and half a pasture for a horse in the Burne Greene as it is now divided.

By surrender of John Watson. Fine 2s. 4d.

Idem

5 May 2 Car. Half of one cottage.

Fine 6d.

Rent for these two copyholds 3s. 2d.

ELIANOR and DOROTHY GRINDY daughters of Robert Grindy deceased

7 May 8 Car. 1 house with a garden containing in length 40 yards in breadth 18 yards lying between the tenement of Henry Wright on the north.

Rent 6d. Fine 1s. 4d.

JOHN WATSON

2 May 18 Car. 1 close lying in Chester Southfield abutting on the lands of Robert Oliver on the east and the lands of George Clarke gentleman on the west and north and the common called Steward-shipp on the south

By surrender of William Pearson.

Fine 1s. od.

Idem

3 April 18 Car. One close containing 1 acre of land on the north of the west loaning.

By surrender of William Pearson. Fine 4d.

Idem

dat ut supra. A pasture for 4 beasts in Holmehill.

As heir to his father. Fine 1s. 0d.

Idem

16 May 15 Car. 6 acres of land in Southfield.
   As heir to his father. Fine 2d.

Idem

19 September 21 Car. 6 acres of land lying in Newbriggfield on the east part of the lands of Charles Fletcher on the south the lands of Robert Smith on the west and the lands of Thomas Turner and the half of a pasture for one horse and the half of a first part of one pasture for one horse in the Burne Green.
   As heir to his father. Fine 1s. 4d.

Idem

16 May 20 Car. 5½ acres of land lying in Boldon Crooke adjacent upon the Newbridge and Water of Wear on the south and the Spittle closes on the north.
   As heir to his father. Fine 1s. 8d.

Idem

14 October 15 Car. 5 acres 20 perches of land lying upon the lands of John Humble on the south and on the north of the lands of Thomas Dickenson and William Punshon and Robert Clugh and on the westside the maine dikes on the east.
   By surrender of Richard Taylor. Fine 6d.

Idem

6 July 15 Car. Half of one messuage with a garden on the backside on the north containing in length 42 yards in breadth 10 yards.
   By surrender of Richard Taylor. Fine 6d.

Idem

20 April 6 Car. 1 rood of land late the Lord's waste lying at Waldridge Greene on the south of a close called Brenne Nook there as heir to his grandfather John Watson and June Elianor his daughter.
   Fine 1d.

Idem

dat ut supra. ½ acre of land parcel of 4 acres of land lying on the north of one close of John Harrisons one parcel of land of the said John on the west one close called Morley on the east Chester Moor on the south.

By surrender of his grandfather John Harrison. Fine 3d.

Idem

16 May 19 Car. One parcel of land containing 1 rood between the lands of John Wardell on the south and of the north of William Sheddert.

As heir to his grandfather. Fine 8d.

Idem

18 April 10 Car. 1 messuage with a garden on the backside adjacent to a parcel of 1 messuage and 12 acres in Chester.

By surrender of William Pearson and Phillipp Wheatley. Fine 6d.

ELIZABETH MOWBURNE

4 May 13 Car. 4 acres of land in a close adjacent to the lands of John Watson on the north and west and the south loning on the east.

By surrender of Raiph Hedworth and Phillip Hall. Fine 1s. 4d.

Idem

dat ut supra. 4 acres 2 roods 28 perches of land lying in a close adjacent to the lands of John Watson on the north and west Richard Davison on the south and the south Loning on the west and half a pasture for a beast on the Burne Greene.

By surrender of Raiph Hedworth and Phillip Hall. Fine 1s. 4d.

Rent for these two copyholds 2s. 4½d.

RAIPHE COOK

18 April 13 Car. One messuage and one garden.

By surrender of John Hodgson. Rent 3d. Fine 6d.

ISABELL CHILTON widow relict of George Chilton

5 June 8 Jac. One messuage in Chester late in the possession of George Chilton (parcel of a tenure vzt. one messuage) half a husbandry lands.

In widdowright. Rent 1s. 4d. Fine 1s. 4d.

KATHERINE PORTER widdow relict of Charles Porter
13 April 14 Car. 10 acres of land parcel of 20 acres and 2 roods of
land lying in westfield.
  In widdowright. Fine 4s. 4d.

Eadem

dat ut supra. 10 acres of land lying in the westfield.
  In widdowright. Fine 3s. 4d.

Eadem

dat ut supra. 1 messuage with a garden and 10 acres of land parcel
of a close lying in the westfield.
  In widdowright. Fine 3s. 4d.

Eadem

dat ut supra. 5 acres and 11 perches of land parcel of a close in
westfield.
  In widdowright. Fine 1s. 8d.
  Rent for these four copyholds 8s. 2d.

ROBERT PARKINSON gentleman
27 April 11 Jac. 2 messuages 1 orchard and 1 garden in Chester
parcel of 2 messuages and 3 acres of Exchequer land of the rent
of 3s. 4d. with free entry and passage to the same.
  By surrender of Michael Hall gentleman. Fine 1s. 10d.

Idem

dat ut supra. parcel of land lying between the bridge and bank
of the Mill of Chester.
  By surrender of Raiphe Oliver. Fine 8d.
  Rent for these two copyholds 2s. 10½d.

JOHN COTESWORTH
13 April 11 Car. One house with a garden in Chester.
  By surrender of William Storey. Rent 2d. Fine 1s. 8d.

JOHN GIBSON
2 May 19 Jac. Pasture for 2 beasts in a close called Holme Hill.
  By surrender of Phillip Wheatley. Rent 1s. 8d. Fine 8d.

WILLIAM GIBSON son of Anne Gibson widdow

30 May 22 Car. 1 acre of land in Chester abutting on the land of George Clarke gentleman on the west John Watson and Roger Watsons on the north the Kings Streete on the east and the lands of Robert Allenson on the south (parcel of one oxgang of land in 3 parts divided) And the third part of a pasture for 2 beasts in a close called Holme Hill in 3 parts divided And also the 3rd part of a pasture for one horse in a certain place called Burne Greene in 3 parts divided.

By surrender of his mother Anne. Rent 4s. 8½d. Fine 8d.

MARGARET GIBSON spinster

14 January 20 Car. Half of one cottage with a garden on the backside.

By surrender of Robert Gibson her brother. Rent 4d. Fine 6d.

KATHERINE BROWNE

4 May 13 Car. One messuage in Chester.

Rent 4d. Fine 1s. od.

WILLIAM CHILTON son and heir of John Chilton

16 May 15 Car. One messuage in length 80 yards and in breadth 27 yards and a garden on the backside adjoining.

As heir to his father. Fine 2s. 2d.

Idem

dat ut supra. One house and one garth parcel of the whole tenure late John Hart 2 acres of land lying in west loneing and Mill lands in Chester and 1 acre lying with the moors.

Fine 6s. 8d.

Idem

dat ut supra. One close called Waltons Close on the south of the west loning.

Fine 8d.

Rent for these three copyholds 3s. od.

CUTHBERT PARMELEY

18 October 3 Car. One house containing 9½ yards of land and one garden on the backside containing in length 50 yards in breadth 9

yards and one half of land (parcel of one half of one cottage and of one tenement).

By surrender of Thomas Dickinson. Rent 1s. od. Fine 2d.

HENRY MATHEW

14 October 15 Car. 3½ acres of land adjacent on the lands of Thomas Halliday on the east and the Stell on the south The tenement of Richard Pearsons on the west and Bellam Flat on the north (parcel of one close containing 10 acres of land) and 10 acres of land and 10 perches.

By surrender of Richard Pearson. Rent 6d. Fine 1s. od.

JANE and WILLIAM TEWART

5 October 8 Car. One cottage.

By surrender of Jane Harbottle. Rent 1s. 10½d. Fine 1s. 4d.

JOHN MARLEY

18 April 10 Car. One house called Smyth Shopp containing in length 30 yards in breadth 26 yards in Chester.

As heir to his father Anthony Marley. Rent 3d. Fine 9d.

THOMAS CUTHBERT

16 May 19 Car. One tenement with a garth containing in length 30 yards and in breadth 8 yards abutting upon a tenement of William Lawes on the west and on the east upon the common.

By surrender of Robert Jackson. Rent 1d. Fine 1d.

THOMAS WHELDON

2 September 22 Car. Half of one cottage in Chester.

As heir to his father. Rent 11½d. Fine 2s. 6d.

JANE now wife of Robert Somerside relict of Roger Pearson

2 September 22 Car. Half of one cottage and the half of one garden as it is now divided and lying on the north of a tenement late in the possession of Thomas Smith.

In widdowright. Rent 11d. Fine 10d.

ROGER ROBINSON

13 April 16 Car. Half of one cottage late William Dunns

By surrender of Francis Denham and Mary his wife. Rent 11d.

Fine 4d.

ROBERT ROBINSON
3 November 22 Car. Half of one parcel of land late in the waste of the Lord which half with another half contains 24 yards in length and 18 yards in breadth of land 18 yards of land in Chester.

By surrender of Roger Robinson his brother. Rent 2d. Fine 1d.

THOMAS ROBINSON
dat ut supra. The other half.

By surrender of his brother Roger. Rent 2d. Fine 1d.

THOMAS ROBINSON son and heir of Robert Robson
2 September 22 Car. 2 acres of land late of the Lord's waste adjacent to the close of the said Robert Mastclose.

As heir to his father. Rent 8d. Fine 8d.

MICHAEL ASKELL son and heir of Leonard Askell
19 May 15 Car. One messuage one orchard and one garden between Linghouse on the north and the tenement of John Rutter on the south.

As heir to his father. Rent 6d. Fine 3s. od.

RICHARD CROFTON son and heir of Nicholas Crofton
2 September 22 Car. The south part of one cottage containing 7 yards in length and the half of one fold to the said cottage belonging.

As heir to his father. Rent 11¼d. Fine 2d.

ROBERT ANDREW
17 October 14 Car. The west half of one cottage with a garden containing in length 18 yards in breadth 18 yards as they are divided (parcel of ½ acre of land at Hawside).

By surrender of John Dawson and his wife. Rent 1d. Fine 1d.

GEORGE JOBLING son and heir of Edward Jobling
19 May 5 Car. One rood of land with one house thereupon built lying at Waldridge Greene upon the garth of John Curney.

By surrender of Edward Curney. Rent 1d. Fine 1d.

JANE YOUNGER widdow relict of John Younger
31 March 22 Car. The half of a cottage vzt. the north part of the same cottage vzt. to the 4th syle in the said cottage from the north or cottage aforesaid and the half garth to the same belonging vzt. the north part aforesaid as it is now covered with Deals.
Rent 11¼d. Fine 4d.

CHRISTOPHER WATSON
12 April 13 Car. A half of one cottage.
As heir to his father Henry Watson. Rent 11¼d. Fine 1s. 0d.

ROBERT OLIVER
4 May 13 Car. 5 acres of land adjacent to the lands of Richard Hedworth on the north and Stewardside on the south.
By surrender of Raiph Hedworth and Phillip Hall. Fine 1s. 8d.

Idem
4 May 13 Car. 3 acres 2 roods and 31 perches of land adjacent to the lands of William Pearson on the west the lands of John Watson on the east the lands of Richard Hedworth on the north and Stewardside on the south and half of one pasture for a beast.
Fine 1s. 0d.
Rent for these two copyholds 1s. 8d.

ROBERT PUNSHON son and heir of William Punshon and Mary Richardson.
20 April 6 Car. The part of a whole tenure
By surrender of Richard Hedworth and Phillip Hall. Fine 1s. 4d.

Idem
20 September 22 Car. One house containing 12 yards of land with a garth containing 10 yards in length and 8 in breadth parcel of the 7th part of a whole tenure lying between the tenement of Anne Sanderson on the east and the tenement of Christabell Punshon on the west.

As heir to his grandfather. Fine 4d.

Idem
dat ut supra. A parcel of a garth on the backside adjacent to the house late the said John's his grandfather containing 24½ yards in length from east to west and in breadth to the west end 12 yards.
As heir to his grandfather. Fine 1d.
Rent for these three copyholds 5d.

JANE HEDLEY late relict of John Hugill
10 September 21 Car. The 3rd part of one cottage in 3 parts divided.
In widdowright. Rent 7½d. Fine 1s. 1d.

KATHERINE late relict of Peter Gowland
21 April 11 Jac. One dwelling house with a little garden to the same adjacent containing in length 11 yards and in breadth 8 yards (parcel of one dwelling house late in the tenure of Robert Humble and Cicillie his wife with the half of one garth).
In widdowright. Rent 4d. Fine 3d.

JOHN MATHEW
18 April 14 Car. One cottage with a garth in Chester.
By surrender of John Reed. Rent 1s. 0½d. Fine 2s. 0d.

ROBERT ALLANSON son and heir of Margarett Allenson deceased
2 September 22 Car. 3 parts of one half of an oxgang of land.
Rent 1s. 1d. Fine 2s. 3d.

TIMOTHY ALLENSON
2 September 22 Car. Half of 3 parts of one oxgang of land abutting upon the lands of Anne Gibson on the south side of the common street on the east part the land of George Clarke gentleman on the west the land of Robert Allenson on the north.
By surrender of Robert Allenson. Rent 1s. 8d. Fine 1s. 8d.

ANNE GIBSON
4 May 13 Car. 4½ acres of land and 6½ parts lying upon John

Watson on the north the lands of Margaret Allenson on the south and the end of the garden on the East and the lands of George Clarke on the west and 2 acres of land adjacent upon the lands of Roger Simpson on the north.

By surrender of Raiph Hedworth and Phillip Hall. Rent 2s. 6½d. Fine 1s. 4d.

ROBERT MARLEY
13 May 20 Jac. One house of Exchequer land.

By surrender of John Fetherstonhaugh. Rent 8d. Fine 1s. 8d.

RICHARD HASWELL
16 May 15 Car. One close of Exchequer land late William Baly as it is divided into parts by ancient foggage on the south of another tenement of Robert Darnell containing 40 yards in breadth 110 in length.

By surrender of Richard Somerside. Fine 1s. od.

Idem
18 April 15 Car. ½ rood of land called the Delfe.

By surrender of William Foster. Fine 1d.

Idem
5 May 1 Car. Half of one cottage.

By surrender of Roger Haswell his father. Fine 6d.

Idem
26 April 7 Car. Of the Lord's waste one parcel of land containing in length 7 yards of land and in breadth 5 yards of land parcel of the common street of Chester being opposite to the house of the said Richard by demise from the Bishop as of new increase.

Fine 1d.

Rent for these four copyholds 2s. 2¼d.

WILLIAM HALL supervisor of Richard Hall
20 October 12 Jac. 5 acres of land lying at Pelton late Robert Snowlands And also 1 rood of land lying upon the north side of Chesterburne on the south of the said 5 acres of land (parcel of one acre of land late in the Lord's waste).

By surrender of William Hall. Rent 2s. 2d. Fine 1s. 9d.

THOMAS HOLLIDAY

4 May 13 Car. 2 acres of land in the west field at the end of his garden the land of Charles Fletcher on the north and parcel of the land belonging to the Baliffe of Chester on the south and Leonard Rutter on the west and 17 acres 3 roods 5 perches Le Maine land on the west and the land of Richard Pearson on the west Pelton Loaninge on the north and Hall Close on the south and pasture for one horse on Burne Greene.

By surrender of Ralph Hedworth and Phillip Hall. Fine 8d.

Idem

18 April 14 Car. One messuage parcel of one messuage and of one husbandland.

Fine 6d.

Rent for these two copyholds 4s. 8½d.

GEORGE FORCER

5 October 8 Car. One little meadow close called Hartside parcel of the lands and tenements called Earlehouses.

By surrender of George Wadell. Rent 6s. 8d. Fine 3s. 4d.

MICHAEL HALL son and heir of John Hall

27 April 11 Jac. The half of a field called Newfield as heir to his father and brother Thomas deceased.

By surrender of Christopher Skepper. Fine 6s. 8d.

Idem

dat ut supra. 1 parcel of land called hillside lying in the north field of Chester And also the whole tenure formerly Isabell Milne And also 2 messuages and 3 acres of Exchequer land.

As heir to his father. Fine 7s. 6d.

Idem

5 October 8 Car. One close called Walkers Close parcel of one messuage one orchard one garden and one husbandry lands.

By surrender of John Wilson. Fine 4d.

Rent for these three copyholds £1. 13s. 11½d.

HUGH STOTT

9 October 13 Car. One close called Coronatoris well close lying near the City of Durham.

By surrender of John Browne. Rent 2s. 2d. Fine 1s. 8d.

THOMAS BEWICK gentleman

6 October 17 Car. 3 acres of moor or waste of Urpeth on the north of the Town of Urpeth nigh the bridge there at the garth of Robert Robson.

By surrender of Sir William Darcy knt. Fine 1s. od.

Idem

dat ut supra. 6 acres of land now inclosed upon Urpeth Moor.

By surrender of Sir William Darcy knt. Fine 1s. od.

Idem

dat ut supra. 10 acres of land adjacent to the hedges of the Free tenement called Ryding on the west and one close called Whitting Ryding on the south.

By surrender of Sir William Darcy knt. Fine 3s. od.

Idem

dat ut supra. 3 cottages and 3 gardens upon Urpeth Moor called Potthouses.

By surrender of Sir William Darcy knt. Fine 1s. od.

Rent for these four copyholds £1. 4s. 8d.

The names of such tenants who pay the Rents hereunder written but have placed no writing copies deeds or other evidences how they hold the same

Chester Township	Copyhold		
Anne Bennison	£0.	0s.	3¾d.
Blaxton Mrs.	£0.	3s.	4d.
Robert Harrison gentleman for the Crownery Close	£0.	5s.	0d.
Richard Darling for Andes land	£0.	0s.	7d.
Idem: for Wheatley land	£0.	1s.	4d.
John Fletcher	£0.	0s.	11d.
Abraham Fowlett	£0.	0s.	4d.

Ralph Millott	£4.	14s.	od.
Thomas Postgaite	£0.	os.	10d.
Ewr Road	£0.	2s.	od.
	£5.	os.	0¾d.

WHITBURN AND CLEADON,
EAST & WEST BOLDON

An answer unto 25 Articles given us in charge by the Survey of the Bishop's lands within the County Palatine of Durham 10th May 1649

Memorandum

Mr. Chapman holdeth the parsonage of the gift of the late Bishop of Durham who had the free donation and presentation of the same and it is worth per annum £80 Mr. Robert Chapman Minister for his Tythes and Glebe payeth no rent his Glebeland containing 60 acres of land lying in the 3 corn fields of West Boldon with a pasture close and a Meadow Close called by the name of Crooke More Dykes with all houses belonging to that Parsonage which is a Free gift of the Bishop.

Sir William Lawson for Strodderhouse Freehold 6s. 8d. Mr. William Fenwick for Newton Garthes Freehold 20s. William Atkinson of West Boldon Freehold 6s. 8d. Thomas Carnaby and Margarett Sparrow for a Gillie Tythe in East and West Boldon paying no rent The copyholders of the Mannor of Boldon oweth no service to the Bishop but in paying our rents at 2 times a year by equal portions and to appear at the Hallmott Court two times in the year if they are summoned. We have a common belonging to East and West Boldon which is appurtenances to our Fines with Borders on Scotts house and Follonsby on the south side Werdlie on the west and Hedworth on the north. Also all the whole Mannor standeth upon limestone which we have always held as our own We have nothing more to present to any of the Articles

Jurors:
Ralph Lumley
George Wake

John Bell
William Atkinson

Cuthbert Baynbrigg
Thomas Lettany
Thomas Wright
Anthony Wright
Richard Chambers

William Atkinson
William Humble
John Smailes
Charles Trewhitt

Boldon Township Leaseholds

ANNE SHARPE deceased Thomas Sharp the younger and Alice Sharpe children of William Sharpe late of Cold Hesleden deceased 4 August 13 Jac. A close or pasture called the Fatherless Field near Boldon.

For the lives of the said Anne Thomas (who is now about 40) and Alice Sharpe (now about 41).

The said premisses contain 2 closes the one being pasture the other meadow.

Rent £1. 3s. 4d. Improvement £8. 0. od.

Boldon Township Copyholds

WILLIAM ATKINSON son and heir of Thomas Atkinson deceased

25 October 17 Car. One quarter of husbandland.

Fine 3s. 4d.

Idem

dat ut supra. One messuage with 3 lands of husbandland called Coateland.

Fine 1s. 8d.

Idem

28 December 22 Car. One house and a backside of the said house abutting upon the house of one William Wayne on the west and the house of William Briggs on the east parcel of the quarter part of one messuage and of one Barne with 2 closes containing 6 acres of land also part of the quarter of one messuage.

By surrender of William Readhead. Fine 2d.

Rent for these three copyholds £2. 2s. 11¾ d.

GEORGE BRIGGS son and heir of William Briggs
13 April 16 Car. A moitye of the 4th part of a messuage with a
barn 6 acres of land and also ½ of the 4th part of one messuage.
    By surrender of William Briggs. Rent 6s. 4½d. Fine 1s. od.

JOHN HODGE
25 October 18 Car. One parcel of land called Crakes Garth lately
built.
    By surrender of William Hodge his father. Rent 6d. Fine 1s. 4d.

WILLIAM READHEAD son and heir of Margaret Robinson
deceased
9 May 18 Car. The 4th part of one messuage the half of a barn
with 2 land cottage containing 26 acres of land and also the 4th
part of one messuage and of one husband land.
    Fine 5s. 10d.

Idem
12 October 21 Car.   The 4th part of a messuage and a barn with 2
closes containing 6 acres of land And also the 4th part of a
messuage.
    By surrender of Margaret then the wife of James Moody. Fine
6s. 10d.
    Rent for these two copyholds 18s. 11½d.

THOMAS WOOD son and heir of Anthony Wood
26 June 21 Jac. One rigg of arable land lying in the tofts, one other
rigg of arable land with the meadow to the same belonging lying
at Bishop Meadow one other Rigg of arable land lying in the dypes
and 2 other riggs of arable land lying the dypes ½ rood of arable
land lying at the Crose Lawes one rood of land Berry Flatt and 2
roods of arable land lying in the heap parcel of the half of one
messuage called Easterhouse the half of one husbandry land.
    Fine 8d.

Idem
dat ut supra. One cottage with a garden to the same belonging
containing 30 roods in length and 12 roods in breadth and in the
occupation of the said Anthony parcel of the half of one land in
West Boldon.

As heir to his father. Fine 2d.
Rent for these two copyholds 2s. 6d.

JOHN WELSH son and heir apparent of Richard Welsh
16 May 13 Jac. One cottage and 18 acres of land with one parcel
of land called Hall Greene Garths.
Rent £1. 13s. 6d. Fine 5d.

MARGERY WELSH, widdow relict of William Welsh deceased
4 May 13 Car. One cottage lying on the south of the town of
Boldon late in the occupation of Anne Chamber one garden lying
on the north of the town there adjoining of the tenement of Robert
Smailes and the half of the half of one land husband parcel of 3
messuages and 2 acres of land husband and the half of one land
husband.
In widdowright Fine 4d.

Eadem
dat ut supra. One ¼ of land parcel of the 3rd part of parts in 3
parts divided (vzt) the 5th part of arable land.
In widdowright. Fine 1s. 5d.

Eadem
dat ut supra. One messuage and one barn and 3 parts of one
husband land containing 36 acres in the fields there in 4 parts to
be divided.
In widdowright. Fine 10s. 0d.
Rent for these three copyholds £1. 15s. 9d.

THOMAS, youngest son of John Todd
24 May 12 Car. One messuage and one barn 2 gardens lying between the tenement of Sibell Smith and John Newlands and 3
acres of land (vzt) one acre in each field of East Boldon and pasture
for 2 beasts in the west pasture from the feast of St. Michael until
the Invention of the Cross yearly.
By surrender of the said John Todd. Rent 1s. 0d. Fine 1s. 0d.

JOHN TODD and Janett his wife
4 May 13 Car. One messuage with a garden on the backside
adjoining on which John Welsh lately dwelt and the half of one

land husband late in the tenure of the foresaid John Todd by the demise of John Welsh for their life.

Fine 2s. 6d.

Idem

17 October 14 Car. The 4th part of 1 acre of land and also the 4th part of one husbandland.

By surrender of Thomas Todd. Fine £1. 10s. 0d.

Rent for these two copyholds £1. 9s. 3d.

JOHN SMAYLES brother and heir of George Smailes deceased 2 May 18 Car. One messuage one barn and one husband land and a half containing 44 acres of land lying in 3 fields late belonging to Richard Pearah.

Rent £2. 3s. 2½d. Fine 12s. 4d.

CHRISTOPHER TREWHITT

9 October 13 Car. 2 cottages 30 acres of land 2 messuages and 4 Cole lands containing 72 acres of land in 3 fields.

By surrender of William Hedworth. Rent 10s. 0d. Fine 10s. 0d.

JOHN son and heir of Robert Turner deceased 2 September 22 Car. One messuage and the half of 30 acres of land.

Fine 4s. 0d.

Idem

dat ut supra. The half of one messuage and the half of 30 acres of land.

Fine 4s. 0d.

Rent for these two copyholds £1. 6s. 8d.

JOHN SHARPE enfeofed for
ALICE TODD spinster

4 November 22 Car. One husbandland lying in the upper field nigh Pasture Strabb Close Coate Flatt and the Moor.

Rent £1. 8s. 8d. Fine 5s. 0d.

RICHARD RAWE son and heir of Richard Rawe deceased

16 May 15 Car. The 4th part of 36 acres of land in 4 parts to be divided.

By surrender of his mother Jane Rawe. Fine 1s. 3d.

Idem

dat ut supra. One messuage called the Headhouse with the half of one oxegate and one kilne and one garner lying on the west side of the fold there with the half of the said garth called the Stack-yard the west half of the ..... there lying on the backside the messuage aforesaid and the half of one husbandland parcel of 3 messuages and 2 lands husband and the half of one land.

By surrender of his mother Jane Rawe. Fine 1s. 3d.

Rent for these two copyholds £1. 9s. 9d.

THOMAS son and heir of Thomas Plumbton
15 May 13 Jac. All that tenure late of Nicholas Younger and one messuage one farm one cottage 72 acres of land lying in 3 fields within the territories of East Boldon.

Rent £3. 13s. 9d. Fine £1. 0s. 0d.

WILLIAM HUMBLE
14 May 13 Car. One messuage and one husbandland.

Rent £2. 7s. 8¾d. Fine 12s. 4d.

HENRY MATHEW son and heir of William Mathew
3 November 16 Car. The 3rd part of the 15th part in 3 parts divided (vzt) 5 quarters of arable land.

Rent £1. 8s. 2½d. Fine 7s. 0d.

MARGARETT SPARROW
5 May 1 Car. The 5th part of the 5 parts of arable land late of William Mathew.

By surrender of Henry Mathew. Rent 7s. 0½d. Fine 1s. 0d.

JOHN BROTHERSTON
25 April 8 Car. One cottage lying in the north side of the town there lying by the tenement of Robert Smayles.

By surrender of John Lodge. Rent 2d. Fine 2d.

WILLIAM son and heir of William Hodge deceased
21 April 23 Car. One messuage one barn and one husbandland

and a half containing 54 acres of land lying in 3 fields with meadow and pasture belonging.

Rent £2. 7s. 1¾d. Fine 16s. od.

JANE ATKINSON the elder

5 October 6 Car. One cottage and a garden.

As widow of William Atkinson. Rent 1s. od. Fine 1s. od.

RICHARD CHAMBERS son and heir apparent of George Chambers

4 May 13 Car. One messuage, one barn, one husbandry land and a half one husbandryland containing 54 acres in 3 fields and a half of one husbandland with moors and demeasnes.

Rent £3. 6s. 8d. Fine £1. 10s. od.

THOMAS CARNABY

19 May 4 car. One house with a garden on the backside adjoining in East Boldon.

By surrender of Thomas Newland and Elianor his wife. Rent 4d. Fine 6d.

WILLIAM CHAMBERS son of William Chambers

9 October 13 Car. One cottage with a garden and a fold and a barn with all houses to the same adjacent called Wallfront adjoining to the east of West Bouldons on the east of Thomas Atkinson.

By surrender of William Chambers his father. Rent 6d. Fine 6d.

ELIZABETH wife of Robert Ayton and Anna wife of Richard Harrison coheirs of Elizabeth Puncheon deceased

23 November 40 Elz. One messuage and one husbandland in East Boldon One cottage and 3 acres of land and ½ one husbandryland in West Boldon.

Rent £3. 12s. 2d. Fine 13s. 4d.

JANE HODGE widdow relict of Thomas Hodge

13 April 11 Car. One cottage with a garden late in the possession of Richard Bateman.

In widdowright. Rent 4d. Fine 2d.

THOMAS TWEDDELL and Dorothy his wife and John Tweddell son and heir apparent

10 March 22 Car. One cottage and one garden in East Boldon.
By surrender of John Atkinson. Rent 6d. Fine 1s. 0d.

RALPH brother and heir of John Newland
18 April 14 Car. The half of half the messuage called Westhouse
and the half of half a husbandry land and half of half of one
quarter of husbandland.
As heir to his brother. Rent 3s. 4d.

Idem
dat ut supra. Half of half a messuage and half of half a husband
land and half of half a quarter of husbandland.
As heir to his brother. Fine 3s. 4d.
Rent for these two copyholds £1. 9s. 8½d.

JANE the wife of William Atkinson late Jane Hodge
24 May 12 Car. One husbandland in Midleshelfield Langley and
Brockley Whyns.
By surrender of William Atkinson. Rent £1. 10s. 0d. Fine 5s. 0d.

The names of such tennants belonging to the Township of East
and West Boldon and pay the rents underwritten but have showed
no deeds, evidences, copies or other writings whereby they hold
the same

William Hinde	£5.	4s.	5½d.
William Hodge	£0.	0s.	2d.
Mathew Waire	£0.	0s.	4d.

Whitburne cum Cleyton Copyholds

ELIZABETH relict of Robert Chambers
2 September 22 Car. One messuage and 5 acres of Coateland.
In widdowright. Fine 13s. 4d.

Eadem
dat ut supra. One messuage and one husbandland and one other
messuage and a half of land husband.
In widdowright. Fine 10s. 0d.

Eadem

dat ut supra. One messuage and one husbandry land and ½ messuage and ½ husbandry land late of Robert Hall and one messuage lying on the east end of the town on the south side One husbandland with the moor late belonging to John Leigh and known by the name of Easter Hallfield Middle Hallfield and Wester Hallfield late in the occupation of Thomas Chambers deceased And also known by the names of one tenement and garden lying at the east end on the northside of the town of Cleadon And also of 3 closes lying within Whitburne and Cleadon of which one is called the Hall Leaze the other called the East Farr Moore End and the 3rd called the West Farrmore End And also 16 riggs of land in Cleadon in a certain place there called Farthing Slayde and of a certain piece of land there called Milstobb and 15 riggs of land to the same adjoining within Whitburne and Cleydon and the whole arable land of meadow and pasture within the 3 fields called East, West and Middlehall field.

In widdowright. Fine £1. 6s. 8d.

Rent for these three copyholds £12. 9s. 8d.

All the said lands are to descend and come after the death of the said Elizabeth unto Mary Chambers and Barbary daughters and coheirs of the said Robert Chambers deceased.

JANETT wife of John Roxby
25 September 9 Jac. The half of one messuage with a garden on the backside adjoining and containing ½ acre of land. By surrender of Thomas Chambers and Barbary his wife. Rent 2d. Fine 6d.

ELIONER wife of Robert Sharpe and Isabell wife of William Maxwell
20 May 18 Car. One messuage and the half of one land husband parcel of one husbandland.

By surrender of Cuthbert Baynbrigg. Rent 5s. od. Fine 6s. od.

ISABELL relict of Humphrey Taylor
16 May 13 Jac. One cottage and 3 acres of arable land lying in Whitburne (vzt) in every field one acre and pasture for one beast in Le Lezures and pasture for another beast and 10 sheep in the moor.

In widdowright. Rent 2s. 2d. Fine 2s. 6d.

THOMAS CHILTON senior
2 October 34 Elz. One messuage and one husbandland and the half of a husbandland.

By surrender of John Chilton. Rent £3. 9s. 4d. Fine 10s. od.

MATHEW GEORGE
2 May 18 Car. 2 parts in 5 divided of one cottage and 8 acres of the demesne lands and 12 acres of the demesne lands and one cottage late of William Chambers And also one messuage and 14 acres of land in Cleadon By the demise of John Cooke William and Thomas Mallet Tutors and Guardians of Susan Lawson Mary and Elizabeth Lawson.

Rent £2. 11s. 10d. Fine 4s. od.

ELLIANOR MATHEW relict of Michael Mathew
12 April 8 Car. One messuage one husband land and one land lying on the east of the whole town there.

In widdowright. Rent £2. 6s. 6d. Fine 16s. od.

ANTHONY MATHEW son and heir apparent of Michael Mathew
20 October 2 Car. One tenement called a Coateland in Cleadon.

By surrender of his father. Rent £1. 18s. 6d. Fine 10s. od.

THOMAS COLSON
13 May 20 Jac. The half of one husbandland and 2 cottages with one garden on the backside adjoining parcel of one messuage and of one husbandland.

By surrender of William Roxby. Rent £2. 2s. 6d. Fine 10s. od.

GEORGE WAIKE son and heir of Richard Waike
17 October 14 Car. One messuage and one husbandry land.

By surrender of his father. Rent £2. 6s. 8d. Fine 10s. od.

ISABELL wife of Richard Readhead
25 October 17 Car. The 3rd part of the whole tenure.

By surrender of Thomas Heppell her brother. Rent £1. 8s. 4d. Fine 4s. 6d.

JOHN PATTISON in right of Isabell his wife one of the daughters and coheirs of James Mathew

24 May 12 Car. One messuage one barn one oxhouse and one parcel of Cotesland and 2 closes called the Tofts in Halfield (parcel of one messuage and 2 Cotes in Cleadon).

By surrender of James Mathew. Rent 19s. 3d. Fine 2s. 0d.

WILLIAM son and heir apparent of William Chapman gentleman 17 October 14 Car. 2 halves of one messuage and the half of half of one land husband and also the half of one other messuage and the half of half of one other land husband and also the moiety of another oxgang and also one messuage and one husband land and also one other messuage and a half of husband land.

By surrender of William the father. Rent £6. 1s. 0d. Fine £1. 0s. 0d.

WILLIAM son and heir of Katherine Atkinson 20 April 6 Car. The whole tenure with Katherine his mother.
Fine 10s. 0d.

Idem

25 October 17 Car. One house now or late in the occupation of Richard Helcoate and one parcel of land called the half land containing 18 acres of land parcel of half of one land which Thomas his late father had.
Fine 2s. 6d.
Rent for these two copyholds £3. 0s. 0d.

THOMAS son of Thomas Wright
The half of one messuage and the half of one husband land which Grace Wright ought to hold the foresaid tenement by her widdow-right being the relict of the foresaid Thomas deceased.
Fine 13s. 4d.

Idem

One land husband paying 40s. and another parcel of land called Utlaw paying 2s. lying near the common lees and also one house near the tenement of Robert Kitchin.
Fine 13s. 4d.
Rent for these two copyholds £3. 2s. 0d.

CUTHBERT BAINBRIGG
24 October 41 Elz. One cottage and the half of one land husband

parcel of one messuage and two acres of husband with the increase to the same belonging in Whitburne.

By surrender of Thomas Calverley. Rent £3. 18s. 0d. Fine 3s. 4d.

JOHN ROXBY

10 October 20 Jac. One messuage and one acre of husband land.

By surrender of Richard Mathew. Rent £2. 0s. 0d. Fine 10s. 0d.

THOMAS COLSON

13 May 20 Jac. Half of one husband land and 2 cottages with one garden on the backside (parcel of one messuage and of one husband land).

By surrender of William Roxby. Rent £1. 0s. 0d. Fine 10s. 0d.

RALPH son of Michael Lumley

27 April 11 Jac. One messuage and one husbandland in Whitburne.

By surrender of John Merryman. Rent £2. 0s. 0d. Fine 13s. 4d.

THOMAS PRESTON

19 October 11 Car. The whole tenure which Agnes his late mother held.

Rent 13s. 2d. Fine 13s. 4d.

RICHARD WRIGHT

18 April 14 Car. One close of land arable containing 4 acres by the south of Ann Bell widdow and pasture for 12 beasts upon the West Moor parcel of the 40 acres of arable land and 40 acres more in Whitburne.

By surrender of Richard Hedworth. Rent £2. 1s. 6d. Fine 2s. 0d.

EDWARD son and heir of Stephen Kitchin

20 April 6 Car. One land of husband in Whitburne.

By surrender of Henry Hilton and Elizabeth his wife. Fine 13s. 4d.

Idem

dat ut supra. One other land husband in Whitburne.

By surrender of Henry Hilton and Elizabeth his wife. Fine 13s. 4d.

Rent for these two copyholds £4. 0s. 0d.

ROBERT son and heir of Anthony Johnson
16 May 15 Car. The half of one messuage and husband land with
the moors and demesnes belonging and one messuage and one
husband land with moor and demesnes and one backhouse.
Rent £3. os. od. Fine 10s. od.

JOHN LETTANY
6 May 13 Car. The moytie of one husband land called Halland and
the 3rd part of land called Fletcher land and another 3rd part called
Fletcher land.
By surrender of Richard Bell gentleman. Rent 13s. 4d. Fine
10s. od.

THOMAS LETTANY and Isabell his wife
5 May 13 Car. The half of one husband land called Halland and the
2nd and 3rd part called Fletcher land by demise of Richard Bell
gentleman.
Rent £1. 13s. 4d. Fine 5s. od.

JOHN WRIGHT
17 October 14 Car. One messuage and one husband land.
By surrender of Thomas Sharpe. Rent £2. os. od. Fine 10s. od.

JOHN son and heir of Cuthbert Bell
7 October 10 Car. The half of one land called Husband land.
By surrender of ... Bell widdow. Rent £1. os. od. Fine 6s. 8d.

THOMAS son and heir of William Hutchinson
11 May 10 Jac. One messuage and one husbandland.
By surrender of his father. £2. os. od. Fine 10s. od.

The names of such tennants in Cledon and Whitburne as pay the
rent hereunder written but have produced no writings copies deeds
or other evidences whereby they hold the land

Ann Cornford	£0. 19s. 3d.
Thomas Colson	£1. os. od.
John Taylor	£0. 2s. 6d.
John Lettany senior	£0. os. 8d.

The town of Whitburne for one wind mill which they hold by copy of Court Roll for the use of the town and pay for her yearly £2. os. od.

RYTON LORDSHIP

An answer unto 25 Articles given unto us in Charge by the Surveyors of the Bishop's lands within the County Palatine of Durham 10 May 1647.

Imprimis to the first, second and third we have neither mannor house castle nor park within the Lordship.

To the fourth Article we have no forrage outwoods forest or chase, but one moor called Ryton Fell which contains about 1000 acres whereof the most part of it was improved and inclosed for divers years for which there were paid to the Bishop of Durham 4d. per annum for every acre untill such time as it was violently pulled down by a multitude of adjacent towns.

To the fifth there is no woods and therefore no rent nor bayliffe but for the Halmott Court there is both.

To the 6th there is no game of swans no pools or fish ponds save only an ancient fishing within the River of Tyne belonging to the coppyholders of Ryton as appurtnent to their tenements and payeth to the Lord of the Mannor 10s. per annum for the same to the Coronor which usually collected the same.

To the 7th Article there is no mills of any sort which in this Lordship save only one water corn mill now in the tenure or occupation of the Lady Troth Tempest by virtue of a lease made by John Bishop of Durham unto Sir Thomas Tempest Barronett dated the 24th October 1631 for the natural lives of Richard Tempest Nicholas Tempest and Thomas Tempest who are all living this present day and payeth to the Lord of the Mannor for the said mill 40s. per annum, the Lady Tempest being whole Executrix to the said Thomas Tempest Barronett and so we think is worth at the rack 20 markes per annum with the Lord's Rent.

To the 8th Article we hear no complaint by the Miller of the said mill so that we can present none.

To the 9th Article there are no salt boilers nor any mines of tin, lead, iron, allom or other use within our Lordship save only one Coal mine which as we hear is holden by lease for tenure of 3 lives which lease we could not see and therefore the value thereof we know not.

To the 10th and 11th Articles there is one Freeholder lying within the Lordship namely Francis Hedworth gentleman who payeth to the Lord of the mannor the yearly rent of 17s. 6d. included in the rental of Ryton and likewise a certain rent called the Fee Farme of Crawcrooke being 10s. per annum which goeth in with the rental aforesaid.

To the 12th Article there is no Customary Tennants and for the coppyholders they have all returned in their coppies with their rents and duties thereunto belonging for custom and service they pay to the Lord of the mannor 10s. per annum mentioned in their rental.

To the 13th Article there is a certain fine due to the Lord of the mannors at the death of a tennant as by his copy may appear which is upon record.

To the 14th Article there is some decayed timber in the copyholders land of the said Lordship but not sufficient to repair the houses within the copyholders lands of the said Lordship for the mines and quarries we have answered in the 9th Article.

To the 15th Article we have answered unto in the 12th Article.

To the 16th Article the cottages hath delivered in their coppies heretofore with their rents and several fines as for services they owe none.

To the 17th Article we have no intacks but such as we have formerly mentioned in the fourth article.

To the 18th Article we have no markets or fairs.

To the 19th Article we have one Halmott Court commonly holden twice in the year at Chester in the Streete but what the profit thereof is worth to the Lord we know not nothing being estreated and where any extracts are they are paid into the Exchequer from time to time.

To the 20th we have no free warren.

To the 21st Article there is a parsonage belonging to this Lordship which was in the gift of the Lord of the mannor One mansion house thereunto belonging which is indifferent repair there is certain glebe land belonging to the said Rectory of Ryton and payeth to the Lord of the mannor and certain accustomable rents of 10s. per annum in the rental of Ryton aforesaid.

To the 22nd Article the whole rectory or parsonage of Ryton is worth £100 per annum.

To the 23rd Article there is a house belonging to the parsonage and the same is indifferent repair together with the chancel.

To the 24th there is no woods as is before answered.

To the 25th Article we know no rents or services to be paid save only 30s. per annum which hath been paid to the school of Houghton out of the said rectory of Ryton.

Alice Coulson and Margaret Coulson holdeth one house and one garth which they hold by coppy of Court Roll which copy cannot be gotten at this time and pay for the same 4d. John Sander hath one house likewise pay 4d. Isabell Codling widdow hath one house and pay 4d.

The names of the Jurors

Cuthbert Walker   John Lensay
William French   John Greene
William Jolly   Nicholas Newton
Cuthbert Jolly   William Dodd
Thomas Greenway   Thomas Greene
George Hawxley   Nicholas Best
John Humble

Ryton Township Leasehold

LADY TROTHE TEMPEST

24 October 7 Car. Water corn mill of Riton

For the lives of Richard Tempest then 11, Nicholas Tempest then 6 and Thomas Tempest then 2 years sons of Thomas Tempest Barronet.

Rent £2. os. od.

Ryton Township Copyholds

LADY TROTHE TEMPEST

22 August 21 Car. One messuage and 30 acres of land.

In widdowright. Fine 3s. 9d.

Eadem

27 August 21 Car. 3 riggs of meadow lying in Ryton Haugh And one rood of meadow lying at Bogle Hole and also 2 riggs of meadow lying near Netlehaugh and one rood of meadow lying at Boglehole.

In widdowright. Fine 5d.

Eadem

dat ut supra. One cottage with a garden and 3 acres of arable land in several fields of Ryton in every field one acre and also pasture for 2 beasts in a certain pasture there called Welgreene and also other 3 acres of land arable within the several fields of Ryton and pasture for 2 beasts in a close called Browne Close and pasture for 10 sheep in the fields aforesaid.

Fine 1s. 8d.

Eadem

dat ut supra. 2 riggs of meadow lying in Riton haugh in a certain place there called Bogglehole between the riggs of her the said Trothe on the east and a parcel of meadow called Powle acre on the west containing ½ acre of land.

Fine 1d.

Eadem

dat ut supra. One messuage with a garden containing 1 acre.

Fine 3d.

Eadem
dat ut supra. One messuage with a garden containing 1 acre.
   Fine 3d.

Eadem
dat ut supra. 1 acre of land lying on the west part of Murreygate.
   Fine 3d.

Eadem
dat ut supra. 2 acres of land near the Lord's mill one close containing 1½ acres of land called the North Close as it is inclosed with hedges on the back of the dwelling house of John Hunter parcel of the premisses late in the tenure of Thomas Newton of Crawcrooke (excepted and reserved) and also 1½ acres of land lying on the west side of Ryton millhouse of Faddenbreg being near a close of the said John Hunter.
   Fine 6d.

Eadem
dat ut supra. One rigg of land lying on the west part of waterbanks in Riton haugh ½ rigg lying in the broad meadows and ½ rigg there and one rood of land parcel of half of half an acre called the Wheele Hole acre lying at Ritonhaugh.
   In widdowright. Fine 1d.

Eadem
dat ut supra. ½ rigg of land nigh Bogleholegate ½ rigg of land nigh broadmeadow and ½ of one parcel of land called Wheele halfacre nigh the said broad meadows now in the tenure of the said Trothe parcel of one messuage and 36 acres of land late in the tenure of William Laverocke
   In widdowright. Fine 1d.

Eadem
dat ut supra. One dale of meadow lying in waterbanks in Ryton haugh between the lands of Robert Walker on the south and the lands of William Foggatt on the north 5 riggs lying in Ryton Haugh near the Blacktree and one beastgate in broome field pasture pasture for one beast in broome field aforesaid and a forefogg for one beast pasture for one cow or oxe in the common pasture called Hole

Greene 3 riggs of land lying together at Whitlaw in Riton haugh and another rigg of land in Riton haugh aforesaid upon the gallis lying on the south of the lands of the said Thomas And also 3 riggs of meadow lying in Lowe Hettifield upon Rowbanck on the east the lands of the said Thomas pasture for one beast in the willy pasture and pasture for one beast in the foreFog 6 little riggs or butts of meadow and 2 other longer riggs of meadow to the said 6 little riggs in part adjacent together with a certain hedge and soile and ground of the same hedge scituate at the higher part of the same riggs and also a certain parcel of meadow called a half dale of meadow lying in a field called Nether Hattifield and also one rigg of meadow lying in Riton Haugh in a certain place called Gallis and one other little rigg of meadow called a Butt in Riton haugh aforesaid, parcel of the whole tenure late John Turners.

Fine 1s. 9d.

Eadem

dat ut supra. A pasturegate in cow pasture and one foggate one rigg of arable land lying in Riton haugh between the rigg of John Walkers on the East and a rigg on the west fogage for 2 beasts feeding through all the fields in Riton and 4 riggs of land containing by estimation one rood in a certain place called Whaley in Riton haugh late parcel or belonging to one tennant and 24 acres of land in Ryton.

In widdowright. Fine 4d.

Eadem

dat ut supra. 4 little riggs or butts lying at Speckton Wharfe in Riton haugh and half of one rigg lying at Gallis in Ritonhaugh aforesaid and also one rigg of meadow in Hattifield upon Rowley and also pasture for 2 beasts in the forefogg in the fields there 6 riggs of land lying in the westfield (vzt) 2 riggs upon peppermoor poole 3 riggs upon overside banks and foggage for one horse in the fields of the town of Riton pasture for 2 beasts in Reafley Field and pasturing parcel of 12 acres of land sometimes William Sander.

In widdowright. Fine 6d.

Eadem

dat ut supra. 12 acres of land and one messuage to the same belonging.

In widdowright. Fine 2s. 6d.

Eadem
dat ut supra. The half of one town called the husband half of one messuage and half of 12 acres of husbandry land.
   In widdowright. Fine 2s. 2d.

Eadem
dat ut supra. One platt of land Exchequer late Robert Wrighte.
   In widdowright. Fine 1s. 0d.

Eadem
dat ut supra. One parcel of meadow called a dayle of meadow lying in Ritonhaugh between the riggs of the lands arable called Water Banks on the south and one parcel of meadow of John Sanders on the north parcel of 6 acres of land called Shallocke land late William Collings.
   In widdowright. Fine 2d.

Eadem
dat ut supra. One parcel of land and meadow called Maines acre and two riggs of arable land lying in Netlehaughfield parcel of one messuage and 20 acres of land in Riton.
   Fine 3d.

Eadem
dat ut supra. One rigg called Crookes rood one butt lying at Plawstile one little butt in Swable meadow one rigg in Cashett Low Myers and one piece of meadow at How Burne and pasture for one beast in the Faugh and one piece of meadow lying at Hattifield.
   Fine 2d.

Eadem
dat ut supra. One parcel of land late the Lord's waste called Bradleys Crooke also Sower Myers and Birkley Close containing 30 acres of land
   Fine 6s. 8d.

Eadem
dat ut supra. One acre of land lying in Riton haugh called Mayes

acre and one rood of meadow called Crooked Rood and one rigg lying on the south part of Brode Meadow.
    Fine 2d.

Eadem

dat ut supra. One messuage and 24 acres of land in Riton.
    Fine 2s. 6d.

Eadem

dat ut supra. One rigg containing one rood of land lying in Brode Meadows and 2 riggs of land whereof one rigg lies in longland and another in Gallies parcel of the third part of 35 acres of land.
    Fine 2d.

Eadem

dat ut supra. 2 riggs of arable land lying upon Langlands in the haugh 2 riggs in Gallis pasture for one beast in the Broomefield and pasture for one beast in the wallies 2 riggs and one parcel of Meadow called Reay Balke lying in Hettifield one balke descending from the Kings Street at Holburne 2 riggs of meadow upon Longland and 3 riggs called Little butte upon Sheeles bread in Ritonhaugh 2 riggs of land between the lands of the said Thomas on the west and the lands of John Laveroche on the east half of one parcel of meadow called half of a dale lying in water banks in the occupation of Richard Colson parcel of 6 acres of land.
    Fine 8d.

Eadem

dat ut supra. 11 riggs of land lying in over Hettis and 8 riggs of land lying in Broomefield and 6 riggs of land lying in Risleyfield and 11 riggs in Westfield and 7 riggs in Eastfield and foggage for a horse in the former foggage in the lands aforesaid and foggage for one beast there and pasture for 2 beasts in the Faugh in Ryton and pasture for 2 horses there and one parcel of meadow lying near Boglehole 1 rigg lying in low Hettifield Banckes and 2 butts lying in Tittin deanehead And also one butt lying in Tittin deanehead aforesaid and one Balke lying on the west part of Tittin deanehead aforesaid and one butt of land lying in broken Shaw one pasturegate in a pasturegate called Holegreene in Ryton 2 riggs of land arable lying upon the meadow land lying between the lands of John Johnson on the west the lands of Roger Coulson on the east one parcel of land called Wester playdaile and one other parcel of meadow called Easter playdaile and one rigg of land lying upon the high acre parcel of a tenure late Cuthbert Goarleys grandfather of Roger Coulson.

Fine 3s. od.

Eadem
dat ut supra. One rigg in the broad meadows in Riton haugh and one daile of meadow in the water banks of Riton haugh containing ½ acre of land and 3 riggs of land lying in Hattesfield and 1 rigg lying in the haugh and 10 buttes on the west of Riton haugh and 2 riggs of meadow land and 1 little butt in Ryton haugh parcel of one messuage and 21 acres of land which were late James Pickering.

Fine 4½d.

Eadem
dat ut supra. Once close called Gawens Close.

Fine 4d.

Eadem
dat ut supra. One messuage with a garden and 2 closes called Slades also Whittell Closes.

In widdowright. Fine 4d.

Eadem
dat ut supra. 33 acres of land within the Bishop's woods on the west of the water called Stanley Burne and the lands of Pruddoe on the south and east common of the Lord on the north of one pasture and another tenure of land late John Lyons of Bradley and the tenure of Thomas Humble called Channells.

Fine 5s. 6d.

Eadem
dat ut supra. One parcel late the Lord's waste of the land called Bradley greene also le loaning adjacent to the tenure late of John Lyons there containing 3 acres.

Fine 6d.

Eadem
dat ut supra. One parcel of land abutting on the Chappell contain-

ing 4 acres of land and a garden with a half built upon the premisses.

Fine 1s. od.

Rent for these thirty copyholds £7. 19s. 11d.

GRACE widdow relict of John Sanders

31 May 22 Car. Half of one messuage and half of 12 acres of land. In widdowright. Fine 2s. 6d.

Eadem

dat ut supra. The third part of one messuage and 21 acres of land. In widdowright. Fine 10d.

Rent for these two copyholds £1. 0s. 10d.

ISABELL wife of George Hauxley and Elizabeth wife of Nicholas Newton sisters and coheirs of Margaret Foggatt

21 April 23 Car. 2 riggs of meadow lying on the west of water banks in Riton haugh 4 little butts of meadow lying there extending itself to the River of Tyne on the north one other rigg of arable land lying upon .... high acres pasture for one beast and former foggage of the town another great rigg of arable land lying in Riton haugh another rigg of arable land upon Longland parcel of 12 acres of land.

Fine 8d.

Eadem

dat ut supra. 2 riggs lying upon the layor and 2 riggs in Smetcroft-hill in the field of Ryton aforesaid called Hettesfield and also 2 riggs lying in Middlecrooke Hill there in the field there called Broome-field 2 other riggs of pasture lying near Sanders Close nooke in another field called Refley field and also 2 riggs in Nettlehaugh parcel of 20 acres.

By surrender of John Hauxley. Fine 4d.

Eadem

dat ut supra. Half of one toft half of one croft half of one messuage being an ancient house garden and fold late in the occupation of Andrew Poyd and ½ of 6 acres of land called Shecklocks land late William Cotlings and also the half of 6 acres of land late Robert Paxtons and also half a parcel of one messuage and the half of 13 acres of land parcel of 24 acres of land and also the half of 2 acres of land and 2 roods of land (2 of the Leazes lying at the head of the croft one rigg of arable land lying upon Milburne pasture for one beast in Howle Greene one rigg of meadow lying in the Croft Flatt the west half of one rigg lying in Ryton haugh in the bushes and foggage for one beast in the fogage in town meadows formerly granted to James Nixton excepted) (and also except 4 riggs of arable land lying in Hettifield nigh Doublegate and pasture for 2 beasts or common pasture formerly granted to William Follie only excepted).

By surrender of John Hauxley. Fine 5s. od.

Rent for these three copyholds 4s. 11d.

CHRISTOPHER NEWTON

5 May 1 Car. One messuage 24 acres of husbandryland and 4 acres of exchequer land.

As son and heir of Anne Newton. Rent 12s. od. Fine 5s. od.

JOHN COOKE

2 May 18 Car. One cottage with a garden and 3 acres of land called Roperland and also 2 acres of land and also other two acres of land and one rood of land with pasture for one beast in the fallow (except and reserved 2 acres of land called Eastmoore Spott and one rigg of land on the east of Blacktree in Ryton Haugh on the west of Elands (parcel of the premises formerly granted to Thomas Hauxley).

As heir of William Sander his uncle. Rent 2s. 6d. Fine 2s. 6d.

MARGARET HAUXLEY widdow

26 May 14 Car. 12 acres of land one messuage and 6 acres of husbandrie.

As relict of John Hauxley. Fine 7s. od.

Eadem

dat ut supra. Half of the 4th part of 5 acres of land and pasture for 2 beasts in the foggage and pasture for one beast in the Summer Pasture and ½ pasture in the faugh and after fogge.

Fine 3s. 4d.

Eadem

dat ut supra. 2 riggs or butts lying at Milburne Flat (parcel of one messuage and 6 acres of land).
Fine 2d.
Rent for these three copyholds 9s. 4d.

JOHN GRENNOE of Crawcrooke
20 April 12 Car. Half of half of 36 acres of land (one messuage excepted).
By surrender of Nicholas Newton. Fine 1s. 3d.

Idem

2 May 19 Jac. 2 riggs of land called Longlaine lying in Riton Haugh adjacent between the riggs of Roger Colson on the east and Thomas Tempest Esq. on the west (parcel of one tenement and 24 acres of land) and also fishing there in the water of Tyne.
By surrender of John Follie. Fine 4d.
Rent for these two copyholds 3s. 4d.

MICHAEL BEST in right of Isabell his wife relict of Thomas Hauxley
31 March 22 Car. 2 acres of land called Eastmoore Spott and one rigg of land on the East of Blacktree in Riton Haugh and the west of the Eland.
Fine 4d.

Idem

dat ut supra. One house upon the green and the half of one rig lying upon the Floores and 2 west riggs Riggs upon the Crakes 2 butts upon the Stainmers and 3 riggs of arable land in the playes one rigg in Blacktree of either side of the gate and 2 butts in the Styes meadow and the north riggs at Short Croft and one parcel of meadow at Birkshaw and pasture for one beast in the Faughs and latter foggage (parcel of 36 acres of land).
Fine 1d.

Idem

dat ut supra. One rigg of arable land on the North of blacktree at the east end of the same extending itself to the Hand another rigg of arable land lying at Milburne Flatt parcel of a whole tenure late John Turners.

Fine 1d.

Idem

dat ut supra. One pasture in the Holegreen and pasture in the forefogg one pasture in the faugh 3 pastures in the latter foggage one headland and 2 butts in the East Croft one rigg in the Staward 2 butts in the stawes one dale of meadow in the small deane one parcel of meadow in the Church dean with a parcel of a balke in the leame and another rigg in the short crop (parcel of one messuage and 21 acres of land).

Fine 4d.

Idem

dat ut supra. One dale of meadow in the water banks 2 riggs of arable ground lying in Middlecrooke in Broomefield 2 other riggs of arable land lying on the east of Loneside and 2 riggs of land lying on the south of Linghy hill And pasture for one beast in a pasture of the North there with a former foggage for the land parcel of one tenement and 24 acres of land arable.

Fine 4d.

Idem

dat ut supra. One messuage and one parcel of meadow called the Fallowemeadows.

Fine 4d.

Idem

dat ut supra. 2 riggs of land lying upon Gallies in Ryton haugh one butt and parcel of meadow in Hettifield Reynds late in the possession of Isabell Stowe and pasture for one beast in the ox pasture (parcel of 22 acres of land).

Fine 3d.

Rent for these seven copyholds 6s. 8d.

NICHOLAS NEWTON

3 March 17 November. One messuage and 20 acres of land (parcel of 30 acres).

By surrender of William Walton. Rent 3s. 4d. Fine 6s. 8d.

EDWARD HENDERSON in right of his wife
22 April 23 Car. One house with a garth on the backside containing ½ acre.

    As relict of Thomas Holcoate her husband. Fine 1d.

Idem

dat ut supra. The 4th part of 30 acres of land (one messuage parcel of the premisses excepted and reserved)

    Fine 1s. od.

Idem

dat ut supra. One messuage with a garden on the backside lying at Newgate and one other rigg lying at the Hall flat near peach head (which premisses are part of one messuage and 6 acres of land late in the possession of Roger Coulson).

    Fine 1d.

    Rent for these three copyholds 4s. 8d.

JOHN son of John Dodd
13 May 20 Jac. One close called Newfield containing 1 acre.

    By surrender of John Dodd his father. Fine 1s. od.

Idem

dat ut supra. The half of one tenement called Woodishouse By surrender of Nicholas Newton.

    Fine 5s. od.

    Rent for these two copyholds 17s. 4d.

CUTHBERT WALKER and Jane his daughter
9 October 13 Car. The half of the half of one messuage and the half of the half of 30 acres of land.

    By surrender of Robert Saunders. Fine 8d.

Idem

16 April 7 Car. The 4th part of 25 acres and the half of one rigg of land in the Hall Flatt, one rigg and one little rigg called a butt in Thincrooke one parcel of meadow in Le Playe first granted to one Robert Walker.

    By surrender of Edward Briggs. Fine 6d.

Idem

15 October 8 Jac. The half of one toft, the half of one croft the half
of one messuage the half of 6 acres of land Skellett land late of
William Colling And also the half of 6 acres of land late of Robert
Payton.

By surrender of Andrew Poyd. Fine 4s. 2d.

Idem

26 June 21 Jac. The half of the whole tenure of 36 acres of land and
14 acres of land and one rood of land and pasture and one beast
in Fallow of the same half one close Laverock Bank parcel of the
premisses excepted.

By surrender of William Laverock. Fine 2s. 6d.

Idem

17 October 14 Car. The half of the half of one messuage and the
half of the half of 30 acres of land late in the occupation of Margarett Saunders.

By surrender of Robert Saunders. Fine 8d.

Idem

20 October 12 Car. The half of the half of one Messuage and the
half of the half of 30 acres of land in Ryton. By surrender of Robert
Saunders. Fine 8d.

Rent for these six copyholds 15s. 11d.

MARY wife of Robert Cooke one of the daughters and coheirs of
Robert Humble deceased
24 January 14 Car. A tenement or pasture called Greeneside.
Fine 4d.

Idem

dat ut supra. One parcel of meadow lying on the water banks called
water bancke daile late in the occupation of the aforesaid Robert
containing 1 acre of land parcel of one messuage and 24 acres.
Fine 4d.

Rent for these two copyholds 2s. 7d.

JOHN son and heir of Robert Lindsey
25 September 15 Jac. The whole tenure sometimes of John Thirner.

By surrender of John Thirner. Rent 3s. 11d. Fine 6s. 8d.

ROBERT STOCKETON

5 October 8 Car. One messuage and 21 acres of husbandry land.
  As heir to his father. Rent 9s. 11d. Fine 5s. 0d.

JOHN STOKOE

13 April 11 Car. 3 acres of land.
  As heir to his father. Fine 3s. 4d.

Idem

dat ut supra. One close called Laverock bank.
  As heir to his father. Fine 1d.
  Rent for these two copyholds 1s. 9d.

WILLIAM son and heir of William French

15 April 19 Jac. One cottage with a garden.
  Fine 2s. 0d.

Idem

dat ut supra. One parcel of land late the Lord's waste containing
16 acres of Moor nigh the Lordship of Pruddoe
  By surrender of George Nixon and Elizabeth his wife. Fine 5s. 0d.

Idem

dat ut supra. A parcel of meadow lying in water banks late in the
occupation of Robert Humble containing 1 acre.
  Fine 1d.

ELIZABETH SANDER now wife of William French

23 April 3 Car. One messuage and 10 acres of land in Ryton Woodside.
  By widdowright. Fine 4d.

Eadem

dat ut supra. A kilnestead with a garden and a parcel of ground
late of the Lord's waste at Newfield containing 1 acre.
  Fine 10d.

Eadem

dat ut supra. The half of a half of a tenement called Wood House.

Fine 6s. 8d.
Rent for these six copyholds £1. 0s. 10d.

MARGRETT wife of William Coulson
25 April 8 Car. One parcel of land called Channell containing 20 acres formerly the Lord's waste.
   By surrender of Thomas Humble. Fine 6s. 8d.

Eadem
19 May 5 Car. One messuage and 2 acres of land.
   By surrender of Thomas Humble. Fine 2s. 0d.

Eadem
dat ut supra. One parcel of land at Hishophill containing 3 acres.
   By surrender of Thomas Humble. Fine 1s. 8d.
   Rent for these two copyholds 7s. 2d.

WILLIAM FOLLIE
20 April 6 Car. Half of a tenure vzt. half of half of 36 acres of land (one rigg called Wheele half acre and 2 riggs in broad meadows (one bridge nigh the water bank excepted).
   By surrender of William and Alice Follie his parents. Fine 1s. 3d.

Idem
10 Car Re. One parcel of meadow in the lower ford of water banks late in the tenure of William Walker with fishing in the water of Tyne.
   By surrender of William and Alice Follie his parents. Fine 2d.
   Rent for these two copyholds 3s. 3d.

WILLIAM FOLLIE the elder
22 October 22 Jac. One parcel of meadow called broadmeadow swaith one other parcel of meadow called Crawcrooke Heapes 1 rigg of meadow called Halfon Rigg in Low Hettifield 3 riggs in short croft 2 riggs in east croft in the carrs one rigg in Broomefield on the back of Middlecrooke one rigg in Cushotts low car in the middle of the same and 2 other riggs in Cushett Law to the west of a rigg there towards Rifley Field bank 2 riggs in Ryfley Field in the highest part of Pethside one parcel of meadow in the westfield at the holme doves 2 pasture gates in the Faugh.

By surrender of William Jolley the younger. Rent 8s. od. Fine 1s. 8d.

WILLIAM WALKER son and heir of Marie Pickering and cousin and heir of Jane Pickering

31 May 22 Car. One messuage and 21 acres of land.
As heir to Mary and Jane. Rent 8s. od. Fine 6d.

CUTHBERT JOLLIE

4 May 13 Car. One dale of meadow lying in Crawcrooke heapes one little rigg lying in East Flatt and pasture for 2 beasts on the haugh.
As heir to his father. Fine 4d.

Idem

dat ut supra. One parcel of meadow lying on the south of water bank dales between the lands of James Pickering on the south and Margarett Briggs on the north and pasture for one beast in a pasture of the town of Ryton called Holegreene with a pasture for the same beast in the former foggage and after foggage there.
As heir to his father. Fine 4d.

Idem

dat ut supra. 3 butts and one headland lying on the east of the garth of William Jollie and of the north of a garth of Roger Colson's and adjacent to certain riggs of John Hauxley on the west and 2 riggs of Margaret Briggs on the north parcel of 6 acres of land.
Fine 2d.

Idem

dat ut supra. The 4th part of 35 acres.
Fine 1s. 8d.

Idem

dat ut supra. 4 riggs of arable land and meadow lying in Hettifield nigh doublegates and pasture for two beasts in an open pasture (parcel of 6 acres called Shellocke land formerly William Collins).
Fine 6d.
Rent for these five copyholds 7s. 4d.

ROBERT WALKER

3 November 16 Jac. The 3rd part of one messuage and 21 acres.
   As heir to his mother Christabell Walker. Fine 1s. 8d.

Idem

17 October 2 Jac. The 4th part of 35 acres.
   As heir to his father George. Fine 1s. 8d.
   Rent for these two copyholds 8s. 4d.

MARY WRIGHT widdow

31 March 22 Car. One cottage as it is divided in the possession of George Colson.
   As relict of Edmond Wright. Rent 4d. Fine 2d.

MARGARET MIDDLETON

2 May 18 Car. One house with a garden.
   As sister and heir of Edward Briggs. Rent 4d. Fine 1s. 0d.

CHRISTOPHER GREENE

26 June 21 Jac. 3 riggs in Ryton Westfield, one rigg in Steppings Close 2 riggs in Croft 3 riggs in High Acres pasture for 2 beasts in one pasture and pasture for 2 beasts in the forefog (parcel of 24 acres).
   By surrender of William Follie. Fine 8d.

Idem

3 November 16 Jac. 2 riggs of land lying upon the flowers in Ryton Westfield half of one rigg of land upon the burne banks one rigg and one butt lying upon Todhorse Flacke one rigg and one butt lying upon Hettifield bank one parcel of meadow upon Birkinshawe and ½ rigg of arable in the Gallies and one rigg in Bogglehole and one parcel of Meadow in Riton haugh and another parcel of meadow lying at water banks pasture for one beast in ox pasture with former foggage for the same and pasture for one horse in the faugh (parcel of one oxgang of land in Riton).
   By surrender of William Colson. Fine 2s. 6d.
   Rent for these two copyholds 7s. 10d.

ANTHONY SANDER

21 March 22 Car. Half of one messuage and half of 13 acres of land (parcel of 24 acres).

By surrender of Robert Sander. Rent 2s. 1d. Fine 6d.

ROBERT TODD

21 March 22 Car. 4 acres of land late the Lord's waste called the Intacke lying between Rickley Ford on the north part of the Lordship of Chopwell.

As heir to his father William Todd. Rent 4s. od. Fine 1s. 4d.

JOHN HUMBLE

17 October 14 Car. One messuage and 24 acres of land.

By surrender of George Humble and Jane his wife. Rent £1. os. od. Fine £1. os. od.

JAMES GREENE

19 May 4 Car. The 8th part of a parcel of land called Crakley.

By surrender of Thomas son and heir of William Greene. Rent 6d. Fine 2s. od.

ROBERT LABURNE

21 May 22 Car. One parcel of land lying at Slades with a house thereupon.

By surrender of Frances Wren. Rent 8d. Fine 1s. od.

GEORGE NIXON

18 April 10 Car. One parcel of land late the Lord's waste lying in Greenside containing 3 acres.

As heir to his father. Fine 1s. 6d.

Idem

dat ut supra. One house lately built lying at Easter Greenside and one parcel of land extending itself on the north of the house and south of his tenure.

Fine 4d.

Rent for these two copyholds 2s. od.

WILLIAM DODD

21 April 23 Car. The west half of 16 acres of land called Rickefield.

As heir to his mother Alice Dodd. Fine 4s. 4d.

Idem

22 October 22 Jac. One parcel of one house built together with half

a rood of land to the same belonging adjacent along on the east of the Kings way there to brown house late the Lord's waste.

By surrender of Richard Clugh. Fine 2d.

Rent for these two copyholds 1s. 10d.

GEORGE DODD

21 October 23 Car. The east part of 16 acres called Rickefield.

As heir to his mother Margaret Dodds. Rent 1s. 8d. Fine 3s. 4d.

RALPH NEWTON and Jane his wife

4 March 15 Car. One parcel of land thereupon built containing 3 roods of land on the east of a little piece of land late in the occupation of the Parson of the Church of Ryton and of the north part of a piece of land late in the occupation of Richard Rennison.

By surrender of Stephen Coulson. Fine 4d.

Idem

9 May 18 Jac. One parcel of land containing 2 parts of one close called Hobsclose in Ryton woodside containing 2 acres late the Lord's waste with the houses thereupon built.

By surrender of Robert Newton. Fine 1s. 0d.

Rent for these two copyholds 4s. 8d.

JOHN BELL

10 October 20 Jac. One cottage 1 barn and 1 parcel of land adjacent in Ryton woodside.

As heir to his father Alexander. Rent 6d. Fine 1s. 0d.

JOHN DODD

25 October 18 Car. The 3rd part of a tenure late John Holmes vzt. the 3rd part of 11 acres of land.

As heir to his father John Dodd. Fine 5s. 0d.

ISABELL JACKSON

16 May 19 Car. 1 house 12 yards in length 5 yards in breadth with a garden 16 yards in length likewise breadth (parcel of half a tenement called Woodishouse).

By surrender of John Dodd. Rent 4d. Fine 4d.

THOMAS BOWETT, WILLIAM RAYNE, JOHN STOKOE and GEORGE HAUXLEY

25 October 18 Car. One piece of meadow being ½ of a dale upon

waterbanks in Ryton haugh parcel of a messuage with a garden 10 acres of land and 2 of pasture in the townfields of Ryton.

By surrender of Stephen Coulson. Fine 5s. 4d.

Idem

dat ut supra. 16 acres of land late the Lord's waste lately built.

By surrender of Stephen Coulson. Fine 5s. 4d.

Rent for these two copyholds 4d.

THOMAS BOWETT, Elizabeth his wife and Lancellot their son 9 October 13 Car. One messuage and 10 acres of land lying between the town and territories of Ryton and also 2 acres of land lying on the south part of the house of William Wright called the first part of Newfield.

By surrender of Anthony Humble. Fine 7d.

Idem

7 — 10 Car. Half of one messuage and 24 acres of land.

By surrender of Margaret Dodd and Anthony her son. Fine 5s. 0d.

Idem

dat ut supra. Half of one messuage and 24 acres.

By surrender of Thomas Rough. Fine 5s. 0d.

Rent for three copyholds 16s. 6d.

ROBERT SANDERS

21 April 1647. Half of half a tenement called Woodhouse.

As heir to his father George Sanders. Rent 4s. 0d. Fine 4s. 0d.

JOHN LIDDLE

5 October 20 Car. One parcel of land lying at Ryton Woodside containing 10 yards in length and 3½ in breadth upon which a little house lately built And also one other parcel of land to the same adjacent belonging containing ½ acre.

As heir to his father. Fine 4d.

Idem

30 May 19 Car. One parcel of land containing the 3rd part of Hobsclose in 3 parts divided and now being in one close containing 1 acre of land.

As heir to his father. Fine 6d.
Rent for these two copyholds 2s. 4d.

ISABELL STOKOE widdow
9 May 4 Car. One house with a garden and pasture for one beast in Holegreene.
By surrender of Robert Walker and Margaret his wife. Rent 4d. Fine 4d.

CHRISTABELL STOBERT widdow
9 May 4 Car. Half of half of one tenement called Woodhouse.
By surrender of Robert Todd. Rent 4s. 0d. Fine 4s. 0d.

JANNETT COULSON widdow
20 October 5 Car. 1 house with a croft to the same adjacent called a Bank.
As relict of Roger Coulson. Rent 1s. 8d. Fine 4d.

JANNETT NIXON
23 May 12 Jac. 2 Leazes lying at the head of the croft 1 rigg of arable land lying upon Milburne Flat one other rigg of arable land lying at the end of Milbourne Flat parcel of 6 acres of land called Shellocke land.
By surrender of Andrew Poyd. Rent 2s. 6d. Fine 2s. 8d.

ELIZABETH HUMBLE
22 April 3 Car. A certain tenement or pasture called Greeneside.
As daughter and heir of Robert Humble.

Eadem
dat ut supra. One parcel of meadow lying in the water banks dale late in the possession of Robert Humble daughter and heir of the said Robert her father.
Fine 4d.
Rent for these two copyholds 2s. 7d.

JANE COLLESON
19 May 5 Car. One cottage with a garden on the backside.
By surrender of Thomas Hilcoate. Rent 4d. Fine 4d.

The names of such tennants belonging to the township of Ryton and pay the rent underwritten but have showed no deeds, evidences, coppies or other writings whereby they hold the same.

Codlin Isabell	£0. 0s. 4d.
Anne Hinde	£0. 12s. 0d.
Hopper Grace	£0. 1s. 0d.
Middleton Margarett	£0. 0s. 4d.
Newton John	£0. 5s. 0d.
Stapleton John	£0. 16s. 8d.
Sander John	£0. 0s. 4d.
Walker Jane	£0. 0s. 4d.
Ann Humble	£0. 12s. 0d.
Nicholas Newton	£0. 3s. 4d.

Here followeth the full and perfect account of the total sums of the several rents entered and charged in this Survey of Chester and which are to be collected by the Bayliff or Collectors of the several towns hereunder named and are payable at the Exchequer in Durham.

Chester in the Street £54. 15s. 8¾d.	54	15	8¾
East Boldon	35	10	5½
West Boldon	10	13	11
Whitburne	51	0	2
Cleadon	21	10	4
Ryton	27	3	6
	£200	14	0¼

Out of which is paid by patent to the Bailiffe of Chester at 26s. 8d. per annum and as keeper of Cockburne Wood at 13s. 4d. per annum In toto £2.

So the remainder de Claro is £198. 14s. 0¼d.

The improved rents of all the leased lands contained in this Survey

The 12 cavills in Chester le Streete	£51. 16s. 3d.
The ures and fleweres there	7. 0s. 8d.
Chester Mill and Bakehouse	21. 12s. 0d.
The pasture called Bedom Flatt	12. 3s. 4d.

Ryton Mill   15. 0s. 0d.
Fatherley Fields   8. 0s. 0d.
                                                    ────────────────
                                                    £115. 12s. 3d.

The Survey was taken by us

John Duncalfe
John Husband
Christopher Mickleton

SURVEY OF THE MANOR OF WHICKHAM

A true and perfect Survey made and taken of the Manor of Whickham with the appurtenances in the County of Durham by us George Lilburne, Thomas Saunders, George Grey, Samuell Leigh, amongst others appointed Surveyers by Commission from the Hon'ble Committee of Trustees for the disposal and sale of the late Bishops' lands within the Kingdom of England and Dominion of Wales by Several Ordinances of Parliament Authorised

The verdict of the Jury impannelled and sworn at the Court of Survey held at Whickham for the Manor of Whickham with the appurtenances in the County of Durham the 31st August A.D. 1647 before the Commissioners of Survey for the said Mannor held by the said Jurors delivered in Signed and sealed on the 12th October Anno supradict.

To the first Article we say That there is no Manor house or Mansion house wthin this Lordship which belongs to the Lord of the Mannor, Neither any Barnes Stables Granaryes or other houses or Tennant houses other than belongs to the Copyholders And the arrable and meadow grounds wthin the said Mannor and estimated to contain 828 acres besides Comons Moores and Waist Grounds which are not inclosed And there is at this present no groweing or standing timber upon this Mannor And for the Improvement we referr ourselves to our Verdict and Answer given to the succeeding Articles And the said Mannor is scituate about Two Miles from Newcastle which is a great Markett Towne And part of the lands and grounds do extend unto the River of Tyne which is a Navigable River which doth Ebb and Flow above the said Mannor

To the second Article we say That the severall closes or parcells of ground hereafter menconed are demeasne lands wthin the Mannor of Whickham (vzt) The Millen Meadows Containing 3 acres worth 10s. an acre p.a. one wth another besides Cole stayths therein and houses for the Staythmen to dwell in The great Midgem the Little Midgem and the Broad Meadows containing 30 acres worth 10s. an acre p.a. And also a Water Corne Milne known or called by the name of Swalwell Milne formerly letten for £16 p.a. but now quite decayed and fallen to the ground And there is also half an acre of meadow grounds belonging to the said Milne and parcell of ground above mentioned in this Article have been occupyed and injoyed by the Grand Lessees of Newcastle or their Assigns as parcell of there Grand Lease for which as we are informed Together wth other things graunted by the said house The Grand Lessees have paid to the Bishops of Durham £14. 10s. od. p.a. And we knowe of no stock of cattle to be left on any the premisses at the expiration of the Leases in being

To the Third Article we say There is not free warren or Parke within this Mannor Neither any Deere or Conyes belonging to the Lord thereof

To the fourth Article we say There are no forrein or outwoods wthin this Mannor or pastures other than are Moore and Comon belonging to the same Mannor wch Moore and Comon doth lye on the Southwestside of the Towne of Whickham wherein diverse Freeholders near adjoyning have right of Comon as belonging to their freehold lands as well as the Copyhold Tenants of the said Mannor of Whickham have, And the names of the Townefields of Whickham within which the meadow graunds arrable land and pasture do lye are comonly called and knowen by these names Morras field, the Lowfield, Whickham meadows, Dunston Westerhaugh, Matphens haugh, Coloway haugh, Eastonhaugh the High, Whitefield, Symonds Crooke, Rowlands Close, Eastfield, Easter south field, Wester southfield, Corne Moore, Wheatleys, Marshallands, Whaggs, Newfield, and Goose Moore. And the said Mannor of Whickham doth bounder as followeth (vzt) To the East upon the Water of Tame and the grounds of Furnace To the south upon a Beck called Blackbourne which divides the said Mannor of Whickham from Ravensworth Lordship And the Moore or Common called Hedley Fell To the southwest upon Ridinghouse Self field Rideing field and Greenelawe To the west upon part of Gibside grounds To the north west upon Hollingside Oxclose and Summerfield To the North upon the ground of Clockborne; Also to the North goeing Eastwards upon the grounds of Axshells till it come at Swalwell And then upon part of the ground belonging to Winlawton Lordship till it come to a Runner of Water called the Dock and part of Darwin dame to Darwin mouth And so along the River of Tyne untill it come to the River of Tame. And the said Comon or Moore is known by these severall names of Brealme, Haydons, Whinneyhill, Crosse Moore, Frances Hill, Gleaneley Hill, Talbotts greene and Longsettles. All which with Cole Carriages and other Carriages are totally spoyled wth great beaten and worne ways Except onely Talbott greene which said Comon or Moore doth conteyn in all by estymation 100 acres butt the said Comon is so straight and little that no parte thereof can be Improved or taken in wthout the great prejudice of the Tennants and Freeholders thereunto adjoyning.

To the fifth Article we say that the Lord of this Mannor hath no outwoods wthin this Mannor And therefore the tennants of this mannor can have no Pannage, Mastage or herbage there And we say that one Thomas Milburne of Newcastle is reputed to be Bayliffe of this Mannor And one Robert Laraine of Whickham is his deputy.

To the sixth Article we present That there is a Comon Fishing within the River of Tyne which the Grandlessees of Whickham and Gateside now have and is injoyed by them their Tenants or assigns as belonging to this Mannor And is of the ancient rent of £1. 13s. 4d. p.a. which is worth by year 20s. over and besides the said ancient rent.

To the seaventh article we Answer That there is no other Milne of any kind whatsoever belonging to this Mannor save only that decayed water Corne Milne mencioned in our second Article.

To the Eighth article we say That the Copyholders of this Mannor ought to grind at the said Milne if it were in repaire which now they cannot do it being utterlie decayed and fallen to the ground to the great prejudice of the said Tenants.

To the Nynth Article we present and say That there are diverse

Cole mines Cole pitts and seames of Cole within this Mannor part whereof are wrought and destroyed And other parte whereof are unwrought and in workeing by several undertenants who Clayme severall meane Conveyances from the forementioned Grandlessees of the Manor of Whickham and Gateside And the names of the particular owners or possessors of the said Mines and Coles are as followeth vzt:

Mr. Ralph Maddgson	¼ pte
Mr. Thomas Bewick	⅙ pte
Mr. Edward Mann	⅛ and $^1/_{36}$ pte
Mr. Thomas Davison	⅛ pte
Mr. John Claveringe	$^1/_{12}$ pte
Mr. Robert Shaftoe	$^1/_{12}$ pte
Mr. Henry Eden	$^1/_{18}$ pte
Mr. Robert Bewick	$^1/_{24}$ pte
Mr. Ralph Grey	$^1/_{24}$ pte

And the said Colyerye is worth to the owners thereof £2500 p.a. over and above the Rent reserved upon the whole Mannor And diverse Quarries of stone wthin the said Mannor but they are of little or no valew, nor are there any particular farmers thereof but the said Quarries are belonging to the Maior and Burgesses of Newcastle as farmors of the said Mannor or Lordship of Whickham who make the profitt of the said stone quarryes if any be And other Mynes of any sort there are none wthin this Mannor that we know of

To the tenth and Eleventh Article we say There are diverse Freeholders wthin the precincts of this Mannor or Townshipp but they do not owe their suite or service to the Mannor but are held in capite of the Bishop of Durham and pay rent to the said Bishop but not to the Maior and Burgesses of Newcastle who pretend themselves to be Lords of the said Mannor onely by virtue of the Grand Lease aforesaid

To the twelfth and thirteenth Articles we present and say There are diverse and severall Copyholders and Freeholders who do belong to and owe service to this Mannor whose names and severall rents which they pay are Contained in a Rentall herewithall returned And amounteth in all to £43. 1s. 7d. And the fynes as they pay for the same upon death or Alienacon are certain and not arbitrary And the several Fines do or will appeare upon every several Copy or admittance whereunto we referr ourselves, and to the severall Entries thereof made by the Surveyors

To the fourteenth Article we can make no further or other Present-ment or Answer Than what we have made to the first and Nynth Articles, And so for the Copyholds Tennants they are in good Repaire

To the fifteenth Article we say there are no works customs or services due for the Copyholders to do or perform to the Lord of the Mannor; save onely suite at the Halmote Court holden for the Lord at Whickham And payment of their Rents at the dayes usuall and accustomed.

To the sixteenth Article we say There are diverse Cottages within this Mannor whose names are inserted in a Rentall herewithall Returned together wth the Rents which they are to pay, which Rents are called the Smalls or small rents but they are to do no service or Customes save onely suite at the Court of the Mannor, and payment of theire severall and respective rents

To the seventeenth Article we present and say That there are diverse and severall Intacks houses and Lodges taken of and builded on the Comon and waists of this Mannor for the use of the Grand Lease Coleworks which the Grandlessees pretend they may do by virtue of their lease wthout Impeachment of waste.

To the eighteenth Article we say That the Proffitts of the Halmott Courts held within this Mannor And the Fines and Amerciaments and other the like Casualties there are of small yearely valew, and are as we beleeve worth (communibus annis) to the Maior and Burgesses of Newcastle 20s p.a. And the said perquisits are yearely collected by their Bayliffe of the said Mannor or his deputye And the same are not letten to farme at a yearely rent And the waifes and estrays did belong to the late Bishop of Durham and now by the Sherriffs Bayliffe collected and taken but of small worth, but of what valew we know not.

To the Twentyeth Article we say there is no Free warren belonging to this Mannor neither any other previledges Royaltyes Franchises, Immunities or other profitts that do of Right belong unto this Mannor, other than are before sett down to our knowledge

To the 21, 22 and 23rd Articles we present and say That the Bishop of Durham whose predecessors were anciently Lords of the said Mannor had the Right of Presentacon free gift, nomination disposition and Advowson of the Rectorye or Parsonage of Whickham And there is a Parsonage house one barn one Stable and other undertenants houses thereunto belonging And there are certein Glebelands belongeing to the Rectorye which Together wth the Tyeths thereof are worth £50 p.a. And the said parsonage house and other buildings, thereunto belonging are in good repair but the Chancell of the Church stands in need of repaire which ought to be done by Thomas Wood Dr. of Divinity now present Parson there.

To the 24th Article wee say There are neither woods nor coppies in this Mannor

To the 25th Article wee present and say That there hath been anciently paid to the Coronor of Chester Ward 22 Threaves and 2 sheaves of Oats at Michelmas onely or about that time yearly which are worth £1. 13s. 4d. p.a. but how the same becomes due we know nott And likewise there hath been anciently paid certeine hennes now called Foster hens together with 2d or 3d in monye wth any hen paid also by those who paid the same henns which were in number about 15 henns yearly And in default of any hen Then 4d. in money Together also with the said 2d. or 3d. in money worth p.a. 7s. 6d. or thereabouts.

Whickham Township Copyholds

MARGERYE JACKSON widdow relict of Richard Jackson
19 May 5 Car. One parcell of land now built upon containing in length 24 feet and in breadth 24 feet lyeing in Swalwell.
  By surrender of Henry Winshapp. Rent 8d. Fine 8d.

GEORGE YEWTON son and heir of Rich Yewton
27 October 17 Car. One cottage.

As heir to his father. Rent 3s. 4d. Fine 3s. 4d.

AGNES late wife of George Hindmires

11 May 11 Car. 6 acres of land lying in all the several fields of Whickham And also one parcell of land lying at the west end of the Town abutting upon the lands of the Rectory there containing in length 14 ells and in breadth 5½ ells.

In widdowright. Fine nihil.

MARY LEY daughter of George Ley

11 May 6 Car. 6 acres of lands (parcell of one oxgang of lands called Myntings Oxgang).

By surrender of George Watson. Rent 2s. 0d. Fine 2s. 0d.

JOHN RENETT

30 April 16 Car. One messuage late built upon parcell of a peece of land at Swalwell containing in length 40 foot and in breadth 60 foot which messuage conteineth in the whole length 10 yards.

By surrender of Thomas Morley. Rent 2d. Fine 2d.

JOHN PATTISON

6 November 34 Elz. One cottage with a garth called Hicks Garth (one half acre excepted).

By surrender of Thomas Hedworth and John Hedworth. Rent 1s. 0d. Fine 1s. 0d.

ANNE RICHARDSON

11 May 6 Car. The third parte of one Messuage near the Church.

By surrender of George Watson. Rent 4d. Fine 4d.

JAMES YOUNG

13 June 18 Jac. One house called the Whitehouse and one parcell of land adjacent containing in length 60 yards and in breadth 12 yards now in the occupation of Nicholas Watson (parcell of one messuage and 21 acres husband land).

By surrender of Robert Matfen son and heir apparent of Nicholas Matfen. Rent 1s. 0d. Fine 8d.

JAMES YOUNGE son and heir of Jane Young (vzt) daughter and heir of John Merriman decd.

4 May 2 Car. One parcell of land called Brode Puddle containing in length 11 ells and in breadth 11 ells.

As heir to John Merriman. Rent 2d. Fine 2d.

JAMES YOUNGE, younger son of James Younge

30 September 4 Car. One house adjacent on the north of a house called Whitehouse wth one parcell of land to the same house belonging containing in length 60 yards and in breadth 15 yards.

By surrender of Edward Bellaby. Rent 4d. Fine 4d.

WILLIAM NATTRES

22 May 17 Car. One house containing in length 10 ells and in breadth 6 ells with one parcell of land in length 60 ells and in breadth 12 ells (parcell of one cottage and one garth formerly in the tenure of Nicholas Matfen (except 10 ells in length and 14 ells in breadth (pcell of one house containing in length 10 ells and in breadth 6 ells) with one parcell of land containing in length 60 ells and in breadth 12 ells (parcell of one Cottage and of one garth formerly in the tenure of Nicholas Matfen (wth Wm. Atkinson held as heire of his brother Anthony).

By surrender of the said William Atkinson. Rent 4d. Fine 4d.

SUSAN CRAWFORTH relict of John Crawforth

24 May 10 Jac. One parcell of land built upon containing in length 25 yards and in bredth 16 yds of land.

By surrender of Archibold Gibson. Rent 4d. Fine 4d.

JOHN JOHNSON

12 October 20 Jac. The moytye of 2 parts of one Messuage divided into 5 parts.

By surrender of William Morley without the Ct. held at Newcastle 20. Nov. 20. Jac. Rent 1d. Fine 1d.

JOHN WHELTON son and heir of Cuthbert Whelton

5 June 8 Car. One garth of a waste now built upon in Whickham which his father Cuthbert Whelton held.

By surrender of Lancellot Mallam. Rent 1s. 4d. Fine 1s. 4d.

CUTHBERT SHAW

5 June 8 Car. The third parte of one tofte and crofte formerly Will Maynards.

By surrender of Hugh Walton gent. Rent 3d. Fine 3d.

GEORGE HARRISON in right of Anne his wife and during the minoritie of Jane and Mary Walton daughters and coheirs of Ann another daughter and heire of Richard Archer and Anne his wife A house called Woodwell house (parcell of an Oxgang of land called Mintings Oxgang).

By surrender on 19 July 12 Car. Rent 1s. 0d. Fine 1s. 0d. dat ut supra. 6 acres of arable land and meadow lying in the several fields of Whickham wth pasture for 2 beasts in the high And also pasture in the severall fields of Whickham to the said 6 acres of land belonging wch.

By surrender of Anne Archer (ut supra). Rent 6s. 8d. Fine 6s. 8d. dat ut supra. One messuage (parcell of one Oxgang of land called the Mintings Oxgangs) containing in length 22 yds and in breadth 14 yards.

By surrender of Anne Archer (ut supra). Rent 1s. 0d. Fine 1s. 0d.

STEPHEN MURREY Tutor and Gardian of Richard Murrey son and heir of Mathew Murrey during his minority
30 September 10 Car. One parcell of a messuage containing in length 18 yards and in bredth 21 yards of ground late belonging to one Messuage and 2 oxgangs of land in Whickham.

By surrender of Robert Hindmers. Rent 2d. Fine 2d.

RALPH FOWLER Marchant
10 October 14 Car. One parcell of land late of the waste of the Lord called Hadder Whaggs and one parcell of land called Wester Whaggs containing 7 acres of land.

By surrender of Nicholas Blaxton. Rent 13s. 4d. Fine 13s. 4d.

BARTHOLOMEW PESCOD Clerk son and heir of Thomas Pescod decd.
12 May 1 Jac. The moytye of 2 parts of 35 acres of land divided into 5 parts (vzt) the Moytye of 14 acres of lands.

By surrender of Mathew Matfen. Rent 5s. 3d. Fine 1s. 8d.
25 October 18 Car. One house now built containing in length 17 yards and in bredth 4 yards (parcell of the Moytye of one Tenemt.).

By surrender of William Newby. Rent 2d. Fine 2d.

GEORGE PESCOD, brother and heire of Nicholas Pescod
30 September 11 Car. One parcell of land lyeing between Swalwell
Loaning called little Parock.

As heir to his father. Rent 4d. Fine 4d.

CATHORINE now wife of Ralph Temple late widdow of George
Rudderforth
14 October 15 Car. One part of one Cottage containing in length
32 yds. and in breadth 28.

As heir to her late husband by surrender of Thomas Rudderforth. Rent 6d. Fine 6d.

EDWARD BELLARBY
12 May 16 Jac. One house wth a garth upon which is a barn lately
built (which premisses are parcell of 3 parts of one Messuage
divided into 5 parts and 3 parts of 3 acres of land divided into 5
parts late in the possession of Thomas Hollyday.

By surrender of Anthony Robson. Rent 6d. Fine 1d.

WILLIAM MADDISON tutor and gardian of Richard Home son
and heir of Richard Home deceased during his minority
25 October 7 Car. 2 parts of one cottage and a garth formerly
Richard Matfens which his said father Richard Home held.

By surrender of Cuthbert Wheldon. Rent 1s. 2d. Fine 6d.
29 March 14 Car. One parcell of land called Roberts Meadow
containing 4 acres of meadow lyinge in the territories of Whickham.

By surrender of William Tempest. Rent 1s. 4d. Fine 1s. 4d.

THOMAS GIDERYE
25 October 7 Car. One peece of ground containing in length 14
yards and in breadth 10 ells lying nigh a close of the Rectory there
(pcell of 20 ells in length and in bredth 10).

By surrender of Thomas Hurst. Rent 2d. Fine 2d.
28 May 3 Car. One parcell of land built and containing in length
25 yards and in bredth 10 yards.

By surrender of Archbold Gibson. Rent 4d. Fine 4d.

ROBERT HARRISON son and heir of Robert Harrison
12 October 21 Jac. One messuage (parcell of 7 acres of land formerly
William Stringers).

By surrender of Jane Kirsopp to his mother Elizabeth Harrison. Rent 4d. Fine 4d.

MICHAEL PESCOD

7 October 15 Car. The west part of one messuage containing 11 yards in length and 4 yards in bredth and the west part of a garth containing in length 16 yards and in bredth 11 yards And also the moytie of one garth lying in the town and territories of Whickham.

By surrender of Richard Bulman. Rent 4d. Fine 6d.

PHILLIS SHAFTOE late relict of Tho Shaftoe

14 April 18 Car. One tenement containing in length 24 yards and in bredth 6 yards of ground with a garth lying on the backside of the said tenement containing in length 24 yards and in bredth 30 yards as it is now inclosed.

In widdowright, the rent being paid by Isabell Shaftoe mother of the said Thomas deceased.

SUSAN JACKSON relict of Richard Jackson deceased

18 April 13 Car. 6 acres of land lyeing in the Fields of Whickham which her said husband held.

By surrender of George Moore and Elizabeth his wife. Fine 3s. 6d.

29 March 14 Car. 7 parts of one close in 8 parts to be divided lying nigh Rydings in Swalwell containing 2 acres of land which her said husband held.

By surrender of Christopher Clerkson. Fine 4d.

5 June 8 Car. The moytie of a moytye of one Messuage and the moytye of 30 acres of grounds in Whickham which her said husband held.

By surrender of John Kirsopp. Fine 2s. od.

30 September 10 Car. One tenement wth a Croft on the North of Whickham containing in length 40 feet lyeing opposite to the Rectorye there and 12 acres of land.

By surrender of William Dalton. Fine 3s. 4d.

20 June 20 Jac. The moytye of one Messuage and the half of 30 acres of land in Whickham which her husband held.

Fine 11d.

12 October 20 Jac. 6 acres of the Lord's land in Whickham in which Robert Kirsopp had Right which her husband held.

Fine 2s. od.

1 June 3 Car. 18 acres of land in which Thomas Liddell had right wch her husband held.

Fine 6d.

17 May 7 Car. One tenement and 9 acres of land parcell of one tenement and 15 acres of land in Whickham which her said husband held.

By surrender of William Barras. Fine 3d.

12 October 22 Car. 6 acres of land parcell of a third part of one Oxgang of land and a half lying in the town of Whickham which her husband held.

By surrender of John Dalton. Fine 3s. 4d.

THOMAS HARRISON

25 October 18 Car. The moytie of one Cottage and half a pasture gate for one beast in a Field called the High and half a pasture gate for another beast wthin Whickham.

By surrender of Nicholas Harrison. Rent 4d. Fine 4d.

ELIZABETH Relict of Richard Hodgshon

9 October 14 Car. The moytye of a third parte of a Moytye of a Moytye of 6 acres of ground And the moytye of a third parte of a moytye of a moytye of 4 acres And also the moytye of a third parte of a moytye of a moytye of one acre of land lying at the west end of the towne opposite to the tenant formerly Cuthbert Reafleys and Alice his wife.

In widdowright. Fine 4d.

dat ut supra. The moytye of a third parte of one parcell of land containing in length 20 ells and in bredth 15 ells and a third parte of a third parte of a messuage and the moytye of the 3rd parte of a moytye of another messuage formerly Cuthbert Leafleys and Alice his wife.

In widdowright. Fine 1s. od.

dat ut supra. The third parte of 6 acres of ground lying in the town and territory of Whickham And the third parte of one parcell of ground containing in length 20 ells and in breadth 15 ells formerly Cuthbert Legetts.

In widdowright. Fine 9d.

dat ut supra. The third parte of 6 acres of grounde lying in Whickham and the third parte of the moytie of a tenement of a waste in

Whickham formerly Cuthbert Legetts.

In widdowright. Fine 9d.

dat ut supra. The third parte of one Messuage and the Moytie of one Oxgang of land and the third parte of the Moytie of 6 acres of grounde and the third parte of the Moytie of 4 acres of ground in Whickham formerly her husbands.

In widdowright. Fine 2s. 6d.

dat ut supra The third parte of the moyety of one Messuage And the Moytye of a Moytye of one Oxgang of land And the third parte of the Moytye of the Moytye of 6 acres of ground and the third parte of the Moytye of the moytye of 4 acres of ground And also the third parte of the Moytye of the Moytye of one acre of ground lying at the West end of the town opposite to the tenure of Cuthbert Legetts.

In widdowright. Fine 8d.

dat ut supra. The third parte of one Messuage and the moytye of a Moytye of one Oxgang of land and the third parte of the Moytye of the Moytye of 6 acres of grounds and the third parte of the Moytye of a Moytye of 4 acres of ground And also the third parte of a Moytye of a Moytye of one Acre of ground lying at the west end of the Town against the lands late Cuthbert Legetts.

In widdowright. Fine 8d.

dat ut supra. A third parte of 6 acres of ground lying in the fields of Whickham And also a third parte of one parcell of land containing in length 20 ells and in breadth 15 ells late William Robinsons.

In widdowright. Fine 8d.

dat ut supra. One Moytye of a third parte of 6 acres of land lying in the fields of Whickham and the Moytye of a third parte of a parcell of lands containing in length 20 ells and in breadth 15 ells which her husband held.

By surrender of Edward Austin and Christabell his wife. Fine 8d.

dat ut supra. One moytye of a third parte of 6 acres of land in Whickham once Edward Austins and Christabell his wife which her husband held.

In widdowright. Fine 6d.

dat ut supra. The moytye of a third parte of a moytye of 6 acres of land and the moytye of a third parte of a moytye of 4 acres of land in Whickham once Edward Austins and Christabell his wife.

In widdowright. Fine 1s. 3d.

dat ut supra. One moytye of a third parte of one Moytye of one Messuage and the Moytye of a Moytye of one Oxgang of land And the Moytye of the third parte of the Moytye of a moytye of 4 acres of land And the Moytye of the third parte of the Moytye of the Moytye of one acre of land lyeing in the west end of the town against the lands once Edward Austins and Christabell his wife.

In widdowright. Fine 8d.

dat ut supra The moytye of the third parte of a Moytye of a messuage and the Moytye of the Moytye of an Oxgang of land And the moytye of the third parte of a Moytye of a moytye of 6 acres of land and to the moytye of one acre of land lying at the west end of the Town against the lands of the late Edward Austins and Christabell his wife.

In widdowright. Fine 4d.

dat ut supra. The one moytye of a third parte of 6 acres of land lying in the Whickham fields and the moyety of a third parte of other 6 acres of Whickham aforesaid late Cuthbert Reafleys and Alice his wife.

In widdowright. Fine 8d.

dat ut supra. The moytye of the third parte of a moytye of 6 acres of land And the moytey of the third parte of the moytye of 4 acres of land in Whickham late Cuthbert Reafleys and Alice his wife

In widdowright. Fine 1s. 3d.

dat ut supra. The moytye of the third parte of a moytye of a moytye of one Oxgang of land And the moyety of the third parte of a moyty of 6 acres of land And the moyety of the third parte of the moyety of a moyty of 4 acres of land And also the Moytye of the third parte of a moytye of a moyte of one acre of lands lying at the west end of the Town against the lands late Cuthbert Reafleys and Alice his wife.

In widdowright. Fine 4d.

dat ut supra. A 3rd parte of a moytye of one messuage And the moytye of a moytye of one Oxgang of land and the 3rd parte of a moytye of a moytye of 6 acres of land And a 3rd parte of a moytye of a Moytye of 4 acres of land And also a 3rd parte of a Moytye of a moytye of one acre of land lying at the west end of the Towne near William Robinsons land And a 3rd parte of 6 acres of land lyeing in Whickham and a 3rd parte of a Moytye of one Tenement waste in Whickham late William Robinsons in which the said

Richard Hodgson had right And also a 3rd parte of the moytye of 6 acres of land and a 3rd parte of the moytye of 4 acres of land in Whickham also late William Robinsons in which Hodgson had right.

In widdowright. Fine 3s. 11d.

ISABELL WAKEFIELD widow relict of Thomas Wakefield

22 August 33 Elz. One parcell of ground containing 4 yards in breadth and 7 in length which her husband had.

By surrender of Richard Dainey and Margery his wife. Fine 2d. dat ut supra. One messuage which her husband had.

In widdowright. Fine 4d.

6 May 3 Jac. One parcell of land containing in length 24 yards and in breadth 16 yards lying in the fields of Whickham in which her said husband had right.

By surrender of John Hall. Fine 1s. 0d.

RICHARD JACKSON

2 June 7 Car. One parcell of land lyeing in Whickham containing in length 10 yards and in breadth 9 yards and also a 3rd parte of a Toft with a croft late William Maynards (One house parcell of the premises referred) in which Will Dalton had right.

Fine 10d.

JOHN ARMSTRONG

23 May 6 Car. The half of one parcell of land in Swalwell containing in length 40 foote and in breadth 60 in which Roger Stott and his mother had right.

Rent 4d. Fine 6d.

GEORGE HERON and Jane his wife and John Thompson heir

of the said Jane One messuage containing 7 yards in length and 5 yards in breadth in Swalwell.

By surrender of John Armstrong. Rent 2d. Fine 2d.

Mem. That this fine is part of the preceeding fine.

GEORGE LEWIN

by several copies. One oxgang of land in Whickham parcell of 2 oxgangs and 6 acres of land late in the tenure of Henry Harrison in which Richard Harrison has right. And also 6 acres of land with a garth called Stackgarth which premisses with the appurtenances are parcell of 2 messuages and 2 oxgangs of land in Whickham As also one messuage and 9 acres of land parcell of one Oxgang of land And also one house now built containing in length 9 yards wth one peece of land lying to the aforesaid house containing in length 6 yards and in breadth 6 yards as also 6 acres of land parcell of a Moytye of a Messuage and a Moytye of one Oxgang of land and a half wth a moytye of one other Oxgang of land and a half And also one Messuage wth a garth on the backside of the same containing in length 20 yards.

Fine £1. 0s. 4d.

EDWARD NEWBYE and Jane his wife
30 September 11 Car. The moytye of 12 acres of land in Whickham.
Fine 4s. 6d.

GEORGE WATSON
by several copies. One messuage and one Oxgang of land in which Peter Harrison and Isabell his wife have right And also the half of 7 acres of land late William Pendreth and 15 acres of land late Thomas Cants in which Peter Harrison and Isabell had right.
Fine 13s. 6d.

ISABELL FREIND
15 October 5 Car. The half of one tenement of waste with the Moytye of one garth lying on the backside of the said tenement and belonging to the said tenement as it is now divided and possessed wch Cuthbert Freind her late husband had right.
Fine 2d.

AGNES late wife of George Harrison, daughter and heir of Thomas Matfin deceased.
15 August 13 Car. One cottage wth a garth in which Thomas her father had right.
Fine 3s. 4d.

JAMES HARRISON son and heir of George Harrison deceased
24 December 22 Car. The moytie of one messuage and 10 acres of husband land wth which Anne Harrison his mother had in widdow-right.
Fine 1s. 8d.

ROBERT HARRISON

30 September 10 Car. The moytie of two partes of one Messuage devided into 5 parts And the moytye of two parts of 35 acres of land devided into 5 parts *vzt* the Moytie of 14 acres of land which John his late father had in right.

Fine 1s. 8d.

ROGER FRAME

18 April 15 Car. One messuage containing in length 20 feet and in breadth 30 feet in Swalwell in which Thomas Morley and Isabell his wife had right.

Fine 2d.

MARY LEA widdow relict of George Lee

9 October 14 Car. 9 riggs of pasture containing 2½ acre of ground lyeing in Whitefield.

In widdowright. Fine 10d.

dat ut supra. One Messuage

In widdowright. Fine 4d.

dat ut supra. The moytye of a moytye of one messuage

In widdowright. Fine 8d.

dat ut supra. The moytye of one messuage and the moyety of one Oxgang of ground and a half And also the moyety of one other Oxgang of ground and a half.

In widdowright. Fine 10s. 0d.

dat ut supra. 6 acres of grounds parcell of 3 acres of land and one Messuage and 21 acres of husband lands.

In widdowright. Fine 1s. 8d.

dat ut supra. The third parte of one oxgang of land and a half.

In widdowright. Fine 2s. 0d.

dat ut supra. 10 acres of land parcell of 2 Oxgangs of land.

In widdowright. Fine 2s. 0d.

dat ut supra. 6 acres of land (parcell of one Oxgang of land called Mintings Oxgange.

In widdowright. Fine 2s. 0d.

dat ut supra. 6 acres of land lying in all the severall fields of Whickham formerly in the tenure of Rowland Blenkinsop.

In widdowright. Fine 2s. 0d.

RALPH BEDLINGTON

22 July 13 Car. One messuage or house and one parcell of ground

containing in length 23 ells and in breadth 23 ells in Whickham.

By surrender of Robert Merriman son and heir of Robert Merriman deceased. Fine 2d.

SYMON JACKSON son of Lancellot Jackson

13 June 18 Jac. 12 acres of land parcell of one messuage and 18 acres of land in Whickham.

By surrender of Andrew Rodham. Fine 5s. od.

JOHN CLAVERING

14 May 9 Car. A certeine peece and parcell of land in Whickham of the waste of the lord lying on the south side of Axwell between Axwell Banke and Clockburne containing 18 acres of land.

Fine 5s. od.

17 May 7 Car. One tenement and 2 Oxgangs of land.

By surrender of Lawrence Watson. Fine 9s. od.

dat ut supra. One oxgang of land.

By surrender of Lawrence Watson. Fine 3s. 6d.

18 April 13 Car. One tenement. parcell and belonging to 3 oxgangs.

By surrender of Robert Carudder. Fine 4d.

dat ut supra. The moytie of 2 parts and 18 acres of land in 3 partes to be divided formerly the lands of Marke Cocken.

By surrender of Thomas Pescod. Fine nil.

several copies. 6 acres of lands being the moytie of one Oxgang of land now in the possession of Richard Watters or his assigns in which Richard Watter late had right. And also one tenement And 2 oxgang of land in whch Richard Whelton and Isabell his wife had right And also 8 acres of land parcell of one messuage and 15 acres of land parcell of 21 acres of land As also 7 acres of land formerly William Stringows in which William Newbye had right And also 9 acres of land parcell of one oxgang of land formerly William Knocks in which Henry Hodgshon had right And also 6 riggs of land lying in the Morrifield of Whickham containing 2 acres of land in which John Crawforth had right and also one tenement. with 3 oxgangs of husbandland and 3 acres of Exchequor-land

By surrender of Ralph Robinson and Margery his wife. Fine £1. 13s. 4d.

Rent for these six copies 6s. 4d.

JAMES CLAVERINGE
24 December 22 Car. One messuage near the church and one Oxgang.
>   By surrender of John Dalton. Fine 3s. 4d.
>   Now demised to the said John.

GEORGE HARRISON youngest son of George Harrison
25 October 7 Car. One pasture in the South field and other pastures in the Ley wth the Foggish. And also one rood of meadow near the new Dyke And 1½ acres of arable land lying in 3 several fields of Whickham (parcell of two Oxgangs of land in which George Harrison, father of the said George has right.
>   Fine 1s. 4d.

ANTHONY BARRAS
18 April 13 Car. One house and a gardenne belongeing to Penderith Oxegange for the tenure of 21 years.
>   By surrender of Henry Robinson. Fine 2d.

WILLIAM HALL
23 May 12 Jac. One cottage and half a pasture gate for one beast in the Field called the Leigh As also half a pasture gate in the Average in the Fields of Whickham.
>   By surrender of Hugh Walton. Fine 4d.

ROBERT JACKSON
by several copies. 2 tenements wth 2 garths near adjoining parcell of a messuage and 15 acres of land in Whickham late Thomas Carrs And also 3 acres of land in which Lancellot Jackson father of the said Robert had right And also 12 acres of land parcell of one Messuage and 31 acres of land and one other Messuage and 15 acres of land in which Lancellot Jackson father of the said Robert had right.
>   Fine 5s. od.

ROBERT LORAINE
5 October 18 Car. One messuage with a gardeine lying on the backside One rood of land parcell of 12 acres of land In which Anthony Huetson had right.
>   Fine 3d.

MATHEW HODGSON younger son of Nicholas Hodgson
21 July 6 Car. One parcell of one Messuage containing in length
13 yards and in breadth 7 yards of ground then built and used for
a kitchin And a gardeine lying on the south side of the said messuage By surrender of Nicholas Hodgson and Elizabeth his wife,
Henry Hodgson and Jane Jackson. Ut patet in Rotie Cuo Halmott.

NICHOLAS HODGSON and Elizabeth
One messuage and one husband land (except a kilne and a garth
scituate on the North and East end of the said kilne And also
except a Court yard as it is now inclosed wth a stone wall And a
horse milne and a wind milne and 4 butts of land lying between
the same all which excepted are parcell of the Messuage and
husbandry lands).
   Fine £1. 1s. 3d.

ISABELL SHAFTOE widow and Relict of William Shafto
14 April 18 Car. One messuage 31 acres of land and one messuage
and 15 acres of land and one cottage and 4 acres of land.
   In widdowright. Fine 8s. 8d.
dat ut supra. One messuage and 2 Oxgangs of land and One messuage and 18 acres of land.
   In widdowright. Fine 10s. 8d.

KATHERINE BLAYCKLOCKE widow relict of Miles Blaick-
lock
11 June 14 Jac. A 3rd parte of a Messuage lying near the Church
And a 3rd parte of one Oxgang of land and a half in Whickham.
   In widdowright. Fine 2s. 4d.

EDWARD SURTIES
13 June 18 Jac. The half of 15 acres of land lying in Whickham.
   By surrender of Bartram Dodds. Fine 5s. 7d.

ROBERT HARDEING
12 October 22 Jac. One messuage and 21 acres of land.
   By surrender of Dorothy and Isabell Hardeing. Fine 13s. 4d.
9 October 33 Jac. One parcell of waste land upon parte whereof
there is a house built near the land called Northburne in Whickham containing 200 yards in length and 40 in breadth.

By surrender of Dorothy and Isabell Hardeing. Fine 3s. 4d.

29 March 21 Jac. One parcell of waste land upon parte whereof there is a house built lying in Whickham containing 33 yards in length and 18 in bredth.

By surrender of Dorothy and Isabell Hardeing. Fine 3s. 4d.

Rent for these three copies 1s. 0d.

WILLIAM DAWSON and Eliz. his wife

18 April 13 Car. Parcell of one Messuage containing in bredth 23 yards and in length 8 yards.

By surrender of George Carr and Elizabeth his wife. Rent 3d. Fine nil.

ELIZ DAWSON vid

20 April 16 Car. One little backhouse And the west half parte of a garth parcell of one messuage in which her husband had right while he lived.

By surrender of George Carr and Elizabeth his wife. Rent nil. Fine nil.

Mem. The Rent of this Copy is paid by William Dawson.

ELIZABETH CARR widdow relict of George Carr

4 May 2 Car. The moytye of a Messuage and the Moytye of one Oxgange of land and a half And also the Moytye of one other Oxgang of land and a half which her husband had of right while he lived.

By surrender of James Carr marchant. Fine 10s. 0d.

RALPH KENNITIE son and heir of George Kennitye

3 September 11 Car. The moytye of one Messuage.

By surrender of Edward Newbye and Jane his wife. Fine 2d.

JOHN HARRISON son and heir of John Harrison decd.

18 January 21 Jac. One cottage and 9 acres of land parcell of one Oxgang of land formerly William Knocks and 6 acres of land formerly William Martins which John his late father had in right And which Agnes the relict of John had in widdowright.

By surrender of Agnes Hodgson. Fine 3s. 4d.

9 October 4 Car. The moytye of a messuage on the west parte of a tenement now in the tenure of George Ley And the moytye of an

Oxgang of land with a gardein to the said Messuage belonging which premisses are parcell of 2 messuages and 2 oxgangs of land and 6 acres of land

By surrender of George Hodgson. Fine 3s. 4d.

14 April 18 Car. The moytye of one Messuage on the West parte of a tenement now in the tenure of George Ley wth a gardeine to the said Messuage belonging which are parcell of 2 messuages and 2 oxgangs of land and 6 acres of land.

By surrender of Robert Applebye. Fine 1s. 0d.

AGNES HODGSON now wife of William Hodgson and late wife of John Harrison deceased.

24 September 5 Jac. One cottage and 9 acres of land late William Kudes and 6 acres of land late Wm. Martins which the said John Harrison had in right while he lived.

In widdowright. Fine 3s. 4d.

WILLIAM HODGSON and Agnes his wife

31 January 4 Jac. One messuage and 15 acres of land.

By surrender of Nicholas Matfen. Fine 6s. 8d.

ELIZABETH HEDLEY widdow relict of Anthony Hedley

14 April 18 Car. One messuage and also the moytie of 12 acres of land in Whickham in which the said Anthony had right.

In widdowright. Fine 3s. 6d.

dat ut supra. The third parte of a toft with a croft late William Manners in which her late husband had right.

In widdowright. Fine 4d.

WILLIAM JOPLINGE

27 March 11 Car. One peece of land late of the Lord's waste at Swalwell Milne upon which one house is built containing in length 12 ells and in bredth 8 ells.

By surrender of William Herst and Anne his wife Samuell Hancok and Jane his wife which Anne and Jane are coheirs of John Longstaffe. Fine 4d.

ROBERT SAUNDERS

28 May 3 Car. 3 houses as it is now inclosed wth a gardeine on the

backside of the said houses containing half an acre of land late of the waiste of the lord called Wester Whaggs.

By surrender of William Porter gent. and Margery his wife. Fine 4d.

THOMAS PALMER
14 May 9 Car. The moytie of a parcell of land called the Galloway meadows lying wthin the fields of Whickham.

By surrender of Robert Porter. Fine nil.

19 May 4 Car. 3 houses lying in the town of Whickham with a gardeine belonging to the same and pasture for one beast in the Easter southmoore of Whickham.

By surrender of Cuthbert Stevenson. Fine 2d.

Rent for these two copies 2d.

JANA MATFIN late relict of Mathew Matfin and now wife of Claudius Hambleton
25 October 18 Car. One cottage and 14 acres of land late Allin Arres which the said Mathew had in right.

In widdowright. Fine 4s. 8d.

dat ut supra. The moytye of one Tenement and one Oxgange of land in Whickham which the aforesaid Mathew had.

In widdowright. Fine 6s. 8d.

14 October 15 Car. One messuage and 30 acres of land wth 3 acres of meadow and the Moyty of one Messuage and the Moytye of 24 acres of land which her husband had.

In widdowright. Fine 13s. 4d.

DOROTHY WELTON sister of Ralph Welton decd.
24 November 12 Car. One messuage with a gardein thereunto belonging and 6 small butts of land in which Ralph Whelton her brother had right.

Fine 4d.

BARBARY EMERSON vid relict of William Emerson
30 April 9 Jac. The moytye of one Messuage and 10 acres of husband land.

In widdowright. Fine 3s. 4d.

MARGARETT LEGETT vid heire of Cuthbert Legett

25 October 18 Car. The moytye of a tenement of waiste in Whickham
In widdowright. Rent 2d. Fine 2d.

MARGARETT HARRISON
9 October 14 Car. One parcell of land containing 40 yards in length and 15 yards in bredth parcell of a tenement called Doddisgreane in the South parte of Swalwell in which Thomas Walker heir of Edward Walker deceased had right.
Rent 4d. Fine 4d.

THOMAS RUTHERFORD
19 May 1 Car. One cottage in which Margarett his mother had right while she lived.
Rent 1s. 1d. Fine 1s. 1d.

JANE HARRISON wid relict of William Harrison
11 June 14 Jac. One house with a parcell of land containing in length 25 yards and in bredth 8 yards (parcell of one Oxgang called the Mintings Oxgang).
In widdowright. Rent 4d. Fine 4d.

ELIZABETH PURDIE wife of Thomas Purdie
27 October 17 Car. One peece of land containing 10 ells in length and 14 ells in bredth parcell of one house containing in length 10 ells and in bredth 6 ells wth one parcell of lands containing in length 60 ells and in bredth 12 ells pcell of one Cottage and one gardeine late in the tenure of Nicholas Matfin in wch William Atkinson brother of Anthony Atkinson deceased and brother of the said Elizabeth had right.
Rent 2d. Fine 2d.

HENRY REAFLEY
12 May 16 Jac. The moytye of one Tenement of Waist in Whickham in which Agnes Brownden, William Robinson and Cuthbert Legerd had right
Rent 4d. Fine 4d.

WILLIAM CARR and Dorothy his wife
29 March 14 Car. One peece of land containing in length 18 yards

and in bredth 14 yards parcell of one Messuage and 9 acres of land in which Richard Harrison and Charity his wife had right.

Rent 2s. Fine 2d.

GABRIELL RICE who married Mary the daughter and heir of William Craggs decd.
12 October 22 Jac. The moytye of one tenement and the moytye of one gardeine which William Craggs father of the said Mary had in right while he lived.

Rent 6d. Fine 6d.

WALTER WATSON son and heir of Lawrence Watson deceased
14 May 9 Car. The moytye of one Messuage and one Oxgang of husband land which Richard Watters his Grandfather had in right.

By surrender of Lawrence Watson. Fine 9d.
13 June 18 Jac. 4 acres of land in Whickham in which his Grandfather Richard Watters had right.

Fine 1s. 4d.

WILLIAM NEWBYE son and heir of William Newbye deceased who was son and heir of Christopher Newbye decd.
4 May 2 Car. One tenement or mansion house in Whickham lying in the east parte of the town near the Crosse late in the possession of Bartram Bowes containing in length 43 yards and in bredth 6 yards of land with one parcell of a gardeine containing in length 14 yards of land and in bredth 19 yards lying on the backside of the said Mansion House which his father had in right.

By surrender of Christopher Newbye. Fine 1s. 0d.

THOMAS DALTON son of Ralph Dalton decd.
30 April 9 Jac. One messuage wth a garden in Whickham.

By surrender of Katherine Stobbs widdow. Fine 3d.

ELIZABETH MERRIMAN widdow Thomas Merriman senior and Mary his wife and Thomas Merriman the younger
29 May 14 Car. The moytye of 15 acres of land lying in the Fields of Whickham to hold for the longest lives of them.

Fine nil.

THOMAS LAYTON
13 December 11 Car. By command of the Lord Bishop a parcell of

land called Streategate containing in length 40 ells and in bredth 20 ells upon which parcell of land there is one Cottage now built which formerly was Charles Shawe's but now in the hands of the Lord in regard no heir of kinsman in blood came to fine for the premisses a long time according to custom.

Rent 6d. Fine 6d.

dat ut supra. One parcell of land lying at the end of (*torn*) field containing ½ acre which was formerly William and Robert Morleys deceased but now in the hands of the Lord aforesaid.

Rent 2d. Fine 2d.

The Names of those persons who have not showed their coppies but pay rent p.a. as followeth

Thomas Crome gent	9s. 9d.
Richard Brimdon	3s. 3d.
Anthony Dalton	4s. 0d.
Idem Anthony	4s. 6d.
William Hirst	2d.
Alexander Blenkinsopp	1s. 0d.
Robert Drydon	4d.
William Atcheson	6d.
John Swann	4d.
Jane Stott	6d.
Robert Anderson gent and his heires	1s. 4d.
William Smith	14s. 0d.
William Godskirke	4d.
Taylor Flowse	3d.
William Huntley gent.	6d.
Jeffrey Rickas	3d.
Mathew Harrison	3d.
Mr. George Lumley	6d.
	————
	£2. 1s. 9d.

Memorandum

That we do find at the present That there are 15 Cole Pitts on work or agoing within this Mannor of Whickham which we do valew at £20 p.a. for every several Pitt over and above the Rent aforesaid in the Grand Lease And we do find That those seames

and veynes of Cole that are now wrought are farr from the River
of Tyne And are wrought very near to the utter bounder And in
our judgment cannot continue and last to afford Coles to the end
or expiration of the present lease But we do find upon view, That
there is another Seame or veyne of Coles, under that Seame or
veyne of Coles which is now wrought: And the said last menconed
Seame or veyne of Coles is already won and wrought near unto the
said River of Tyne And is like to be of Long Continuance And we
do to the best of our judgement grounded upon view and full
information taken, Estymate the said Collyerye after the expiration
of the Grandlease in being, To be yearely worth in Reversion to be
purchased the summe of £1800

Memorandum
Whereas in some Coppyes entered and returned it is said such a one
holdeth such a Messuage or land but no return is made of the date
of the Copy of year of our Lorde The reason is because the present
Tenants who occupy the said lands never yet came to take up the
said lands by Coppy in Court: But we findeing them possessed
thereof do return them as tenants (as in truth they ought to be)
according to the old Copyes The old rents reserved least both
the rents and tenures should be left to the State.

Memorandum
We entered the Copy of Agnes Hindmers and of Philyp Shaftoe
nakedly as they are for findeing therein neither Cesse imposed or
rent returned we suppose it to have been the ommission of the
Steward

Memorandum
Whereas the Jury say there are many Quarryes of stone within this
Mannor But of small or no valew none of them being in lease:
We say This whole Mannor standeth on stone And although every
one wthout controul (for ought we knowe diggeth what him lusteth)
yet we valew the said Quarries worth (Communibus annis) after
the expiration of the grand Lease 20s.
Item we valeiw the Perquisites of the Halmott Courts wthin this
Mannor yearely worth £1. 10s. od.
And the waifes and Estrays p.a. worth 3s. 4d.

Memorandum

That the 6s. 8d. upon John Claverings Esq. is an increase of rent for a new Improvement made, and is not parte of the £30 p.a. Grand Rent essuing out of the Townshipp of Whickham for the 828 acres of copyhold land

Memorandum

Whereas the Jury in their Answer to the 10th and 11th Articles affirme That there are diverse Freeholds within the Precincts of this Mannor which owe suite or service hereto: but do hold of the late Bishop in capite: We say that no deeds Evidences Offices or Liberates upon the death of any such tenants were produced to us (although we have done our utmost to discover the same) that might demonstrate such tenures or Rents

But we think the said lands if any such be are holden in capite And the Rents payable into the Exchequor att Durham as aforesaid, and will be found (as parte thereof) amongst the Regalia.

Memorandum

Whereas in diverse Copyes returned there is no expression of Rent certeine referred: but these words (inter alia) used The reason is, because the Copyes themselves run so And it is to be understood That they are part of the £30 p.a. Grand Rent payable for the Messuages and the 828 acres of Copyhold land within the said Mannour altogether with the Smalls

(Part of page missing)

Memorandum

Whereas in many Copyes the Rent annuall is greater than the fine or Cesse and in others the Rent lesse than the fine: yet it appeares by Ancient Coppyes that by the Custom of the said Mannor the Fine or Cess is and hath bene Certeine as to each particular estate beyond the memory of man.

Memorandum

That that part of the Demeasne lands called the Mill meadows estimated by the Jury at 3 acres upon our view we estymate to be 7 acres whereof there is about 3 acres in grass ground unspoyled which we valew to be well worth p.a. £3 And the residue of the

said Mill Meadows is for the most parte imployed for Stayths to lay
Coles on by the Occupyers of the Grand Lease which said occupyers
of the Grand Lease do lett 3 keele roomes there for Carriage of
Coles to one Mr. Cole of Newcastle for £3. p.a. And we do estimate
that parcell of ground called the Mill Meadows for the use of
Staithes when the Grand Lease is expired to be worth in toto p.a.
£15 And for the ground called Great Midgham, Little Midgham
and the broad meadow which the Jury hath estymated at 30 acres
and have valewed them at 10s. an acre p.a. are with another (*part
missing*) say upon our view They conteine 42 acres—value one wth
another at 15s. an acre £31. 10s. 0d.

(*Part of page missing*)

Memorandum
That of the £117. 15. 8d. Rent referred to the late Bishops out of
the Mannors of Whickham and Gateshead there is no Estimation
of how much Rent is issueing for the one or the other: But that
the Newcastle men: receave as much yearly as will discharge that
everye Rent (what ever it is) vide the Copyhold Rents and free rents
returned As also the Rents and improvements made of the demeasne
lands.

Memorandum
The Towne of Newcastle or their Leassees are subtenants for the
Grand Lease of the Collyeryes did never produce to us any deeds
of Assignment or other writeings to demonstrate their present estate
therein But onely produced to us a copy of the Original Lease from
Bishop Barnes to the late Queene Elizabeth (a copy of which we
ourselves had produced befour) So that

(*Part of page missing*)

Memorandum
We have in this our Survey to our best skill and discovery valewed
all woods rents services customes Canons Fines forfeitures Royaltyes
Fishings fowlings, waifes Estrayes Courts Baron and Courts Leet
And all other possessions and hereditaments whatsoever withall and
every there appurtenances of what nature or quality soever (except
Jura Regalia) which at any time (*missing*) Tenn years before the

beginninge of this present Parliament were belonging to the late Bishop or Bishops of Durham which he or they held or injoyed as parcell or parte of the said Mannor in Right of his or their Bishopricks dignity or office respectively.

SURVEY OF THE MANOR OF GATESHEAD

Manerium
de Gateshead
cum Membris

A true survey made and taken of the Mannor of Gateshead with the appurtenances in the County of Durham by us Sir George Lilburne, George Grey, Thomas Saunders, Samuell Leigh, John Husband amongst others appointed surveyors by Commission from the honourable Committee of Trustees for the Disposal and sale of the late Bishop's lands within the Kingdoms of England and Dominion of Wales by several ordinances of Parliament Authorised.

A presentment made by the Jury chosen impanelled and sworn by the Commissioners of Survey for the late Bishop of Durham's lands within the Mannors of Gateshead and taken the 11th October A.D. 1647.

To the first Article we present and say that there is no mannor house within this precinct except one house for the farmer to dwell in, which is built with clay and thatched and no timber growing or other things required in this Article that we know of.

To the second Article we present that there are demeasne lands belonging to this mannor called by the name of Gateshead Park (which is part of the Grand Lease of the mannor of Gateshead and Whickham demised by Richard Barnes late Bishop of Durham to the late Queen Elizabeth and now in the immediate possession of George Johnson yeoman), as followeth vzt. In pasture grounds

150 acres worth 5s. an acre per annum, Item in meadow ground 50 acres being in 6 closes worth 6s. 8d. an acre per annum; Item in arable land 150 acres being in 6 closes worth 5s. an acre per annum; which are all of a strong clay ground, but the several names of these closes we know not. Item more of grounds called the Salt Meadows containing 30 acres worth 6s. per annum an acre; which is in the possession of Thomas Wilkinson Shipwright. Item the Broomehill and Hassocks containing 50 acres worth 6s. an acre per annum And is now in the possession of the Grand Lessees, several tennants and assignes. Item 2 meadow closes, one corne close, and 3 small pasture closes containing 30 acres in the several tenures and occupations of Lieutenant Colebury, John Swann and John Newham worth 6s. an acre per annum. Item one corn close called Ectors Close containing 6 acres worth 5s. per acre per annum in the occupation of William Coale or his assigns; Item one small close containing 1½ acres in the possession of Thomas Potts Cordiner worth 13s. per annum. Item one other small close containing 1½ acres in the possession of John Newham worth 15s. per annum. Item 5 keel rooms at Trunck Staithe and 4 keel rooms at the Redhaugh Staithe in the occupation of Sir Thomas Liddell gent. or his assigns worth yearly 40s. Item 4 keel rooms at the Newstaithe in the occupation of Mr. Leonard Car and Mr. Ralph Cole or their assignes, yearly worth 16s. Item one Ballast shore on or adjoining to the Salt Meadows aforesaid in the possession of the Mayor and Burgesses of Newcastle-upon-Tyne who yearly receive Benefit of it and is part of their Grand Lease the yearly value whereof at present is £10 Communibus annis. At the east end whereof there is one house in John Thompson's possession worth 10s. p.a. Item one other house in (*space*) Harrison's possession worth 10s. per annum. Item one house in the possession of Fevell Nicholson worth 13s. per annum. Item one house in the possession of Henry Ord worth 7s. per annum. Item one house in the possession of Thomas Gibson worth 15s. per annum. Item one house in the possession of Thomas Wilkinson worth 20s. per annum. Item one house called Park Staithe house in the possession of widdow Elliner worth 10s. (house and stack) per annum. Item one house in the possession of Thomas Smith worth 13s. 4d. per annum. And more houses and buildings upon the premisses we know not of all which are in the possession of the Mannor and Burgesses of Newcastle, their tennants, farmers, servants or assigns, and they enjoy the premisses mentioned as

parcel of the Grand Lease of Gateshead and Whickham aforesaid; *Item* there are also farmers of several houses and shops built upon Gateshead Bridge over the River of Tyne who hold by the lease from the Bishop of Durham and pay several rents for the same at their Exchequor at Durham, and not to the Grand Lease. As for the several commencements and expirations of the annual rents referred upon the said leases, we refer ourselves to the said leases: And upon view of each several house and shop, we present and say there is one shop belonging to Mr. John Gibson and Mary his wife and is worth 15s. per annum. Item to the said shop on the north part there is adjoining one house and shop belonging to Mr. Thomas Arrowsmith whereof Luke Dobson is the immediate tennant and is worth 20s. per annum. Item adjoining to the northwards there is one other shop wherein John Taylor tradeth worth yearly 5s. Item there is one house and three shops more belonging to Henry Swalwell Cordiner which are worth 20s. per annum. Item there is one other shop belonging to Henry Awder worth 10s. per annum. Item there is one house or chamber with two shops under it belonging to John Gilbert worth 20s. per annum. Item there are two shops and a chamber above them in the immediate occupation of Thomas Turner Cordiner and are worth 20s. per annum. Item there are two shops to the northwards still adjoining in the immediate possession of Francis Farrowe and are worth 13s. per annum. Item there is next to the northwards one shop in the immediate possession of Mr. John Lobett and is yearly worth 10s. Item there are three shops more and a chamber above to dwell in belonging to the said Mr. Gibson and Mary his wife and yearly worth 20s. Item one shop with a room above in Richard Errington's possession worth 10s. per annum. All which are situated upon the westernmost side of the Bridge: but these next ensuing are built upon the easternmost side of the said bridge and are named from the Blewstone successively to the southwards. Item there is one shop and a house wherein Mr. John Gailes now dwelleth worth 10s. per annum. Item there are two shops belonging to Mr. William Henderson worth 10s. per annum. Item there are two shops belonging to Nicholas Wilkinson worth yearly 10s. Item there is one shop and a chamber above it belonging to Lawrence Foster worth 20s. per annum. Item there is a shop in the possession of Richard Swalwell worth 3s. 4d. per annum. Item there is one shop and a chamber above it in the immediate possession of Christopher Sanderson worth 12s. per annum. Item there is a shop with a little room above it in the present possession of Stephen Dunnworth 13s. 4d. per annum. Item there is one shop and a dwelling room over it in Nicholas Wilkinson's possession worth 15s. per annum. Item there is one shop with a chamber above it in the possession and tenure of Thomas Polk Cordiner worth 20s. per annum. Item there is one shop and a room to dwell in above belonging to the aforenamed Mr. Thomas Arrowsmith whereof Mr. Gosse was lately tennant worth 20s. per annum. And there is one shop and a house belonging to Mr. John London, and whereof one Mr. Smith is the immediate tennant and is worth 20s. per annum. And these are the shops and houses that we know of

To the third Article we present and say that there is no park warren nor sheepwalk other than the park formerly mentioned in the second article. Neither are there any deer or coneyes therein or timber growing thereupon so far as we know

To the Fourth Article we present and say that there are no outwoods nor commons within this mannor excepting one common or waste called by the name of Gateshead Fell. The common or herbage whereof belongs to the freeborough men and freemen of the said mannor and borough of Gateshead: containing 1300 acres or thereabouts.*
And we say that the Lord of the mannor cannot improve any part of the same but with the consent of the said freeboroughmen and the freeholders of Gateshead aforesaid

To the fifth Article we present and say that there is no mastage pannage or herbage in the outwoods of this mannor (for there are none) nor anything else in this article presentable.

To the sixth Article we present and say that there is a fishing belonging to the grand lessees, whereof John Chambers is the immediate tennant, And he pays the annual rent of 5s. which is the full value thereof yearly at Rack as we conceive and nothing else in this article presentable.

---

*For a description of the boundaries of Gateshead, vide p. 140

To the seventh Article we present and say that there is one water corn mill called Rocks Mill in the immediate possession of Thomas Wilkinson with a lane or pasturage thereunto belonging and is worth to be let 40s. per annum at the Rack and no more And also one house adjoining thereunto Richard Burrell being the immediate tennant and at the Rack is worth 2s. per annum. And also one wind mill standing on the waste or lane called Wind Mill Hill whereof John Clarke is the immediate tennant and farmes the farm of the Grandlessees and at the Rack is yearly let for 40s. per annum.

To the eighth Article we present and say that the tennants of this mannor are not bound to grind at those mills but where they please themselves.

To the ninth Article we present and say that there are no Boylouries of Salt within this mannor but there are mines of coal and stone within this mannor but not opened or wrought; save only one coal pit lying at a place called Chowden before mentioned, which is wrought by one Mr. Roger Liddell; And the same colliery doth belong to the Grand Lessees and is worth (communibus annis) 40s. per annum; And there is one stone quarry upon Gateshead Fell aforesaid, which also belongs to the Grand Lessees and is farmed by the Maysons of Newcastle who pay £6 rent per annum at the Rack for the same to the Mayor and Burgesses of Newcastle aforesaid.

To the tenth Article and the Eleventh Article we present and say that there are many freeholders or freeboroughmen living within the Borough of Gateshead aforesaid and within the precincts of this mannor who hold several messuages, burgages and tenements freely in burgage tenure there and do owe suit to the Borough Court (which is holden by and in the name of the Mayor and Burgesses of Newcastle as farmers thereof) within the said mannor And do pay certain rents called by the name of land males which amount to and are worth 15s. per annum and no more as we are informed and the Sub-bailiff collects them; But upon death of any tennants or alienation the said boroughmen pay no Harriott or Relief at all to the Lords by their custom.

To the twelfth, thirteenth, fourteenth and fifteenth Articles we present and say that there are no copyholders nor customary tennants belonging to this mannor nor any lands so held within the same that we know of.

To the sixteenth Article we present and say that there are no cotters nor cottages belonging to this mannor, other than burgages whereunto we have answered in the tenth article.

To the seventeenth Article we present and say that there are no inclosures intacks or inchroachments within this mannor, but only two houses built near to Darwin Crooke and upon the common or wastes of Gateshead aforesaid they were built by Mr. Roger Liddell about 10 years ago which are worth 20s. per annum. at the Rack and no more, but they pay no rent to the Lord of this Mannor.

To the eighteenth Article we present and say that although at this present there are no faires nor market days usually kept within this mannor of Gateshead more at one time than another, nevertheless we are informed and do verily believe that formerly there hath been both fairs and markets kept there (vzt) the market days were twice weekly, and the fair days were twice yearly and there is a tollbooth or townshowse there standing And there are (as we are informed) records extant to prove the same, And the late Bishop of Durham did take tolls within the said town of Gateshead within this twelve years past. But the Mayor and Burgesses of Newcastle (as we are informed) do now take the said tolls but by what right we know not For that the said tolls fairs markets are no part of the Grand Lease but are amongst other Royalties (as we are informed) referred by the above mentioned Bishop Barnes from forth the said lease made to the late Queen Elizabeth as aforesaid to which lease for more certainty we referr ourselves, And as for the yearly value of the said tolls belonging to the late Bishop what they amount to we know not.

To the nineteenth Article we present and say that there is a Borough Court holden in Gateshead Tolebooth yearly The profits whereof are recieved by the Mayor and Burgesses of Newcastle-upon-Tyne as being part of the Grand Lease aforesaid or by their Bayliff for the time being And they are worth (communibus annis) 20s. per annum. The Subbayliff collects them; But as for waife estrayes or other casualtyes in this article mentioned we say they did belong to the late Bishop of Durham but the value thereof is very little and altogether uncertain.

To the twentyeth Article we present and say that there is no free warren or other liberties belonging to this mannor That we know of but such as are formerly mentioned.

To the one and twentyeth Article we present that the Bishops of Durham had formerly of Right the free gift, nomination disposition and advowson of this rectory (but now there is no Incumbent) except one Mr. Cuthbert Stott who is elected by the mass of the Parish, and doth preach and supply the place at present). And there hath been a parsonage house with houses necessary, but they are pulled down by the Scotts souldiers in the time of war And there are Gleebe lands belonging thereunto (vzt) 2 acres or thereabouts near Saltwell side in the possession of Thomas Sturfield worth 40s. per annum at the Rack. Item the closes with wayleave in the possession of Barronett Liddell worth 53s. 4d. per annum at the Rack And a small parcel of ground called the Parson's Flatt worth 3s. 4d. per annum.

To the two and twentyeth Article we present and say that there are tyeths belonging to this parsonage of corn Hay, and all other things tythable and are worth £64 per annum (communibus annis).

To the three and twentyeth Article we present and say that the Parsonage house is no mannor house of itself and is ruined aforesaid And the chancell of the church is not in repair but is ready to fall down.

To the four and twentyeth Article we say that there are no woods or copyces within this mannor, and therefore not measurable.

To the five and twentyeth Article we present that there is an hospital worth £40 per annum whereof the Parson is patron and master, out of which three Beedmen recieve yearly £20 And there is also allowed to the Bayliff of Gateshead (for the time being) the salt meadow aforementioned as a fee for his place and office yearly And there are no other reprisals pentions or payments issuing out of this mannor That we know of, but such as are mentioned in the Grand Lease aforesaid, to which we refer ourselves.

Gateshead Bridge Leaseholds

HENRY ALDER
6 October 15 Car. One shop scituate and being on the second pillar of Tynebridge upon the west side thereof.
    For 21 years. Rent 2s. od. Improvement 15s. od.

WILLIAM HENDERSON
18 September 11 Car. Wast or vacant place containing half a Bow lying and being on the east side of Tynebridge betwixt a house of Henry Lawsons on the north and the vacant place (containing the other half of the said Bow) demised to William Noble on the south together with full power and authority to build thereupon house and houses shop and shops.
    For 21 years. Rent 2s. od. Improvement 15s. od.

JOHN GILBERT
11 May 11 Car. Peece or vacant place lying and being upon the south end of Tynebridge containing the breadth of half an arch and is boundered on the west side of the said bridge between a shop of William Ellinor's on the south and a shop of Robert Fosters on the north together with free libertie to build house or houses, shop or shops.
    For 21 years. Rent 2s. od. Improvement 30s. od.

HENRY SWALWELL tutor and guardian of John, Jane and Margery Swalwell, children of Thomas Swalwell during their minority
7 July 11 Car. Moietie and north part of a bow on the west side of Tynebridge betwixt a house of Robert Fosters on the north and a house of John Gilberts on the south together with full libertie to build house or houses shop or shops.
    For 21 years. Rent 2s. od. Improvement 20s. od.

(THOMAS SWALWELL) ANNE HAUKESWORTH widdow and Henry eldest son of the said Anne, scrivener

9 August 14 Car. Waste and vacant place containing one Bow on the westside of Tynebridge between a house in the tenure of Robert Forster or his assigns on the south and a house in the tenure of James Henderson on the north together with authority to build thereupon house or houses shop or shops.

For 21 years. Rent 4s. od. Improvement 15s. od.

NICHOLAS WILKINSON assignee of Lawrence Foster
22 June 17 Car. Messuage or tenement late in the occupation of Michael Goodyear and Nicholas Goodyear 14 September 13 Car. on the east side of the south end of Tynebridge containing in length from south to north 6 yards and bordereth upon a tenement now belonging to the said Lawrence Foster on the north and a tenement belonging unto Thomas Potts on the south

Rent	4s. od.
One fat hen at Martinmas	1s. od.
	5s. od. Improvement 20s. od.

Idem
Nicholas assignee of John King who was assignee of William Noble 12 May 13 Car.
1 February 11 Car.
13 June 11 Car. Waste or vacant place on the eastside of Tynebridge containing the full south part or moitie of one bow betwixt a shop of Robert Foster on the south and a house of Henry Lawson's on the north.

Rent 2s. od. Improvement 15s. od.

Idem
Nicholas Wilkinson assignee of John Gilbert
30 November 19 Car. Moitie of the west side of the pillar and loop mentioned in two several Indentures of lease made from John Bishop of Durham 14 September 1630 and from the Mayor and Burgesses of Newcastle 25 September 7 Car.

For 21 years. Rent 6d. Improvement 5s. od.

HENRY SWALWELL assignee of Richard Swalwell
8 May 17 Car.
6 July 9 Car. House tenement and shop wherein the said Henry

then dwelt and is built upon a part and parcel of the said waste ground on the west side of the south end of Tynebridge.

Rent 4s. od. Improvement 30s. od.

Idem
assignee of idem by his last will and testament
7 July 11 Car. Waste vacant place containing half a bow lying on Tynebridge between a house of Robert Fosters on the south and a shop of Robert Fosters on the north with liberty to build house and houses.

For 21 years. Rent 2s. od. Improvement 15s. od.

LAWRENCE FOSTER

14 September 13 Car. One messuage or tenement on the east side of the south end of Tynebridge being the northwest house upon that part of the said bridge adjoining to a tenement now or late in the tenure of Robert Foster or his assignees And also one other messuage or tenement standing and being on the east side of Tynebridge in the tenure of Michael Goodyear and Nicholas Good-yeare

Rent	5s. od.
Rent	4s. od.
A fat hen for either at Martinmass	2s. od.
	11s. od.

Improvement £1. 15s. od.

Idem LAWRENCE
20 September 6 Car. Messuage or tenement on the east side of the south end of Tynebridge adjoining to the tenement of Robert Forsters.

For 21 years. Rent 4s. od. Improvement £1. 10s. od.

THOMAS POTTS

23 November 9 Car. Messuage or tenement on the east side of the south end of Tynebridge.

For 21 years. Rent 4s. od. Improvement £1. 13s. od.

THOMAS ARROWSMITH

23 January 15 Car. One shop situate and being on the first pillar of Tynebridge upon the west thereof.

For 21 years. Rent 2s. od. Improvement 15s. od.

JOHN GIBSON in right of Mary his late wife who overlived Robert Forster

1 June 10 Car. One messuage or tenement and a shop situate on the west side of Tynebridge.

For 21 years. Rent 4s. od. Improvement £1. 10s. od.

JOHN LONDON

10 October 15 Car. One tenement on the east side of the south end of Tynebridge adjoining to a tenement late in the occupation of Robert Beckwith on the south and the tower upon the same bridge.

For 21 years. Rent 3s. od. Improvement £1. 10s. od.

JOHN GIBSON and NICHOLAS WILKINSON

14 September 1630. Moitie of a shop on the west side of Tynebridge adjoining to the Blewstone The lease whereof is taken in the name of Henry Lambton but not produced.

Rent 2s. od. Improvement £1. os. od.

JOHN GIBSON

13 Car. Two small shops (as they are divided) formerly they were but one on the west side of Tynebridge which Fra Farrer Clother and Fra Milburne Cordiner now occupy which shop apptaines to the said John Gibson in the right of Mary his wife late wife to Robert Foster (the lease itself is not produced but said to be taken away by the Scotts).

Rent 4s. od. Improvement £1. 6s. 8d.

HENRY LAWSON

14 September 6 Car. 2 pieces of voyd ground lying upon the pillar of Tynebridge where the blewstone dividing the lymitts and bounds of Newcastle and the County and Bishoprick of Durham is placed on the west side of the said pillar ten foot and the east side sixteen foot (another small part of which said two pieces of voyd ground by the said division appertaineth to the Mayor and Burgesses of Newcastle) with liberty for the said Henry Lawson to build at his own cash shop and shops or houses A provision that if the said Bishop shall occasion (for the repair of the bridge) to pull down the

said houses, it shall be lawfull for him to do, but then the said Bishop is to build them up again at his own cost and charge.

For 21 years. Rent 2s. od. Improvement £1. os. od.

THOMAS ARROWSMITH

23 January 15 Car. Tenement situate on the south end of Tyne-bridge and also the tower end of the said bridge unto the said house adjoining and all the rooms breadth and height thereof together with the Arch and all houses with the key and staith belonging unto the said house and the iron chain fixed to the said tower.

For 3 lives—

Ralph Graie of Newcastle then 13, said Thomas Arrowsmith then 33, John Ewbanck son of Thomas Ewbank. All in being

Rent	4s. od.
One capon or	2s. od.
	6s. od.

Improvement £2. 10s. od.

JOHN CLERKE of Bowdon Co. Durham, Milne Wright

4 September 21 Car. from the Mayor and Burgesses of Newcastle-upon-Tyne. All that site place or plot of ground upon Gateshead hill where formerly a windmill did stand late in the tenure of Mathew Chapman deceased. The said John Clerke within one year after the date of the said lease at his own costs and charge to erect build and set up upon the site aforesaid one strong and sufficient windmill fitt for grinding And at his own cost and charge during the said term shall repair and maintain whole and keep the same. And at the end of the said term shall, so well and sufficiently repaired and maintained upheld and kept, leave and yield up to the said Mayor and Burgesses of Newcastle.

For 21 years from Michaelmas next ensuing. Rent £2. os. od. Improvement £2. os. od.

Salt Meadow Lease

Cuthbert late Bishop of Durham by Indenture of lease 18 March 1 Phil. and March did demise grant and to farm let to Cuthbert Ellison then mayor and the Burgesses of the town of Newcastle-upon-Tyne and their sucessors all that his piece of ground or meadow called Salt Meadow containing 34 acres of ground in the County of Durham, near the same town of Newcastle. And also all that his part of the water and River of Tyne straight over thereto for and against the said Salt Meadow only. And the soil and ground covered with the same as it lyeth And is within the said County of Durham And other kinds of profits and comodities which may be taken leyved or recieved of the same water or river directly over thereto for and against the Salt Meadow only doth stretch and extend (The fishing only excepted) Together with a way to be appointed and assigned for all manner of persons and conveyance of merchandise wares and other things whatsoever from the said meadow called Salt Meadow to the High Street of the town of Gateshead and from the said High Street to the said Town of Gateshead to the said meadow called the Salt Meadow, And did also grant to the said Mayor Burgesses all and all manner of toll of that his town of Gateshead to be from henceforward levyed gathered and taken up of or for any every kind of merchandise wares and things whatsoever tollable within the precincts liberties and jurisdictions of the same town of Gateshead or anywhere else in the Bishopric of Durham Habend from the feast of Easter then next ensuing for 150 years And so from after the end of the said term of other 150 years then next following and so from 150 years to 150 years during the full term and end of 450 years fully to be complet and ended paying yearly to the said Bishop and his successors for the said Salt Meadows 44s. And for the said toll of Gateshead for themselves and all others £4. 6s. 8d. at the feast of Easter and Michaelmas by equal portions

The Grand Lease

Huiuersis xpi fidelibus pnts bras inspectur Deccanus et Captlm Dunelm Cathis ecclie Xpi et Ste. Marie Virginie salutem in dieo Salvatores Noverint universitae iura nos bras Reverendi in xpo pris et domino Dni Richard dei grat Dunelm epi sub eo quis sequitur verborn tenore inspexisso.

This Indenture made 26 April 24 Elz. between our said Sovereign Ladie the Queen's Majestie on the one part And the Reverend Father in God, Richard by the sufferance of God Bishop of Durham on the other part Witnesseth that the said Reverend Father for diverse great cause and consideration him moving hath given granted demised and to farm letten and by these presents for him and his successors doth give graunt demise and to farm let unto our said Sovereign Lady the Queen's majesty. All those his Mannor lordshipps town and borough of Gateshead in the county of Durham and also all mannor houses edifices buildings barns stables orchard gardens wood underwood milnes mynes quarries moors marshes watesground waters fishing watercourses borough courts perquisitts and said demised and demisable by Copy of Court Roll and all the rent fines and services of the Copyholders and Copyhold lands and also of all the Freeholders and Freehold lands tenements rents and services which are holden of the said Bishop and belonging unto him within the said Mannor town borough and Lordship aforesaid or any of them And also all goods and chattells and fellons and fugatives, fellons of themselves goods of persons outlawed or p'nt in exigent good valued estrayed deedands and forfeitives which shall happen chance or fall within the said mannor Lordship town and places aforesaid or any of them And all fines issues and amerciaments from time to time taxed, affered, set or assessed of or upon any person or persons of by reason touching or concerning any offence of offences whatsoever which shall hereafter be had committed suffered or done within the said Mannor town or Lordship and places aforesaid or any of them And also all the mines of coals as well opened as not opened or already found or hereafter to be sought for rents and sums of money whatsoever heretofore reserved or agreed to be paid to the said Bishop and his predecessors for wayleave in and upon the said premisses mentioned to be demised or any part thereof And all easements perquisits ways commodities advantages and hereditans whatsoever of the said Bishop of what nature kind or quality soever the same be situate lying and being or which heretofore have been used had or enjoyed within the Mannor Lordship towns borough fields hamletts precincts or circuite of Gateshead also Gateshead and Whickham aforesaid or in either of them (except and always foreprised and reserved out of the present Lease) and grant all the liberties and royalties as well of the County Pallatine of Durham and such other rights liberties, jurisdiction power to hold pleas and perogative Royall of the said Bishop and Bishoprick and of the Chancellor Judges Justices Ministers Officers of the said County Pallatine for the time being in the said towns lordships and places of Whickham and Gateshead aforesaid which are not before granted or mentioned to be granted by those presents And except also so much of the Tyne Bridge as is situate standing and being within the said Town Borough or precincts of Gateshead aforesaid and the soil and ground of the same and all houses and edifices thereon erected and built and the toll there used to be taken And also excepted and foreprised out of this present lease and grant all and every the Sheriffe terme fines of Alienation without licence And all Wardships primar seasons of land tenements within the County Pallatine of Durham and lying within the said town and lordship of Gateshead and Whickham And also foreprised and excepted out of this present gift grant and demise the advance and patronage and right to collate and present unto the two parsonages of Gateshead and Whickham and either of them when and how often the same or either of them shall happen or chance to be vacant during the whole and full term of this present grant or demise And because there be diverse customary and copyhold lands and tenements parcel of the demised premises which cannot be kept continued and preserved as copyhold tenants without some Court at which the copyholders of the same may as well surrender their interest as take forth of the Lord's hands their said copyhold lands and tenements which by the special custom there used may be if our said Sovereign Lady shall have of the grant of the said Bishop any one Court whereat the said copyholds have use to take their said copyhold lands and tenements Therefore the said Richard now Lord Bishop of Durham hath granted and for him and his successors by these presents do grant to our said Sovereign Lady one Court commonly called an Halymote or Hallimotte Court to be holden by the stewards of her Majestie and her assignes in Gateshead or Whickham aforesaid at which the said tenants or copyholders shall or may surrender and take the said copyhold land and tenement to have and to hold the said mannor lordship towns boroughs land tenements meadows feedings woods underwoods mynes quarries rent revercons services hereditaments and other the premisses whatsoever mentioned to be demised and granted by these presents (except before excepted) unto our said Sovereign Lady the Queen's most Excellent Majestie and her assignes from the making of this present indenture of lease and demise unto the full end and term of fourscore and nineteen years from thence next ensuing fully to be completed and ended without impeachment of any mannor of waste yielding and paying therefore yearly at or in the Exchequor of Durham during the said term of 99 years to the said Bishop and his successors the yearly rent of

£117. 15s. 8d. of lawful money of England at the Feast of Pentecost called Whitsunday and St. Martin the Bishop in Winter by even portions And the said Reverend father for him and his successors doth grant to our said Sovereign Lady that she and her assigns shall and may during the said term digg, take carry away and convert to her and their own use all and every the mines as well as coals as other things in the said land tenement and hereditament before demised as well such as be now opened and found as also such as are not yet opened or found and shall and may dig the same and do all other things in and upon the same grounds and premisses for the finding and getting of them and every or any of them in witness whereof as well the said Bishop hath to the said Indenture set his seale as our said Sovereign Lady the Queen's Majestie hath caused her great seal of England to be annexed the day and year above expressed.

This lease was confirmed by the then Dean and Chapter of Durham the 15th October 1583, 25 Elz.

Memorandum
That of the ground called Gateshead Parke mentioned in the presentment of the Jury in their Answer to the second Artical estimated to contain 150 acres in pasture 150 acres more in arrable and 50 acres in meadow all in the occupation of George Johnson, we do estimate the premises to contain about 420 acres and we do value them worth (communibus annis) to be letten £200. os. od.

Memorandum
That the grounds called Hassocks and Broomehill same Article mentioned together with a meadow close, called Elliman Close which last mentioned close is ommited in the verdict of the Jury and was anciently accounted only a part of Broomehill but is now divided from the same contains in our estimation about 80 acres vzt. 20 acres more than the Jury presented them to be And we value them worth (communibus annis) £30.

Memorandum
That the 5 keele rooms at Truncke Stayth and the 4 kele rooms at the Redhaugh Stayth in the occupation of Sir Thomas Liddell and others mentioned by the Jury and which they value at 40s. od. per

annum we find there are 18 keele rooms there upon our view And 3 dwelling houses All which we value worth to be letten £18 per annum.

Memorandum

The grounds called the Salt Meadows presented in the same Article to contain 30 acres is by the said Jury valued at £9 per annum. We upon our view do estimate to contain about 60 acres with which the Ballast shore and key adjoyning for the use of shipping to cast thereon their Ballast And being also used for Staythes for coal and other conveniences Together with the five dwelling houses presented by the Jury in their answer to the 4th Article And one cottage called Swillhouse not by the Jury presented we value worth to be letten . . . .

(Part of page missing)

Memorandum

As to the 2 meadow closes one corn close and 3 small pasture closes by the Jury in answer to the said Article estimated to contain 30 acres in the occupation of Lieutenant Osborne John Swann John Newham valued at 6d. an acre per annum We do agree with them as touching the number of acres; But we do value them at 14d. an acre per annum To be letten per annum in toto £21. 0s. 0d. And as to the small close containing one acre and a half in the possession of Thomas Lottie Cordiner valued by the Jury at 13s. per annum We value the same per annum at £1. 5s. 0d.

And that other small close of one acre and a half in John Newham's possession valued by the Jury at 16s. we value per annum at £1. And the corn close called Ectons Close containing 6 acres in the occupation of William Coats valued by the Jury at £30 per annum We estimate the same per annum at £4. 0s. 0d.

(Part of page missing)

Memorandum

As to the house with the 4 keele rooms nigh Thomas Smith lives valued by the Jury in their Answer to the 2nd Article at £1. 9s. 4d. vzt. the house at 13s. 4d. and the stayths (said to be in the occupation of Mr. Leonard Carr, Mr. Ralph Cole at 16s. per annum) We value the said house and stayth (fit to be sold together) at the yearly rent of £10. 0s. 0d. And as to the house which Thomas Wilkinson holdeth valued at 20s. And the corne Milne called Rocks Milne with the house in which Richard Barry liveth valued at 40s. per

annum We value together with a stayth and a small close there not
mentioned by the Jury (All which premisses are in the occupation
of the said John Wilkinson) at per annum £20. And as to the
house and stayth in the 2nd Article mentioned to be in the possession of widdow Ellinor and valued by the Jury at 10s. per annum
we value to be worth per annum £9. As to the stone quarry upon
Gateshead Fell by the Jury in their answer to the nynth Article
valued at £6 per annum we value the same as they have done
at . . . .

(Part of page missing)

Memorandum
The Borough Court of Gateshead is of the nature of a Court Baron
and may be kept from 3 week to 3 weeks and pleas held for any
time under 40s. The yearly profits and perquisites of the said Court
to be worth 20s. per annum we value at 30s. And the waifes and
estrayes at 5s. per annum In toto £1. 15s. 0d.

Memorandum
There are two houses Intacks or Incroachments upon the common
of Gateshead by Darwin Crooke made and built by Thomas Lyddell
for two poor Colliers to dwell in which ought to pay their rent to
the Grand lessees as Lords of the said mannor And we value them
as the Jury doth in their answers to the 17th Article at £2. 0s. 0d.

Memorandum
As to all the formentioned premisses and particulars (except the
Tolls and grounds called the Salt Meadows) they are parcel of the
Grand Lease of the Mannor of Whickham and Gateshead

(Part of page missing)

Which priviledges are (as we hear) at this day by the men of Newcastle devised to the Boroughmen of Gateshead and others the
Bishop's tennants and men of the County of Durham And yet we
find upon examination and report of diverse men yet living That
the late Bishop of Durham vzt. Bishop Neale Bishop Howson,
Bishop Morton have from the port of London and other places
brought wine beer household stuffs and many other things into the
river and Port of Newcastle-upon-Tyne and landed the same at the
Pier called the Bishop's Stayth on Gateshead side without control
of the men of Newcastle their customers or Searchers (who had

notice thereof and paid no Customs or duties for the same The premisses (much more could be said and proved) considered we do not take upon to determin or certify a Right or to set any value thereon but humbly commend the case of the whole and the cause of the oppressed to the Higher powers

(Part of page missing)

Memorandum

The windmill mentioned in the 7th Article to be in the possession of John Clerke and valued to be worth 40s. per annum is parcel of the Grand Lease and we value the same at £4. os. od.

Memorandum

As to the Rectory, Glebeland and tyethes of the Parish of Gateshead in the Juries answer to the 21, 22 Articles mentioned to be worth £64 The collation or advowson and free gift whereof belongeth to the late Bishop of Durham We find and say the same is now void by the death of the late Rector And is in the power of the Trustees for sale of Bishop's lands to dispose to whom they please And we further find That the tythes belonging to the said Rectory have been retained, and not paid in kind for above these 2 years last past— As also the yearly proffits of the said Glebelands in the hands of the Parishoners and occupiers thereof who have allowed to Mr. Cuthbert Stott in the said Articles mentioned, and to other Ministers supplying the Cure, onely so much thereof as they pleased: the certain whereof was allowed we cannot find

(Part of page missing)

Memorandum

Upon the Perclose of this Survey there come to our knowledge a close of pasture called the Owiners adjoining to the forementioned grounds called the Hassocks containing by estimation 8 acres in the possession of Mrs. Maddison widdow And is part of the demeasnes of Gateshead belonging to the Grand Lessees This was ommitted in the presentment of the Jury And is by us valued at per annum £4.

Memorandum

As to the Copy of the Grand Lease with the confirmation thereof taken out of the office of the Records belonging to the Dean and Chapter of Durham As also the Copy of an Inquisition taken out of the said place We last amongst many other things to long to write) may prove the antient right of the Burghers of Gateshead and other the Bishops men for Free Trade Navigation and Fishing upon that part of the River of Tyne which belongs to the See of Durham which Right is now denied them by the men of Newcastle: We humbly request they may be imparted and showed to the Contractors to whome we had sent also had we had time to have transcribed them

(Part of page missing)

To all Christian people to whom these presents shall come or whom these things underwritten do or hereafter shall anyway concern. We William Whittingham, Dean and our Chapter of Durham of the Cathedral Church of Christ and Blessed Mary the virgin wish greeting in the Lord the Saviour undoubted credit to be given to these presents know that at the special desire and request of Richard—of Gateshead in the Diocese of Durham we have searched and looked into the Registers and records remaining which —do know of a surety and have evidently found out amongst other things within the same that is to say in a great book written in parchment called the third Cartinarie of the Cathedral Church of Durham, a certain Inquisition taken by one Simond Eske, Sherrif of Durham the tenor whereof followeth in these words. The Inquisition taken by Simond Eske Sherrif of Durham upon a wrong done by the men of the Town of Newcastle-upon-Tyne: An inquisition taken before Simond Eske Sherrif of Durham at a full County Court held at Durham upon Monday next after the feast of St. Mary the Virgin in the year of the Prelateship of Richard Po Bishop of Durham to enquire for damages oppressions hurts trespasses and wrongs done against the Church and the liberty of the Church of Durham by any person whatsoever by the oaths of John Breton John Gildford John of Broominghill William of Gillsworth John of Hamsheels William o the Spen William Landine Richard of Ravensworth Reynold of Weremouth William of Hilton and Wilkstowe and Robert of Lampton who say upon their Oath that the Bishop of Durham and the men of the Liberty of the same were want to have free passage alongst the midst of the waters of Tyne with Ships and Vessels Carriages or Discarriages wheresoever they would along the coast of the Bishoprick of Durham unto the .. *(space)* .. of the River aforesaid and common Riverage with all manner of there merchandises and whatsoever other things brought in Ships or vessels at the likeing of all persons whatsoever buyers or sellers Also they say that the Borough of Gateshead had a Market two days a week that is to say upon Tuesday and Friday unto the middle of the Bridge and Facres (that is to say) on the feast day of St. Peter ad vincula: Also they say that the Lord Bisshop and the Pryor of the Convent of Durham have there free fishings upon the coast of the River of Tyne there and were want freely to sell their fishes wheresoever they wanted. They say also that the fishermen of the said Lord Bishop and the said Lord Pryor as well in Pipewellgate as in the Sheeles and elsewhere are altogether hindered to sell their fishes which they take as well in the River of Tyne as in the Sea and are compelled and drawn by force of arms unto the Market place of Newcastle if they sell otherwise they are brought back again or they are soundly fined. They say likewise that strangers are not suffered to have riverage to load or unload who are redeemed: And where the Pryor of Durham hath had his own woods coming from Holy Island in some ship delivered in the River of Tyne upon the sale of the Lord Pryor at the sheeles the ship hath been attached for the delivery and brought to Newcastle. And if the fishermen of Sheeles do sell to the Bishop or the Pryor of Durham or to any other at the Sheales upon the south of the said Lord Bishop without the market place of Newcastle The Baliffs of Newcastle do take the said Fishermen and drive them to the town of Newcastle and there they are imprisoned until they be redeemed and they do take custom of the same Futhermore the aforesaid Bailiffs do hinder all that carry wood coal and timber which other things brought in ships to land them on the Bishoprick without redemption: And they say that the Burgesses of Newcastle-upon-Tyne do build at the end of the Bridge upon the Lord Bishop of Durham his ground appropiating to themselves the sale

(Part of page missing)

Bishops of that place and there men might as they ought (*missing*) the River of Tyne and Tease have gone up and down (*space*) of the River of Tyne aforesaid along the whole coast of the said Bishoprick to carry and unload with their ships and vessels fish flesh (*space*) coal and other things whatsoever as well to be sold as not to be sold and the fishermen of the same Bishoprick might (as they ought) have fished in the same water and in the Sea and have taken fishes and carried and recarried at their pleasure all the goods aforesaid and have made their benefit thereof yet have been hindered by carrying them their shipps and vessels to the said town of Newcastle and by inforcing them unduly to unload there to the great prejudice of the said Bishop and his men aforesaid to the apparent hurt of the liberty of his Bishoprick of Durham And because it is our will that no wrong be done to the said Bishop nor to his men in that behalf we do command you that you utterly forbear from doing hereafter the like hinderances to the said Bishop or to his men aforesaid the permit and suffer from henceforth themselves their ships and vessels with their goods and things aforesaid by all the coast aforesaid to carry and unload and their fishermen to take fish and all other there said goods as well for selling as not for selling (*space*) of the water aforesaid.

A particular of the Total Sum of the annual rent reserved on the Mannor of Whickham and Gateshead payable to the late Bishops of Durham with their particular rents reserved And together with the improvement upon the Mannor of Gateshead The Salt Meadow and Tolls as also of the houses built upon the Bridge over a Part of the River of Tyne Rent reserved upon the mannors of Whickham and Gateshead

Rent reserved upon the mannors of Whickham and Gateshead	£117.	15s.	0d.
Rent reserved upon the tolls of Gateshead	4.	6s.	0d.
Rent reserved upon the Salt Meadow	2.	4s.	0d.
Rent reserved upon the Bridge houses	3.	7s.	6d.
Sum total is	£127.	13s.	6d.

Above the
Rent Reserved

The improvement of the Collieries in Gateshead Park and upon the Fell or Moor of Gateshead	£2000.	0s.	0d.
The improvement of the lands in Gateshead Mannor with the Court and waifs and strays	325.	15s.	0d.
The improvement of Tols of Gateshead and Salt Meadows	200.	0s.	0d.
The improvement of the quarries is	6.	0s.	0d.
The improvement of the houses on the Bridge	23.	10s.	0d.
The free fishings being also an improvement		5s.	0d.
The sum total is	£2555.	10s.	0d.

A RE-SURVEY OF THE COLLIERIES IN THE MANORS OF GATESHEAD AND WHICKHAM

Gateshead and
Whickham Mannors
in the Countie
of Durham

A resurvey of the Collieries and Seams of Coals as well opened and wrought as to be opened and wrought within the said Mannor and the several bounds thereof had made and taken as well by information of honest judicious and experienced men in collieries who were by us sent underground. As upon exact examination of several coal-workers above ground as also the view of Edward Colston, John Duncalfe and John Horsell gentlemen nominated authorised and appointed surveyors of the lands and collieries in the said county belonging to Doctor Thomas Morten late Bishop of Durham by virtue of a commission to us in that behalf directed from the Honorable Sir John Wollastor Knt. and others of the Honourable Committee of Trustees for sale of Bishop's lands and for sale of the Mannor and Rectory of Gleebelands bearing date 24th September A.D. 1652 in the month of November in the said year 1652 and followeth in the ensuing pages vzt.

A copy of the Graund Lease as we found the same entered upon records in the office formerly belonging to the Dean and Chapter of Durham.

Huiuersis xpi fidelibus pntes bras inspectur Deccanus et Captlim

Dunelm Cathis ecclie Xpi et Ste Marie Virginie salutem in dieo Salvatores Noverint universitae iura nos bras Reverendi in xpo pris et domino Dni Richard dei grat Dunelm epi sub eo quis sequitur verborn tenore inspexisso.

This Indenture made 26 April 24 Eliz between our said Sovereign Ladie the Queen's Majestie on the one part and the Reverend Father in God Richard by the sufferance of God Bishop of Durham on the other part Witnesseth that the said Reverend father for diverse great cause and consideration him moving hath given granted demised and to farme letten and by these presents for him and his successors doth give graunt demise and to farme let unto our said Sovereign Lady the Queen's majestie. All those his Mannor lordships town and borough of Gateshead in the county of Durham and also all mannor houses edifices buildings barns stables orchard gardens wood underwood milnes mynes quarries moors marshes wasteground waters fishing watercourses barrow-carts perquisits and said demised and demisable by Copy of Court Roll and all the rent fines and services of the Copyholders and Copyhold lands and also of all the Freeholders and Freehold lands tenements rents and services which are bidden of the said Bishop and belonging unto him within the said Mannor town borough and Lordship aforesaid or any of them And also all goods and chattells and fellons and fugatives, fellons of themselves goods of persons outlawed or p'nt in exigent good valued estrayed deedands and forfeitives which shall happen chance or fall within the said mannor Lordship town and places aforesaid or any of them And all fines issues and amerciaments from time to time taxed, affered, set or assessed of or upon any person or persons of by reason touching or concerning any offence of offences whatsoever which shall hereafter be had committed suffered or done within the said Mannor town Lordship and places aforesaid or any of them And also all the mines of coals as well opened as not opened or already found or hereafter to be sought for rents and sums of money whatsoever heretofore reserved or agreed to be paid to the said Bishop and his predecessors for wayleave in and upon the said premisses mentioned to be demised or any part thereof And all easemts perquisits ways comodityes advantages and hereditants whatsoever of the said Bishop of what nature kind or quality soever the same be situate lying and being or which heretofore have been used had or enjoyed within the Mannor Lordship towns borough fields hamletts precincts or circuite of Gateshead also Gateshead and Whickham aforesaid or in either of them (except and always foreprised and reserved out of the present Lease and grant all the liberties and royalties as well of the County Pallatine of Durham and such other rights liberties, jurisdiction power to hold pleas and perogative Royall of the said Bishop and Bishoprick and of the Chancellor Judges Justices Ministers Officers of the said County Palatine for the time being in the said towns lordships and places of Whickham and Gateshead aforesaid which are not before granted or mentioned to be granted by these presents And except also so much of the Tyne Bridge as is situate standing and being within the said Town Borough or precincts of Gateshead aforesaid and the soil and ground of the same and all houses and edifices thereon erected and built and the toll there used to be taken And also excepted and foreprised out of this present lease and grant all and every the Sheriffe turme fines of Alienacon without licence And all Wardships primer seasons of land and tenements within the County Pallatine of Durham and lying within the said town and lordship of Gateshead and Whickham And also foreprised and excepted out of this present gift grant and demise the advance and patronage and right to collate and present unto the two parsonages of Gateshead and Whickham and either of them when and how often the same or either of them shall happen or chance to be vacant during the whole and full term of this present grant or demise And because there be diverse customary and copyhold lands and tenements parcel of the demised premises which cannot be kept continued and preserved as copyhold tenants without some Court at which the copyholders of the same may as well surrender their interest as take forth of the Lord's hands their said copyhold lands and tenements which by the special custom there used may be if our said Sovereign Lady shall have of the grant of the said Bishop any one Court whereat the said copyholds have use to take their said copyhold lands and tenements Therefore the said Richard now Lord Bishop of Durham hath granted and for him and his successors by these presents do grant to our said Sovereign Lady one Court commonly called an Halymote of Hallmotte Court to be holden by the stewards of her Majestie and her assignes in Gateshead or Whickham aforesaid at which the said tenants or copyholders shall or may surrender and take the said copyhold land and tenement to have and to hold the said mannor lordship towns boroughs land tenements meadows feedings woods underwoods mynes quarries rent revercons services hereditaments and other the premisses whatsoever mentioned to be demised and granted by these presents (except before excepted) unto our said Sovereign Lady the Queen's most Excellent Majestie and her assignes from the making of this present indenture of lease and demise unto the full end and term of fourscore and nineteen years from thence next ensuing fully to be complete and ended without impeachment of any mannor of waste yielding and paying therefore yearly at or in the Exchequor of Durham during the said term of 99 years to the said Bishop and his successors the yearly rent of £117. 15s. 8d. of lawful money of England at the Feast of Pentecost called Whitsunday and St. Martin the Bishop in Winter by even portions And the said Reverend father for him and his successors doth grant to our said Sovereign Lady that she and her assigns shall and may during the said term digg, take carry away and convert to her and their own use all and every the mines as well as coals as other things in the said land tenement and hereditament before demised as well such as be now opened and found as also such as are not yet opened or found and shall and may dig the same and do all other things in and upon the same grounds and premisses for the finding and getting of them and every or any of them in witness whereof as well the said Bishops hath to the said Indenture set his seale as our said Sovereign Lady the Queen's Majestie hath caused her great seal of England to be annexed the day and year above expressed

This lease was confined by the then Dean and Chapter of Durham the 15th October 1583, 25 Elz.

There is yet to come and unexpired of this lease in April next which will be A.D. 1653, 28 years A particular of the several borders or the collieries of Gateshead and Whickham demised in the foresaid Grand Lease hereafter followeth vzt.

Whitefield

In this field hath been wrought six pits of the main coal the seam being seven quarters high. One of these pits is also wrought in the five-quarter coal which is the same above the main coal.

There is yet remaining in this field six pit rooms more which will (as judicious men in collieries affirm unto us afford very great quantity of coals)

Eastfield

This eastfield is on the westside of Whitefield and hath in it some places four seams of good coals In other some places three seams and in some places but two they are thus distinguished Two five-quarter seams, the main coal, and in the top coal In the main coal hath been wrought five and twenty pits or thereabouts In the top coal hath been wrought fourteen pits In the five-quarter coal hath been wrought about nine pits In the seven-quarter coal hath been wrought six pits And it is the judgement and opinion of workmen and artist in collieries that three new pits may be sunk and wrought in the main coal And that the five and twenty pits may and will yet cast in the several seams very considerable qualities of good and marchauntable coal.

Leighfield

This field is upon the north side of eastfield and there are three closes in it called Littlewood, Little Woodheads and Allardon fields The main coal is concieved (except the Woodhead and a place called the Leighplaine very inconsiderable) is wrought and yet there is several seams there unwrought which will as is affirmed afford very considerable qualities of coals

Dunstanfield

This field is to the westward of the Leigh And hath yet three pit rooms left at which the main coal may be got, but the rest of the main coal is wrought out There are two several other seams in this field vzt.
The five-quarter seam most of it unwrought A seven-quarter seam part of which is wrought and part unwrought And many considerable quanities of coals may be yet worn and got in this field as we are credibly informed by men judicious in collieries

Lowefield

This field is on the west side of Dunston upon the north of the town of Whickham. There is of late discovered in this field a seam of coal called by the workmen a five-quarter coal, it is underneath that seam of coal (most of which is wrought out here) called the main coal
Note: This seam saieth workmen and other judicious men in collieries lieth (as they verily believe) through the whole mannor of

Whickham And will if the same prove according to their judgement and expectation not only cast very great quantities of coal herself and that without charge of drawing of water (which now the Grand Lease do) but drain all the greatest part of the pits which now stand drowned. This considerable seam as the workmen say lyeth about twenty fathoms beneath the seams termed by the name of the Main Coal.

Norrifield
This field is to the west of the lowfield And hath in her considerable quantities of coal which are now drained but will as we are informed be gained by this new discovered seam when there workings come that way

Longsettles
A parcel of common ground which lyeth on the south of Norrifield and goes westwards by Axewell lands and house a Freehold of James Clavering Esq., unto a Freehold called Hollingshead belonging to Mr. Harding. And Long Hollingshead grounds south and by west to a gate that goes into the grounds of William Blakeston Esq., called Gibside Then southwards again by a Freehold called Marley's land and another Freehold called Whitfield land and the Ridingfield And so to Westfield. There is in this common two several seams of coal vzt. The Main Coal and the Five-Quarter Coal both which seams have been wrought in several places of this common. Yet it is the opinion of men skilful in collieries that there may be very considerable quantities of coal got or won within the circuitts of this piece of common.

Haggdeene
Another parcell of common which lyeth on the east of Westfield which had in her before they were wrought two seams the Main Coal and Top Coal. Many workmen are of opinion that what is left there unwrought may in time be got which will be a good quantity of merchantable coal.

Goose Moore
Another parcel of common which lyeth on the northside of Haggdeene in which hath been twelve pit rooms slightly wrought So as by reason of the goodness of these seams vzt. A seam of ten-

quarters high And another of seven-quarters above it A very considerable quantity of coal may hereafter be got out of the said seams and pits as we are credibly informed by skillful and knowing workmen.

Whaggs
A parcell of Copyhold lands which lyeth on the eastside of Goosemore And hath in it two seams of coal (vzt) The Main Coal and the Five-Quarter Coal both which seams have been slightly wrought Yet it is concieved that considerable quantities of coal may be got out of the said seams.

Corne Moore
A parcel of grounds lying on the northside of the Waggs In which hath been sunk and wrought thirty pit rooms or thereabouts And the Main Coal is much wrought and wasted yet not so wasted but good quantity of coal may hereafter be got there

Marshall Lands
Marshall Lands and Wheateleys these parcels of land lie upon the east of the Whaggs and had some small matter of collieries in them which are wrought out at there pit rooms. Their is some small matters left behind as is believed.
There is likewise upon the south of Marshall Lands a little piece of common the coal of which are very much wrought out and are wasted.

Westmost Southfield
Westmost Southfield abutteth upon Cornemoor on the west In which was collieries but the same as we are informed is long since wasted and wrought at nine several pit rooms.

Eastmost Southfield
Eastmost Southfield adjoining to the Westmost Southfield hath had six several pit rooms which hath been wrought in the Main Coal, Top Coal and Five-Quarter Coal but it is concieved by workmen that considerable quantities of coal more may be got out of each seam.

Blinckensop
Blinkensop is a close adjoining upon the Eastfield And hath in the

Main Coal which hath been wrought in three pit rooms And some small quantities may be got more but not many, the close being but small.

Newfield

This field belongs to a tenement abutting upon part of the common the south and west part in which grounds were two seams vzt. The Main Coal three yards thick much wrought And the Five-Quarter Close wrought in part Yet it is believed and to us affirmed that several hundred ton of coal may be yet got in the said ground

Eastmost Haugh

Eastmost Haugh abutteth upon the River Tame on the east and had collierie in her and still hath as is believed but the same hath been wrought and that which is unwrought is drowned.

Coleway Haugh

Coleway Haugh is upon the westside of Eastmost Haugh in which was and is colliery But the same is wrought out and drowned.

Matfen Haugh

Matfen Haugh is on the west of Coleway Haugh All the Colliery here is wrought and drowned.

Westmost Haugh

Westmost Haugh as the rest lyeth near the River of Tame and therefor were first wrought And what is left unwrought stands drained and not to be recovered as is concieved.

Brockwells

Brockwells lyeth on the Westfield of the Westmost haugh in which close there is but one seam (as we are informed) and that seam is very considerable being seventeen-quarters thick and all unwrought And we are credibly informed that when the Grand Lease shall set on to work the colliery there they will get very great quantity of coal there and that she will last many years. More or other grounds then before mentioned the Grand Lease have not within the said Mannor of Whickham in which any colliery is wrought or unwrought.

Gateshead Bounds are as followeth vzt.

From a Blewstone near Sir Thomas Liddells house in Gateshead which is fixed in the ground or earth near to the high street leading to the Southwoods Close by the Eastside of the Causeway until you come about seventy yards or thereabout from a windmill called Moody's Wynde Mill, from thence southwards to a place called the Whitequarry Thence to the next clod or stone And so to a second third and fourth mark or cross which lyeth to the westward of a Freehold belonging to Mr. Ralph Cole called the Whitehouse And thus far it borders upon a common or waste belonging to Upper and Nether Hewarth on the east. Then southward to a fifth mark from thence to a place called Wrackendike where a cross hath been and a part yet remains with these letters engraven I CHRIST from thence westwards along the said Wrackendike until you come to iton (*eighton*) quarries And thus far also it bounds upon the east of a part of a moor or waste belonging to Barron Hilton his tennants or assignes And from Wrackendike Crosse to Iton Quarries aforesaid to another part of the said waste belonging to the said Barron Hilton and borders upon it on the south part From thence to upper Iton Hedge westwards and so along that hedge untill we come down to the said upper Iton lanesend boundering for the most part upon Iton ground on the south of Chowden And thence to Darwyn Crofte (*Crooke*) ground northwards until you come to go eastwards by the Whinney House ground on the north of it And thence to the Highstreete or way and so to the Blewstone formerly mentioned where we began. This boundary is many miles in length and breadth and all the collieries therein whole and unwrought And though it should be set on and unwrought by the grand lease before the expiration of their term yet their would be collieries left for many ages as all judicious men in collieries affirm unto us.

There is also another parcel of land within this Mannor called by the name of the Parke containing by estimation 479 acres in which the Grand Lease had gained a colliery And have five pits now going there And will as men skilfull in collieries affirm unto us so continue for many ages agoing collieries.

Thus having often and seriously viewed and surveyed the several borders and examined and confirmed ourselves of the true state of the collieries within the aforesaid two mannors of Gateshead and Whickham we concieve and according to our best skill informa-

tion and judgement do value the remaining collieries which may
and will be left unwrought within the bounderys of the said two
mannors at and after the expiration of the said lease termed the
Graund Lease made by the Bishop to Queen Elizabeth for 99 years
to be worth over and above the rent reserved The yearly rent or
value of £1800

Edward Colston
John Duncalfe
John Horsell

6th December 1652.

SURVEY OF THE MANOR OF HOUGHTON LE SPRING

A true and perfect Survey of the said Mannor of Houghton in the Spring and of the several townships of Burdon, Newbottle, High Hayning and Herrington, Ryhope also Ryvehope, Tunstall, Morton and Bishop Weremouth Had and made as well by us George Grey gent, John Duncalfe gent, and John Husband gent and Chr. Mickleton gent In the months of July and August in the year of our Lord God 1647.

The Verdict of the Jury Impanelled and Sworne at the Court of Survey holden at Houghton in the Spring for the said Mannor of Houghton the 26th July 1647.

To the first Article we Present that there is no Mannor house within the said Mannor belonging to the Lord thereof wither any barnes stables granaries Brewhouse Bakehouse Dovehouse and other housing Orchards gardens or other things menconed in this Article belonging unto him Except the pticular Tennants houses and the Parsonage houses and groundes which belong to the particular Tennants or Farmers thereof or to the severall p'sons or Rectors of the Parishes within the said Mannors to which we shall give answer in the 21 Article and other Articles hereafter

To the second Article we present and find that the several persons hereafternamed are farmers and lessees from the late Bishop of Durham and other his predecessors of divers lands and Tenements in their severall leases contayned and for the p'ticulars whereof together with their several Rents which they are by vertue of their severall Leases to pay we referr ourselves to the Entries of their severall Leases and how And the Jury aforesaid do further say that they know not how many acres are or be in the several Townships places or tenements above named nor any of them and that the same lye all in Comon and are not inclosed Except Morton which is a distinct place by itselfe and all inclosed And that the said lands grounds and tenements beforesaid have not heretofore bin demised or letten by the acre and therefore they know not what an acre thereof or one acre accompted with another are worth p.ann. otherwise than as they have formerlie estimated the same And for the rest of the p'ticulars inquired of by this Article we refer ourselves to the several Leases thereof most part whereof we concerne are entered before the Surveyors or some of them and further we cannot present anything to this Article saving that the Tennants abovenamed and their Ancestors have enjoyed the said lands and Tenements by Leases time beyond the Memory of man and do clayme a title and Tennant right in the said premises after the expiracon of their several Leases.

To the 3rd, 4th and 5th Articles we have nothing which we know of to present for that there are no Parks warrens Sheepwalkes or other several grounds belonging to the Lord of this Mannor neither are there any forraigne outwood pastures or comon which the Lord hath in right of this Manor nor any outwood wherein the Tennants have any pannage Mastage or herbages And the Greaves of the several Towns are changable and changed sometimes yearlie (and sometimes not so often) at the Lords Halmott Court held within the saide Mannor by the Steward thereof for the time being.

To the 6th Article we p'sent and find that John Shephardson of Weremouth holdeth a Fishing within the River of Weare by Lease from the Bishop of Durham which he holdeth joyntly in Lease with a Stone quarry there both which are of the yearlie value of £2 besides the Rent 10s. therefore reserved of Improvement £2.

To the 7th Article we present and find that John Rutter of Houghton is farmer by lease from the Bishop of Durham of a water corne milne called Newbottle Milne standing upon a Rivulett called Rainton Burne worth p.a. £10 besides the Lords Rent whereto there belongeth a little Close in Newbottle townshipp and pasturage for one horse in the pasture belonging to Newbottle both Winter and Summer which is valued with the Milne aforesaid which said Milne is in good repaire and for the terme which the said John Rutter hath in the said Milne we referr ourselves to the lease thereof (We likewise present that Martin Watson of Weremouth is possessed of a windmill at Bishop Weremouth being a Corne mill by lease from the Bishop of Durham which hath neither house nor ground belonging to the same neither are any Tennants bounde to grinde thereat and it is worth per ann besides the Lords Rent £4 which is in good repaire. We likewise present that Richard Thompson of Ryhopp holdeth one Windmill being a Corne Mill at Ryhopp aforesaid by Lease from the said Bishop but for what terme we know not nor upon what conditions for he hath not p'duced his Lease to us and it hath neither house nor ground belonging thereunto to our knowledge nor hath it any man tyed to grind at her and the same is worth £2 p.a. over and besides the Lord's Rent which is other £2 p.Ann. as by the Rentall appeareth And the said Mill is but in indifferent repaire

We likewise present that there is a windmill being a Corne Mill at Tunstall which is included in the Lease Tunstall and in the possession of the Tenants of Tunstall who pay rent for the same with their farmes in Tunstall and is valued with Tunstall in our Answer to second Article.

We likewise present that Robert Lambton of Houghton in the Spring is possessed by lease from the late Dean and Chapter of Durham of a water Corne Mill standeing on the ground of the said Dean and Chapter and payeth 53s. 4d. rent to the Bishop of Durham which we conceive is for a watercourse which runneth from and through the said Bishop's land at Houghton to the said Mill.

To the eighth Article we present that none of the Tenants of this Mannor do owe any suite or service or are bound to grind there Corne at any Mill within this Mannor except at Newbottle Mill and that the tenants in Newbottle and East and Middle Herrington do suite and service to the said Mill at Newbottle and we think the tenants doe grind their corne at the said Mill for we heare no complaint thereof And we further present and find that the Tenants of Newbottle and of East and Middle Herrington are bounde by

their tenure to carry and lead stones and timber to the said Mill
and to finde thatch for the repaire thereof and to scoure the Mill
damm or water place of the said Mill.

To the 9th Article we present that there are divers salt panns at
Bishop Weremouth nere Sunderland which are holden of the Lord
of the Mannor by Copy of the Court Roll That the tenants or
farmers of Morton payeth 13s. 4d. Rent for a Myne of coale at
Morton but the same is not wrought nor hath bin wrought for
many yeares last past That there is one stone Quarry at Newbottle
which hath never bin letten but hath heretofore bin used by the
Tenants of Newbottle for their own use And the same may now
be letten for the Rent of £2. p.a. which is the improved valew
thereof.
And there is another stone quarry at Bishop Weremouth with
possession of John Sheppardson which we have presented in our
Answer to the 6th Article.

To the 10th and 11th Articles we present that George Thompson
and Wm. Thompson jun. are Freeholders in Ryhope within the
Precincts of this Lordship and do pay the yearlie rent of 10s. 4d.
John Rutter jun. 6s. 10d. Michael Robinson for another freehold
in Houghton 6s. 10d.
And for the rest of the Freeholders we refer ourselves to the Coroners
Rentall of Easington Ward who is Collector of the said Freehold
Rents.
And we know not what suite or service the said Freeholders are
to do unto this Mannor nor by what severall tenures they hold,
neither what Reliefe or herriott they are to pay

To the 12th Article we say that we know not how many Copyholders or Customary Tenants do belong unto this Mannor but
refer ourselves to the Rentall and to the Entries of their Copies

To the 13th Article we say that the Fynes of the Copieholders upon
death of the tenant or alienacon of their Copyhold Estates are
certaine and are sett downe upon their severall copies at the time
of the Surrendency of their Estates or admission after the death of
their Ancestors and they pay no herryott after the death of the
tenant.

To the 14th Article we say there is no timber groweing upon any of the Coppyholds to our knowledge nor any Quarries or Mynes other than what is before set down

To the 15th we say that the Copieholders are to do no worke nor services that we know of but suite at the Lords Halmott Court and Suite at the Lords Mill for so many as are bound to it.

To the 16th Article we referr ourselves to the several Rentalls and further we cannot present to this Article

To the 17th Article we say that we know of no intacks buildings or inclosures which have been latelie made out of any wasts belonging to this Mannor

To the 18th Article we say that there is a weeklie Markett held in Sunderland by the Sea upon every Friday in every week and there are 2 Faires in the years there held (vzt) May day and Michaelmas day the benifitt whereof belongeth to the Bishop of Durham who hath demised the same with other things by lease for the use of the Town of Sunderland which is a Borough Town and a port or haven for shipps neere adjacent to the Sea and for the Rent we refer ourselves to the Lease thereof but the value thereof we know not.

To the 19th Article we say that the Profitt of the Borough Court of Sunderland belonged to the Bishop of Durham but is demised with other things for the use of the said Inhabitants and others by the lease aforesaide and the profitts of the Halmote Courts belong to the Lord of the Mannor and in like manner all wayfes Estrayes Fellons goods wrecks of Sea. Fynes Amerciements and other like casualties belong to the Bishop of Durham as Lord of the Mannor but what the same are worth unto the Lord of the Manner (communibus annis) we know not and the Collector of the Bishops Rent within the several Townships do collect the same within their several Townes And the Bayliffe of Sunderland doth collect the same within the Borough of Sunderland.

To the 20th we say there is no free warren belonging to this Mannor neither any priviledges Royalties, Franchises immunities

or profitts that we know of other than what are before set down
in our Answer to some of the precedent Articles.

To the 21st and 22nd Articles we present and say that the late
Bishop of Durham who was Lord of this Mannor had the Right of
presentacon free guift, nominacon and disposicon of the several
Rectories of Houghton in the Spring and of Bishop Weremouth
within this Mannor And to the said Rectory or Parsonage of
Houghton in the Spring there is belonging a great large and
spacious Parsonage House with Barnes stables dovehouse and other
outhouses and houses of office gardens Orchard fishpond and
Glebeland and Tythes of Corne hay wooll Lambs Calfe and other
Tythes of all sorts as well Grand Tythes as petit Tythes and other
Ecclesiasticall duties worth p.a. £300 and above And that one
Mr. Reuben Easthorpe is now Incumbent there by Order from
the Parliament upon the delinquency of Hamlett Marshall Doctor
of Divinitie late Parson thereof
And to the Rectory or Parsonage of Bishop Weremouth there is
belonging another great Parsonnage house with Barnes Stables dove-
coates and other outhouses gardens Glebeland and Tythes of Corne
hay wooll lambe Calfe and other Tythes of all sorts and other
Ecclesiasticall duties All which are worth £160 p.a. or thereabouts
And that one Mr. John Johnson is now Incumbent by Order from
the Parliament.

To the 23rd Article we present and say that the Parsonage of
Bishop Weremouth is a Mannor of itselfe and that there are diverse
tenants which hold of the saide Mannor most part of which Tennants do hold by Copie of Court Roll and pay severall yearlie Rents
to the Parson of Wearmouth for the tyme being And the Churches
and Chancells of both the said parish Churches are in good repair
and so are the Parsonage houses for anything we know

To the 24th Article we say there are neither woodes nor Coppices
in this Mannor which we know of therefore we need not to enquire
how the same are measured

To the 25th Article we present that there are certeine Reprises
duties or fees yearlie issuable and to be paide by diverse of the
several Townships within this Mannor to the Coroner of Easington

ward for the time being (vzt) forth of the Townships of Houghton
Newbottle   0. 7s. 8d.
The 2 Herringtons Coppyholders six pecks of
   wheat and no money
Tunstall 14 bushells of wheat and   0. 4s. 8d.
Ryhope 17 bushells of wheat and   0. 5s. 8d.
Burdon 10 bushells of wheat and   1s. 8d.

All which quantities of Corne and somes of money abovemenconed
have and are paid to the Coroner of Easington Ward and his
predecessors Coron's of the said Ward for the time being but for
what we know not and the same hath bin usuallie paid between
Mich and Christmas yearlie

In testimony whereof to this our verdict we have set our hand and
seales at the said Court of Survey held upon Adjournment at the
Cittie of Durham 12th August 1647

Anthony Shadforth	Wm. Thompson
Tho Huntley	Tho. Ayre
George Dale	John Goodchilde
Ralph Dale	Wm. Surrett
Cuthbert Welsh	George Fell
Barnard Robinson	George Homer
Ralph Wilkinson	

Houghton in the Spring Township Freeholds

JOHN RUTTER
29 June 6 Car. 20 acres of land in Houghton from his brother
Robert Rutter.
   Rent 6s. 10d.

MICHAEL ROBINSON
1 May 7 Car. One messuage of land with all houses in Houghton
from Robert Robinson.
   Rent 6s. 10d.

ROBERT LAMPTON
20 July 12 Car. From the Deane and Chapter of Durham a water
corne milne in East Rainton.
   Rent £1. 13s. 4d.

Houghton in the Spring Township Copyholds

JOHN RUTTER

20 April 11 Car. 33 acres of land lying in the East Field adjacent to the free tenement of the said John on the east and extending itself to the Town aforesaid on the west and the leazures and 15 acres of Moore lying on the North of Mooris leaases

By surrender of Sir. Wm. Bellasis knt. Fine 6s. od.

7 November 10 Car. One messuage One close called Hall myers close and one close lying at Willie Dyke One close adjacent to the messuage of Margaret Maltby One parcell of the land lying on the East of the Fourth containing 4 acres of land.

By surrender of Sir Wm. Bellasis knt. Fine 5s. 3d.

Rent for these two copies £3. 4s. 5d.

RALPH IRONSIDE

20 April 11 Car. One close in the long bank on the East of a close of Robert Ranson, one dayle of meadow lying in the broad meadows One close lying upon hallmire hill and adjacent to the water gapp One parcell of meadow lying upon hall mires hill.

By surrender of Sir Wm. Bellasis knt. Fine 2s. 9d.

dat ut supra. One messuage and one Cottage and one close lying in Bradley lying to a close of Robt. Chilton on the west One close on the North of the loaning with leades to the Moore One close in the moore leases One close in the New close lying on the south of the said new close.

By surrender of Sir Wm. Bellasis knt. Fine 11s. 4d.

Rent for these two copies £2. 14s. od.

PETER BRUNTON

27 October 18 Car. One cottage with a garth to the same belonging lying on the East of the Tenement of Christopher Bee on the north of the Tenement called kirkland and on the south of the towne crosse pcell of the 7th part of the whole tenure in 7 parts devided.

By surrender of William Chilton of Houghton. Rent 2s. od. Fine 4d.

JAMES WILD son of Robert Wild
29 April 14 Jac. One cottage and one garth.
  By surrender of Ralph Pendrith. Fine 10d.
20 October 21 Car. One close lying at Howden End near Newbottle hedge.
  By surrender of Ralph Ironside. Fine 2s. od.
9 April 8 Car. One cottage and one garth.
  Fine 1s. 8d.
  Rent for these three copies 6s. 6d.

ELIZ STAFFORD widow sister of Robert Maitland
7 September 22 Car. One parcell of ground containing in length 16 yards and in bredth 15 yds nigh horsepoole in Houghton.
  As heir to her brother. Rent 9d. Fine 4d.

WM. THOMPSON son and heir of Robert Thompson
7 September 22 Car. One house and one close called the kiln close
  As heir to his father. Fine 8d.
dat ut supra. One tenement called Sanderson land and one close called the garth on the South with one close adjoyning upon the foresaid close called Le garth and one close called Sympsons Close head extending itself from the Comon way called Ryhope Streete and one close lying in the new close One close lying under the way called Newbottle way and one close lying in the Moor adjoyning upon the close called Crosse Fyne Close.
  Fine 4s. od.
  Rent for these two copies £1. 3s. 4d.

RICHARD DOBSON
14 July 17 Car. One cottage and one garth.
  By surrender of Wm. Hope. Rent 6d. Fine 6d.

DOROTHY LAMBERT als Hopper widd.
3 October 12 Car. One cottage with a garth.
  By surrender of Ralph Lambert her brother. Rent 7d. Fine 7d.

JOHN RUTTER the elder
10 May 6 Jac. One cottage and one garth.
  By surrender of Ralph Haswell. Rent 7d. Fine 4s. od.

RICHARD TYERS Cosen and heir of John Wilson vzt. son and heire of Margery daughter and sole heire of John Wilson
19 October 11 Jac. 2 cottages.
Rent 4d. Fine 7d.

WM. ATKINSON
27 October 18 Car. One messuage with the garth late in the tenure of John Rosse
By surrender of Ann Rutter wid. and Isabell her daughter. Rent 4d. Fine 4d.

ELIZ. HYND wid. of John Chilton
8 November 6 Jac. One cottage and 3 acres of land
By surrender of Thomas Mathew. Fine 2s. 0d.
dat ut supra. 9 acres of land lying in 3 several fields of Haughton vzt in every field 3 acre arable land (vzt) 2 acres of land lying at the East end of the Towne there upon Jeffrey Flatt and 2 acre of land lying at the water gapp in Howden field and one acre in Corseley hope One acre upon Stony flatt ½ acre upon Beasflatt and ½ acre upon the Maynes in Blinwellfield and one other acre upon upper Saltwell and 3 roodes of land in Nether Saltwell and one rood upon the head of New close and one acre in Bradley at Shelebread dyke nuke and pasture for 3 beasts in the Eastfield with foggage for the same with the oxen of the Town there and pasture for 5 sheepe in the fallowe and pasture for one horse in the Town field pcell of the land called Bryses land which her husband had in right while he lived
By surrender of Robert Ironside. Fine 3s. 4d.
Rent for these two copies 3s. 4d.

GEORGE BARKAS
20 April 11 Car. The moytie of a messuage One close called Halliwell Marsh containing 13 acres of land more or less adjacent upon the broad meadows and 1½ acre of land in the broad meadow and one close called Halliwell Flatt adjacent upon West Howden containing 22 acres of land One close upon Hallmire Hill containing 4½ acres of land One close called West Holden containing 20 acres adjacent upon Newbottle field One close called East Field adjacent upon Warden Law containing 10 acres of land and 3 roods One close upon the Maynes adjacent to the Kings streete called Ryhope

Street containing 16 acres of land one close called Milne Close containing 12 acres of land adjacent on the East part of the New Close.

By surrender of Sir William Bellasis knt. Rent £2. 1s. 8d. Fine 8s. 4d.

MARTIN ROBINSON

1 October 9 Car. 1 cottage with a garth lying at the East end of the house of Robert Ranson parcell of 2 cottages and 12 acres of land formerlie Robt. Kennetts.

By surrender of Peter Sharpe. Rent 4d. Fine 6d.

ROBERT RANSON

20 April 11 Car. One close and one Barne with a garth and one Close lying in the East pasture beyond the water furre and one close upon the moore and one loaning called Raynton miln loaning

By surrender of Sir. Wm. Bellasis knt. Rent 8s. 4d. Fine 3s. 4d.

ALICE wid. relict of Ralph Chilton

11 September 21 Car. One cottage with one garth in Houghton.

In widdowright. Rent 11d. Fine 1s. 8d.

NICHOLAS DOBSON

23 March 15 Car. One cottage with a garth on the backside adjacent

By surrender of John Rutter. Rent 4d. Fine 4d.

ALICE wife of Bartram Smith daughter and heire of Henry Gardiner decd.

22 April 23 Car. One cottage with a garth on the backside adjacent formerlie in the occupacon of James Rutter with a parcell of land late in the tenure of Ellen England.

Rent 4d. Fine 1s. 0d.

ANN WILSON widdow of Wm. Wilson and relict of Ann Chilton her mother

20 April 11 Car. One messuage, One acre, ½ acre of Meadow lying in the broad Meadowes called Stowsdale One close in Slipper Thorne lying neere Newbottle field containing 12 acres of land One close upon West Howden lying neere Newbottle field containing 24 acres One close in Oversaltwell containing 32 acres One

close in the Eastfield pasture lying neare warden meadow containing 10 acres and 3 roods and one close in Bradley adjacent to the close of Ralph Ironside containing 12 acres of land One close in Le loaning adjacent to the close of the Rectory of the Church of Houghton containing 6 acres.

By surrender of Sir Wm. Bellasis knt. Rent £2. 2s. od. Fine 8s. 4d.

MARGARET wid relict of Wm. Chilton

7 September 22 Car. 7 Messuages and 7 Gardens One close called East Whynne and Bracksman hole and parcell of one pasture called Long Bank containing 60 acres of land and 14 acres of land adjacent upon Beaminge Closes and Warden field and parcell thereof adjacent upon the Longbancke and one close called Wettflatt Close and Fuffrie Meadow containing 48 acres lying between the Close belonging to the Rectory of Houghton and one close lying in Bradley containing 20 acres of land lying between one close of Robert Hutton and the close of Ralph Ironside One close called the Hill and containing 3 acres lying on the South of Newbottle East Close and the lands belonging to the Rectory of Houghton aforesaid on the North One close called Crooke Flatt containing 14 acres of ground lying between the close of Robt. Hutton and the close of George Barkas One close in the Low Saltwell containing 12 acres lying between the new close and the close of John Rutter which her husband had in right.

In widdowright. Fine 3s. 4d.

dat ut supra. One close called Pear flatt and Blind well containing 20 acres of ground adjacent upon East Pasture and the close of Thomas Brough One close called Sliper thorne containing 6 acres between the Close belonging to the Rectory of the Church of Houghton and the Close of Ann Chilton widdow and Newbottle field on the west one close in Broad meadow containing 2 acre of land lying between the close belonging to the Rectory of the Church of Houghton aforesaide and the close of Ralph Ironside One close of pasture upon the moore containing 32 acres lying between Newbottle pasture and East Raynton pasture lying on the North of a close late William Belasis knt. called 3 acres pasture and one garth called Crofts adjacent to the Tenement of Robert Chilton.

In widdowright. Fine 3s. 4d.

Rent for these two copies £4. 13s. 3d.

Hereafter followeth the names of the severall persons whose names are Charged with these Rents following but produced no kind of Evidence to show what title they have in the said Estates

Houghton in le Spring
Lease Mr. Robert Hutton for the Mill	£2. 13s. 4d.
Out Rent Mr. Eastropp for the Parsonage	£2. 4s. 5d.
The house belonging nigh to the Free school	11d.
Cop. Mr. Robert Hutton	£6. 2s. 4d.
Elizabeth Browne	13s. 4d.
Grace Cooke	9d.
Ellion Bee and William Unthanke	7d.
John Watson	2s. 0d.
Lambton Robt.	3s. 4d.

Tunstall Township Leaseholds

HIS MAJESTIE
14 January 1 Jac. All those his messuages, lands, tenements, Milnes, Rents, Revercons and Services in Tunstall.
   For a period of 80 years
Who demised to
Dudley Carelton of London Esq. 10 March 1 Jac.
Who demised to
Toby Mathew of London Esq. 26 April 2 Jac.
Who demised to
Edward Easton of Grayes Inn Gent. 22 June 5 Jac.
Who demised to
James Billingham of Levens Knt. 27 February 5 Jac.
Who demised to
Richard Middleton 12 December 6 Jac.
Who demised to
John Shaldforth 9 January 6 Jac.
   Rent for the whole £16 vzt for the Moite or 6th pte.
   Rent £10. 13s. 4d. (Jury). Improvement £48. 0s. 0d. (Jury); Improvement £96. 0s. 0d. (Ourselves)

RICHARD MIDDLETON

14 January 1 Jac. All that Messuage, Farmehold or Tenement in Tunstall with the part and portion of Tunstall Winde Mill p'taining or usually occupied with the same.

For a period of 80 years
Who demised to
John Shadforth
Who demised to
Thomas Ayres
3 February 9 Car.

Rent £2. 13s. 4d. (Ourselves). Improvement £12. 0s. 0d. (Jury), £24. 0s. 0d. (Ourselves).

Warden Law Copyholds

ANTHONY SHALDFORTH

21 October 5 Car. The moitie of the whole towne of Warden wth one house late upon the premisses built by one John Shaldforth the elder late in the occupacon of John Shaldforth younger containing in length 17 yards and in bredth 7 yards of land with half of all other houses, lands, meadows, pastures, mores and other profitts and commodityes to the same belonging.

By surrender of his brother Thomas Shaldforth.

Rent £2. 6s. 8d. Fine £1. 10s. 0d.

East Burdon Leaseholds

THOMAS son and heir of Margaret Huntley

15 October 3 Car. All that messuage or tenement in East Burden.

For the lives of the said Thomas Huntly then 15 years Thomas Huntly the younger then aged 14 son of Richard Huntly of East Burdon aforesaid and of Thomas Ayre the younger then 15 son of Thomas Ayres of Tunstall yeoman

Rent £1. 13s. 6d. Improvement £11. 0s. 0d. (Jury), £16. 10s. 0d. (Ourselves).

ANDREW HUNTLEY

8 October 13 Car. One tenement in East Burdon and one close called Fallop and Fulwell adjoyning on the north side of Isabell Richardson's ground and on the south side Isabell Burdon's and on the East of the King's street and on the west of the grounds of Ryhopp and also one other close called the West End of the Moore boundary on the west side of Isabell Richardson's ground and of the North syde of Wardon's ground and of the East side of Herrington Hayninge and of the South syde of Herrington Moore beinge within the Township of East Burdon aforesaid.

For the lives of the said Andrew Huntly now about 40 years, Wm. Huntly son of the said Andrew now about 8 years and of Robert Foster son of Thomas Foster of Cold Hesledon now 9 years.

Rent £1. 18s. od. Improvement £12. os. od. (Jury), £18. os. od. (Ourselves).

ANDREW HUNTLY in right of Isabell his wife formerlie Isabell Richardson of East Burdon

22 September 7 Car. All that Tenement and a halfe in East Burdon then in the tenure and occupacon of the said Isabell.

For the lives of the said Isabell now 38 years, Isabell her daughter now 16 years and John Lister of Trimdon now about 42 years.

Rent for the tenement	£2. 12s. 8d.
Rent for the ½ tenement	£0. 11s. od.

£3. 3s. 8d.

Improvement £17. os. od. (Jury), £25. 10s. od. (Ourselves)

RICHARD, brother of Tho. Johnson decd.

15 October 3 Car. That tenement in East Burdon

For the lives of the sd. Thomas and Richard and Thomas, younger son of the said Richard Johnson then aged 2 years.

Rent £1. 2s. od. Improvement £7. 10s. od. (Jury), £11. 5s. od. (Oureselves)

WM. ATKINSON in right of Grace his wife, daughter and Executrix of Thomas Johnson deceased heir of Wm. Johnson deceased.

15 October 3 Car. That tenement in East Burdon

For the lives of the said Grace then 3, William then 15 and John

Johnson then aged 10 years son of the said William Johnson.

Rent £1. 16s. od. Improvement £11. 10s. od. (Jury), £17. 5s. od. (Ourselves)

THOMAS BURDON by right of seniorship
27 September 7 Car. One tenement and a half in East Burdon wch Isabell his mother held

For the lives of the said Thomas Burden now 18 years, Edward Burden now 30 and William Burden of the Cittie of Durham now aged 40 years

Rent for the tenement	£2. 4s. 4d.
Rent for the ½ tenement	£0. 11s. od.
	£2. 15s. 4d.

Improvement £14. 0s. od. (Jury), £21. 0s. od. (Ourselves)

Morton Leaseholds

RICHARD BELASIS knt.
16 October 17 Car. All that Manor Farme or Towne of Morton nigh Houghton.

For 21 years Rent £6. 0s. od. Improvement £60. 0s. od. (Jury), £90. 0s. od. (Ourselves)

Middleherrington Leaseholds

GEORGE BARKAS
9 October 16 Car.
Who demised to
Robert Lampton
26 July 4 Car. The full moitie or one half part of 3 Closes and parcels of ground call the high hayning close and also 24 acres of land lying in Bridemoore as the same are now devided.

For the lives of the said George Barkas now aged 60 years Parcivall Barkas then aged about 10 and of Thomas Barkas then aged about 8 years.

Rent £1. 8s. od. Improvement £6. 0s. od. (Jury), £9. 0s. od. (Ourselves)

Newbottle Leaseholds

JOHN RUTTER

30 September 2 Car. Water Corne Mill commonly called Newbottle Milne at Newbottle together with the damm of water and suite and suchen and also one parcell of ground adjoyning to and letten with the same and also the grasse for one carriage horse for the said Milne to depasture and go in such usual place and places at such times and times as any farmer or occupier of the said Milne heretofor enjoyed.

For the lives of Thomas Rutter then 14 years, Robert Rutter then 11 and of William Rutter then aged about 7 years.

Rent £2. 13s. 4d. Improvement £10. 0s. 0d.

MARY STEPHENSON widow and Robert Stephenson executors

of the last will and testament of Robert Stevenson husband of Mary 5 November 7 Car. Messuage or tenement within the townfields and precincts of Newbottle late in the tenure and occupacon of Cicilie Appelby or her assigns and now in the occupacon of the said Mary Stevenson and Robert her sonne.

For 21 years. Rent £1. 17s. 5d. Improvement £7. 0s. 0d. (Jury), £10. 10s. 0d. (Ourselves)

JOHN sonne and assignee of Wm Chilton

5 November 7 Car. Tenement in Newbottle now in the tenure or occupacon of the said John Chilton.

For 21 years. Rent £1. 7s. 5d. Improvement £5. 0s. 0d. (Jury), £7. 10s. 0d. (Ourselves).

ALICE widow of John Chilton and John their son

2 October 6 Car. Tenement in Newbottle wth one outhouse and a garth and 2 acres of land in every field. The lessees shld find a horse wth furniture for the warres.

Rent £1. 19s. 2d. Improvement £6. 0s. 0d. (Jury), £9. 0s. 0d. (Ourselves)

GEORGE WATSON and Margaret his wife assignees of Anthony Surrett

21 September 3 Car. Tenement specified in the lease, in Newbottle.
For 21 years. Rent £2. 6s. 8d. Improvement £8. 8s. od. (Jury),
£10. os. od. (Ourselves)

ANN, widow, and William son of William Wilson
29 October 7 Car. Tenement in Newbottle.
For 21 years. Rent £4. 16s. 10d. Improvement £16. os. od. (Jury),
£14. os. od. (Ourselves)

WM. RANSON
9 May 11 Car. Moytie of one Oxgang of land in the townfields of
Newbottle now in the occupacon of the said Wm. Ranson.
For 21 years. Rent 4s. od. Improvement £4. os. od.

Newbottle Copyholds

WM. RANSON son and heir of Richard Ranson decd.
29 March 23 Car. One cottage and one oxgang of land in Newbottle wch his father had right in.
By surrender of Cicilie Smith late relict of said Richard Fine
5s. od.

Idem

ut supra. One messuage and one oxgang of land and 10 acres of
the lord's land, one dwelling house called a Seathouse in the
occupacon of Garvin Albon and one garth and one barn to the
same belonging 6 acres of arable land in the 3 several fields of Newbottle vizt 2 acres from thence lying in the west field 2 acres from
thence in the North field and 2 acres from thence in the East field
pasture for two beasts in le hall moore wth Foggage through
the whole field of Newbottle pasture for 3 beasts upon the
comon moore called Newbottle Moore wth pasturage for the aforesaid 3 beasts in Newbottle field between Michaelmas and the
Invencon of the Crosse and one close of Meadowe abutting upon
the hall Moore containing 2 acres and pasture for 5 sheep in le
Fallowe To have to the same Cicilie and her Assigns from the Feast
of the Annunciation of the Virgin Mary last past untill 60 years.
Rent for these two £1. 10s. 8d. Fine 10s. od.

GEORGE WATSON and Margarett his wife
4 May 19 Car. 4 partes of one cottage formerlie in the tenure of Wm. Davison and in 5 partes devided.
By surrender of Anthony Surrett. Rent 1s. 1d. Fine 7d.

GEORGE LILBURNE Gent
15 April 13 Car. One messuage and 26 acres of the Lord's land and the third part of two acres of land, one cottage and one Oxgang of land and the half of two acres of land in the Moore.
By surrender of Robert Chilton. Rent £2. 6s. 8d. Fine 13s. 4d.

RICHARD HASWELL
20 October 11 Car. One cottage.
By surrender of John Rogers. Rent 2s. 6d. Fine 1s. 0d.

ROBERT AYTON couzen and heir of Henry Ayton
22 October 10 Jac. One messuage and one acre of lands and one half of five acres of the Lord's land and one acre of Exchequor lands which Henry Ayton his grandfather had in right.
Rent 8s. 2d. Fine 5s. 0d.

ANTHONY RANSON
10 June 21 Jac. One cottage with a garth in Newbottle
By surrender of John Ireland. Rent 2s. 0d. Fine 1s. 8d.

ANN widow relict of Wm. Wilson
1 April 22 Car. One cottage and one acre of land formerlie Richard Franchlands.
In widdowright Rent 3s. 0d. Fine 6d.

ROBERT son and heir of Thomas Chilton
5 April 29 Elz. 33 acres of the Lord's land, three oxgangs of husband land and four acres of moore which his father had in right.
By surrender of Ann Chilton. Rent £3. 6s. 8d. Fine £1. 0. 0.

JOHN son and heir of Robert Chilton
15 June 7 Jac. One cottage and five acres of land which his father had in right.
Rent 8s. 0d. Fine 2s. 0d.

Hereafter followeth the names of the several persons whose names are charged with these rents following who produced no kind of evidence to show what title or clayme they have in their said Estates

Lease Robert Sharpe   Rent £2. 2s. 6d. Fine £8. os. od.
                                                       £12. os. od.

Lease William Surrett   Rent 4s. od. Fine £1. os. od.
                                                       £1. 10s. od.

Lease Bernard Robinson for High Hayning   Rent 6s. od.
                                         Fine £3. os. od.
                                                £4. os. od.

Lease Ellinor Bee for her part in High Hayning. Rent not known.
                                         Fine £3. os. od.
                                                £4. 10s. od.

Cop: Robert Chilton of West Row.   Rent £2. 17s. od.
       William Surrett.   Rent £3. 11s. od.
       Math Smith.   Rent   6s. 8d.
       George Chilton.   Rent   3s. 6d.
       Widd Sanderson.   Rent   6d.
       Nich Blakelock.   Rent   3d.

Ryehope Leaseholds

GEORGE HOLME of Bpp. Weremouth

28 July 14 Car. One messuage or tenement, one land and two parts of a land and one Mayne and half sett in the Towne fields and precincts of Rivehopp.

For the lives of said George Holme now 46 Ralph his sonne now aged 5 and of Robert Goodchilde jun. of Seaton aged 14 years.

Rent £2. 19s. od. £0. 6s. 8d. or one fatt veale at Pent. Improvement £6. os. od. (Jury), £15. os. od. (Ourselves).

JOHN FELL

27 September 3 Car. One messuage or tenement, one land and the 5th pte of two lands and one mayne and a half in the townefields and precincts of Rivehopp. One messuage or tenement.

For the lives of John Fell then 15, Robt Fell then 8, Edward Shephardson son of Wm. Shephardson of Morton now aged 23.

Rent £2. 12s. 8d. Improvement £6. os. od. (Jury), £15. os. od. (Ourselves)

RICHARD son and heir of Nicholas Thompson

30 September 20 Car. One mayne and an halfe and one land in Rivehopp.

For the lives of Richard Thompson then 23 years sonne of the said Nicholas Thompson, Robert Thompson then aged 5 years son of William Thompson the elder and of Robert Thompson also 5 sonne of George Thompson of Rivehopp.

Rent £2. 3s. 4d. Improvement £4. 10s. od. (Jury), £11. 5s. od. (Ourselves).

GEORGE son and heir of John Fell

15 September 30 Car. One messuage or tenement, one land and halfe one Mayne and a halfe and 2 cottages in Rivehopp.

For the lives of the sd. George then 18 years Wm. Fell then 8, Richard Fell then aged 6.

Rent £2. 15s. od. Improvement £6. os. od. (Jury), £15. os. od. (Ourselves).

JOHN sonne and heir of Thomas Rouxby

27 September 3 Car. One tenement, one land and the 3rd parte of one land and one Mayne and one halfe in Rivehopp.

For the lives of the said John Rouxby then aged 8 sonne of the sd. Thomas Rouxby and of William Fell then 10 years sonne of Edward Fell of Rivehopp yeo and of Richard Fell sone of John Fell of Rivehopp.

Rent £2. 11s. od. Improvement £5. os. od. (Jury), £12. 10s. od. (Ourselves)

WM. THOMPSON of Rivehopp

20 November 6 Car. One messuage or tenement one land 1½ maynes in Rivehopp.

For 21 years. Rent £2. 3s. 4d. Improvement £5. os. od. (Jury), £12. 10s. od. (Ourselves).

GEORGE THOMPSON

20 November 6 Car. One messuage or tenement, one land and 1½ maynes in Rivehopp.

For 21 years. Rent £2. 6s. od. Improvement £6. os. od. (Jury), £15. os. od. (Ourselves).

RALPH GOODCHILD by assignment from Robert his father
28 September 6 Car. One messuage or tenement, one land and one mayne
  For 21 years. Rent paid with William Shepperdson

WILLIAM SHIPPERDSON assignee of Robert Goodchild
31 March 23 Car.
18 July 14 Car. Messuage or tenement, one mayne and one land in Rivehopp.
  For 21 years Rent £3. 13s. 4d. Improvement £7. 6s. od. (Jury), £18. 10s. od. (Ourselves)

GEORGE WATSON
29 June 9 Car. Messuage or tenement, one land and the 5th part of 2 lands, 1½ maynes in Rivehopp.
  For 21 years. Rent £2. 12s. 8d. Improvement £6. os. od. (Jury), £15. os. od. (Ourselves).

NICHOLAS THOMPSON of Rivehopp
20 November 6 Car. One land, one mayne, one 4th part of a mayne and half a 3rd part of a mayne being the Moytie or Haffendale of the land late in the tenure and occupacon of Ralph Parkin in Rivehopp.
  For 21 years. Rent £2. 2s. 2d. Improvement £4. os. od. (Jury), £10. os. od. (Ourselves).

Hereafter followeth the names of the several persons whose names are charged with these Rents following who produced no kind of evidence to show what title they have in their said estates vzt:
Leaseholds:
  William Watson. Rent 11s. 8d. Improvement £5. os. od.
  George Thompson. Rent £2. 10s. 9d. Improvement £5. os. od. (Jury), £12. 10s. od. (Ourselves)
  William Sawfield and John Thompson. Rent £4. 5s. 6½d. Improvement £5. os. od. (Jury), £12. 10s. od. (Ourselves).
  Idem Rent £1. os. od. Improvement £4. os. od. (Jury) £10. os. od. (Ourselves)

Richard Thompson for the mill Rent £2. os. od. Improvement £2. os. od. (Jury), £3. os. od. (Ourselves).

William Fyre. Rent £2. 8s. 1od. Improvement £4. os. od. (Jury), £10. os. od. (Ourselves).

Edward Fell. Rent £2. 16s. od. Improvement £6. os. od. (Jury), £15. os. od. (Ourselves).

Copyhold:

Robert Hutton for Warden Law. Rent £2. 6s. 8d.

Bishop Weremouth Copyholds

THOMAS AYRE

4 May 19 Car. Two messuages and 15 acres of land and 12 acres of husband land. One cottage and 12 acres of land formerly William Smith.

By surrender of Thomas his father. Fine 6s. 8d.

Idem

20 March 22 Car. One roode of land in the Milne piece between the land of the foresaid Thomas on the south and a balke on the north. One parcel of land in the west field of Weremouth leading to a Milne there between the land of the said Thomas on the south and the lands of Mary Stevenson widdow on the north, one little rigg or butt lying to the highway lying between the lands of John Hilton on the south and the ground of the said Thomas on the north parcel of the moytie of land called Tunstall demeasnes.

By surrender of Jacob Sanderson also Saundery. Rent (10s. od.) Fine 2d.

Idem

15 October 15 Car. The 4th part of 12 acres of land, the 4th part of 10 acres of the Lord's land and the 4th part of an husband land formerly William Ward's and also the 4th part of 10 acres of the demeasne land in Bishop Wearmouth late in the tenure of John Hilton.

Fine 5s. od.

Idem

dat ut supra. The 4th part of one parcel of meadow lying in small Heaares.

By surrender of John Hilton. Rent £3. 2s. 1d. Fine 4d.

EDWARD HARPER in right of Isabell his wife widow relict of
Thomas Bryan
3 April 3 Car. 9 acres of land and the 3rd part of one house and
of one messuage and of 12 acres of ground with one cottage and one
parcel of a tenement containing ½ roode of land lying in the end
of the Towne there on the north.
  In widdowright Fine £1. os. od.

Idem
dat ut supra. One cottage
  In widdowright. Fine 2s. od.

Idem
dat ut supra. The 3rd part of one Messuage and of 10 acres of land
and 30 acres of land the 3rd part of one messuage and of 30 acres
of bond land and the 3rd part of a 3rd part of one house and of 10
acres of the Lord's land.
  In widdowright. Fine 9s. 6d.
  Rent for these copyholds £4. 4s. 7d.

THOMAS ROBINSON
15 April 13 Car. One messuage lying on the west of a house of
John Shippardson and on the east of a house of John Thompsons
containing in length 6 yards and one garth containing in length 6
yards from the east corner of the house of the said George.
  Fine 1s. od.

Idem
19 October 6 Car. The moietie of the moietie of one cottage containing in length 14 yards of land lying between the tenement and
garth in the tenure of John Colyer on the south and north residue
of the said cottage on the west and the comon street called Litlegate
on the east.
  Fine 3d.
  Rent for these copyholds 3s. 4d.
  By surrender of John Burdon.

JOHN NICHOLSON

11 April 23 Car. The halfe of one messuage and halfe of 12 acres of land and also halfe of one messuage and of one husbandry land formerlie William Ward and half of 10 acres of land lying in Bishop Weremouth, half of one parcel of meadow lying in small myers (6 acres of land, parcel of the premisses vzt. 2 acres lying in the southfield, 2 acres in the westfield, 2 acres in the eastfield and pasture for 2 beasts in the southfield. One house in which Isabell Hilton, widdow, now dwelleth together with another house in which Anthony Bailes now dwelleth with a low barn parcel of the premisses excepted) by demise of the said Isabell Hilton to have to the said John from the Annunciation of the blessed Virgin these last past for 40 years paying yearly to Isabell and her assigns £3. 10s. 0d.

Rent £2. 0s. 10d. Fine 3d.

Idem

22 April 23 Car. 6 acres of land in the 3 several fields aforesaid vzt: 2 acres in the westfield, 2 acres in the eastfield and 2 acres in the southfield (parcel of the moity of one messuage and 15 acres of the Rent 5s. 0d.).

By surrender of Robert Pattison. Rent 6d. Fine 6d.

Idem

dat ut supra. One acre of land in the eastfield and one other acre of land in the southfield and 2 other acres in the westfield.

By surrender of Robert Halliday. Fine 1s. 4d.

Idem

dat ut supra. One little Crosse house (parcel of a dwelling house of one Thomas Taylor of Weremouth aforesaid on the backside of a house extending north and south and one garth adjacent to the said Crosse House north and south containing 15 yards and from the west to the east 18 yards from the southeast nook to the north-east nook 3½ yards adjoining to the house of William Dixon on the north and the house of William Thompson on the south.

By surrender of Thomas Taylor. Fine 1d.

Idem

dat ut supra. One little house extending from the south door cheek of the former house of Robert Thompson towards the north in length ... abutting upon the land of John Nicholson on the north and the lands of Elizabeth Johnson on the west the land of John Shippardson on the south and the common street on the east with a garth to the same belonging.

By surrender of Robert and Richard Thompson. Fine 2d.

ROBERT PATTISON son and heir of William Pattison
7 October 17 Jac. The moytie of one messuage and the moytie of 30 acres of husband land and the moytie of one messuage and of 15 acres of bond land.

By surrender of George Shippardson and Alice his wife. Rent £1. 19s. 10d. Fine 5d.

JOHN JOHNSON Junior
28 April 22 Jac. The halfe of one cottage and the halfe of 10 acres of the Lord's land which John Johnson Senior his father had of right.

By surrender of the said John Senior. Fine 1s. 8d.

Idem
20 May 5 Car. One messuage with a garth on the backside containing in breadth 11 yards to the west end of the same garth and so of the same bredth unto the middle and from thence extend itself to the north nuke of the stable.

By surrender of Thomas Johnson. Fine 4d.

Idem
22 April 23 Car. One cottage, one barn and garth on the west of the same cottage house and barn, parcel of the half of one cottage the half of 10 acres of the Lord's land.

By surrender of Richard Johnson. Fine 1d.

Idem
15 October 15 Car. The 4th part of 12 acres of land and the 4th part of 10 acres of the Lord's land and the 4th part of one husbandry land formerly William Warde and also the 4th part of 10 acres of the Lord's land lying in Weremouth now in the tenure of John Hilton.

By surrender of John Hilton. Fine 5s. od.

Idem

dat ut supra. The 4th part of one parcel of meadow ground lying in Smayle Myers.

By surrender of John Hilton. Fine 3d.

Rents for these five copyholds £1. 13s. 5d.

THOMAS FEWLER and Ann his wife

21 November 12 Car. The 3rd part of 10 acres of land and the 3rd part of 30 acres of bond land and also the 3rd part of a small piece of ground of 10 acres of demesne land by demise of Margarett Jarvis widdow relict of Ralph Jarvice from St. Martin the Bishop in winter for 100 years paying £6 yearly at Martinmas and Pentecost. Fine 4s. 9d.

Idem

dat ut supra. The 3rd part of one plott of ground vzt. the 3rd part of one tenement and 40 acres of land and 40 acres called Westerplace and of one tenement and 10 acres of demeasne land formerly William Hamithorne and Emma his wife by demise ut supra.

Fine 2s. 2d.

Idem

dat ut supra. The moytie of a whole tenure formerly John Roxbyes and the moytie of 6 acres of land by demise ut supra without any rent paying.

Fine 1s. 0d.

Idem

dat ut supra. One messuage late of the Lord's waste and lately built with a croft and 10 acres of land by demise ut supra without any rent.

Fine 1s. 8d.

Idem

dat ut supra. 6 acres of land in every field of Weremouth ut supra.

Fine 1s. 0d.

Rent for these five copyholds £4. 19s. 3d.

JOHN YOUNGER son and heir apparent of John Shippardson the elder.

1 October 9 Jac. One cottage with a garth.
   By surrender as heir to his father. Fine 1s. 0d.

Idem
dat ut supra. One tenement called East Place.
   By surrender as heir to his father. Fine £1. 0s. 0d.

Idem
5 May 16 Jac. The moytie of a tenure formerly John Rowxbye (A dwelling house with barnes, stables, Oxenhouses, dovecotes and a fold or stackgarth parcel of the same tenure excepted and reserved), and also one cottage and Garth lying on the backside and the moytie of 6 acres of land formerly John Colson.
   By surrender of William Roxbye. Fine 2s. 5d.
   Rent for these three copyholds £6. 0s. 0d.
                    (Page missing)

21 October 5 Car. One house containing in length 12 yards of land on the backside adjacent.
   By surrender of George Shipperdson. No rent. Fine 6d.

MARTIN WATSON
20 October 11 Car. One cottage containing in length 20 yards and in breadth 5 yards of ground with a garth to the same adjoyning parcel of one cottage.
   By surrender of George Shippardson. No rent. Fine 1s. 0d.

THOMAS SMITH
13 November 22 Car. The 3rd part of the 3rd part of one messuage lying on the south of the tenement of Edward Harper and on the east of the tenement of Robert Pastmore (parcel of the 3rd part of 2 messuages and of 10 acres of the Lord's land).
   By surrender of Robert Pattison. Rent 9s. 0d. Fine 1s. 8d.

ELIZABETH wife of Edward Chilton and Margarett wife of John Ratcliffe daughters and co-heirs of Thomas Bee
7 September 22 Car. 1½ acres of arable land in 3 several fields of Wearmouth (parcel of 6 acres of land formerly John Colson) as heir to their late father Thomas *(part missing)*
   Fine 6d.

Eadem

dat ut supra. One cottage with one garth to the same adjacent on the backside lying between the cottage of George Shippardson on the south and the cottage of Ralph Holme on the north on Wearmouth.

Fine 2d.

Eadem

dat ut supra. One house scituate in a certain place called below rane adjacent from the tenement of him the said Thomas on the south and 3 roods of land (vzt.) one roode in every field of the same town, parcel of the moytie of one messuage and the moytie of 30 acres of husband land and 15 acres of bond land.

Fine 3d.

Eadem

dat ut supra. 3 roodes of land lying in 3 several fields in the town (vzt) one roode of land in the eastfield lying on the south of Bildon Hill and one rood of land in the southfield lying upon Howden.

Fine 6d.

All which 4 copyholds pay rent included in Thomas Fewler, Robert Pattison, and Robert Ayre being bought as parcel thereof.

RICHARD, brother and heir of Thomas Johnson

1 April 22 Car. One dwelling house vzt. a hall and a chamber and the twixt doors and one shop on the south betwixt doors aforesaid 2 parts of a garth and a fold on the backside adjacent on the south of the same garth and the half of one barn and the moytie of the Moytie of 6 acres of ground Chequer land and the moytie of a parcel of Exchequer land on Wearmouth.

By surrender as heir to his brother. Rent 8s. 9d. Fine 1s. 1½d.

MARTIN WATSON

25 January 22 Car. One dwelling house (vzt) a hall and a chamber and the tweene doors and one shop now made into a chamber on the south of the twixt doors aforesaid, 2 parts of one garth, a fold on the backside lying with a barn thereupon built on the north of the said garden and on the south of the said barn decayed.

By surrender of Richard Johnson. Rent 1s. 1½d. Fine 2d.

WILLIAM COXON
18 April 7 Car. The moytie of one cottage in Wearmouth.
By surrender of Robert Chambers. Rent 3d. Fine 1s. od.

ISAACH WATTSON in right of Jane his wife relict of John Thompson
19 September 14 Car. One messuage adjacent upon the hallgarth in Wearmouth.
By surrender in widdowright. Rent included in Robert Pattison's rent. Fine 6d.

GEORGE LILBURNE gentleman
14 October 15 Car. One parcel of land extending from a street called Pangate from the west to the east end of the town of Sunderland and one house late in the occupation of James Bentley and one other house then in the occupation of Richard Bentflower and one other house now in the tenure of John Scurfield and one other house now in the occupation of Ann Taylor and one Toft then in occupation of Ann Taylor and one Toft then in the occupation of Richard Ourd and one other toft then in the occupation of David Browne and one other house then in the occupation of David Browne and one other house then in the occupation of John Browne and also one other house then in the occupation of Thomas Browne built of and upon the premisses and with all Rents with all houses aforesaid exempted in Sunderland and with other lands belonging to Robert Collingwood and William Power extending itself (*torn*) the south of the Water of Weare from the (*torn*) water mark to the low water mark except the tenement of John Harrison and Adam Burdons and a little parcel of ground then in the occupation of William Dixon
By surrender of Robert Collingwood Esq., and William Power gent. Fine 3s. 4d.

Idem
dat ut supra. One parcel of land now built and containing in length 10 yards and 6 yards in breadth, parcel of one parcel of ground lying to the river or bank of Wear.
By surrender of William Bowes, Esq. Fine 4d.

JOHN HARRISON

5 July 15 Car. One parcel of land with all houses and staithes lying upon the Ash heap near Bishop Wearmouth saltpannes called and known by the name of Wilsons houses and now in the tenure of the said John Harrison and another parcel of land adjacent to the said parcel of ground containing in length from the north to the south 9 yards and in breadth from the east to west 5 yards called Addisons Tenement and now in the occupation of the said John which said parcel of land containing in length from the east to west by the north part of the way leading from the town of Sunderland to the said salt pans 35 yards and in breadth from east to west by water of Wear 50 yards to the lands of Sir William Lambton knt. and the staithe formerly granted to Edward Anderson by William Bowes (*missing*).

By surrender of Robert Collingwood, Esq., and William Power
This rent is included in Sir William Lambton's heirs who show not all their coppies. Fine 4d.

(*missing*) BURDON

10 November 17 Car. One parcel of ground lying in Bishop Wearmouth salt panns containing in length 10½ yards and in breadth 6 yards between the tenement of Henry Babington and William Thompson.

By surrender of George Lilburne gent. Rent—ut supra. Fine 2d.

ROBERT HOLLIDAY

17 October 19 Car. The moitie on the north of one parcel of land containing in length 18 yards and in breadth 18 yards with a house thereupon built.

By surrender of William Church gent. Rent 6d. Fine 4d.

RALPH son and heir apparent of Adam Holme

25 June 20 Jac. 2 cottages and 12 acres of land formerly William Coltmans and 10 acres of the Lord's land in Tunstall.

By surrender of Adam Holme. Rent £2. 2s. 0d. Fine 10s. 0d.

JOHN SURFIELD

4 May 19 Car. One house late in the tenure of the said John Surfield containing in length east to west 13 yards lying on the south of the King's street leading from Sunderland to Bishop Wearmouth

saltpanns and on the north of the land belonging to the town of Weremouth and on the west to the lands of Ann Taylor widdow and on the east to the lands of Richard Bonteflower and also one other house containing in length from the east to the west 8 yards late in the tenure or occupation of Richard Bonteflower lying on the south of the way leading from Sunderland to Bishop Wearmouth saltpanns and on the north to the lands belonging to the town of Weremouth and on the west to a tenement of the said John Surfield and on the east to the tenement of William Dickinson.

By surrender of George Lilburne gent.

These last 6 copies are recorded on fragments and are part of a greater whole.

Bishop Wearmouth Leaseholds

MARTIN WATSON of Herrington Mill yeoman.
20 November 6 Car. Wynd corne milne of Bishop Weremouth.
For 21 years. Rent £5. 0s. 0d. Improvement £4. 0s. 0d.

JOHN SHIPPARDSON of Bishop Weremouth
15 May 11 Car. Fishing in the River of Weare so far as the grounds belonging to the township of Bishop Wearmouth doth extend along the said river together with free way leave to and from the said fishing and libertie to hang their nets to dry upon the ground. And also those quarries of limestone within all and every the wastes or waste grounds within Bishop Weremouth and all lime pits and houses already digged and made within any part of the premisses together with free libertie to dig and make so many lime pits and quarries within the premisses as shall please him the said John Shippardson. And also to build and erect thereupon 2 limehouses for laying and keeping lime in and for the persons employed about the said lime pits to live in and no other (except free libertie for the said Bishop and his successors to dig limestone and burn lime at the quarry of Boldon for repaying their ancient tenements and no otherwise.

For 21 years. Rent 5s. 0d. and also 6 good and fresh salmon in due season. Improvement £2. 0s. 0d. (Jury), £2. 10s. 0d. (Ourselves).

THOMAS SMITH assignee of Robert Pattison
24 August 9 Car.
27 November 22 Car. Cottage and garth and 15 acres of land and meadow in Bishop Wearmouth.

For 21 years. Rent 15s. 4d. Improvement £2. os. od. (Jury), £5. os. od. (Ourselves).

SURVEY OF THE MANOR OF EASINGTON

The manor of Easington with the rights members and appurten-ances thereof in the County or County Palatine of Durham And all rents of assize Free Rents Customary Rents Rents Rents Service and all other Rents and yearly sum or sums of money commonly called Rents of Assize Old Rents Chief Rents or Quit Rents to the said mannor belonging or appertaining per annum £12. 19s. 5½d.

Easington Manor Leaseholds

EDWARD PAXTON and JOHN CLARKE

13 November 10 Car. Bakehouse in the township of Easington late in the tenure or occupation of Edward Paxton and John Clarke.

For the lives of James Paxton, John Clarke and Anne Clarke. All in being.

Rent 4s. 0d. Improvement 10s. 0d.

ROBERT AIRE

5 November 11 Car. Wind corn mill commonly called Easington Wind Mill near Easington aforesaid together with the site ground and sale whereupon the said mill is situated.

For 21 years. Rent £2. 0s. 0d. Improvement £6. 0s. 0d.

ROBERT HEDDRINGTON

2 November 5 Car. Water corn mill within the township of Shotton with all that stream or course of water belonging.

For 21 years. Rent £1. 6s. 8d. Improvement £6. 0s. 0d.

ROBERT DIXON and THOMAS THURSBYE

6 July 13 Car. Water corn mill in the township of Sherburne

For the lives of Richard and Thomas Thursbye and Jane Dixon. All in being.

Rent £2. 0s. 0d. Improvement £10. 0s. 0d.

Thorpe Township Leaseholds

JOHN JURDESON

16 October 20 Jac. Moytie of one half of a messuage or tenement in the township of Thorpe also Littlethroppe being parcel of the demesne lands of Easington.

For the lives of the said John Jurdeson Jane Jurdeson and Richard Jurdeson. All in being.

Rent £2. 4s. 0d. Improvement £9. 0s. 0d.

ROBERT PAXTON

27 March 1 Jac. Moytie or one half part of a messuage or tenement in Thorpe aforesaid and also all those three lands there each land containing 30 acres within the fields and precincts of Thorpe. And also the moytie or one half part of 3 maynes being parcel of arable land parcel of the demesnes of Easington

For the lives of George Paxton Christopher Paxton and James Paxton. Two of the said lives in being.

Rent £2. 7s. 1d. Improvement £9. 0s. 0d.

RICHARD WALKER

31 August 9 Car. Tenement in Little Thorpe aforesaid And also those 3 husband lands and 4 maynes being parcel of the demesne lands of Easington within the several fields there containing in each field 40 acres.

For the lives of Richard, Nicholas and John Walker. Only John is living.

Rent £4. 14s. 2d. Improvement £18. 0s. 0d.

WILLIAM JOHNSON and MILDRED ROBINSON now in the possession of the Trustees

Moytie or one half of a messuage or tenement in Littlethorpe aforesaid and parcel of the demesne lands of Easington.

Improvement £11. 8s. 0d.

ABRAHAM PAXTON now in the possession of the Trustees

Moytie or one half part of a messuage or tenement And all those lands in Littlethorpe aforesaid each land containing 30 acres Also all the moytie of 3 maynes being parcel of arable lands of the demesne of Easington each mayne containing 10 acres.

Improvement £11. 7s. 1d.

Shadforth Township Leaseholds

SYMOND LACKENBYE

10 June 5 Car. All that messuage or tenement in Shadforth

For the lives of Symond, John and Henrye Lackenbye. All in being.

Rent £2. 6s. 8d. Improvement £16. 0s. 0d.

WILLIAM HEDDRINGTON and RICHARD HEDDRINGTON

26 April 13 Car. All that moytie or one half part of a messuage or tenement in Shadforth.

For the lives of John, Robert and William Heddrington. All in being.

Rent £1. 7s. 1½d. Improvement £8. 0s. 0d.

WILLIAM HEDDRINGTON

8 June 10 Car. Moytie or one half of a messuage or tenement in Shaldforth.

For the lives of William, George and Richard Heddrington. Two lives in being.

Rent £1. 2s. 0d. Improvement £8. 0s. 0d.

WILLIAM HALE

16 December 6 Car. Moytie or one half of a messuage in Shaldforth.

For the lives of William, Thomas and John Hall. All in being.

Rent £1. 7s. 1½d. Improvement £8. 0s. 0d.

JANE DENT widdow

13 July 13 Car. Messuage or tenement in Shaldforth.

For 21 years. Rent £2. 5s. 2d. Improvement £16. 0s. 0d.

ROBERT MOABURNE

6 July 9 Car. Moytie or one half part of a messuage in Shaldforth.

For 21 years. Rent £1. 3s. 1d. Improvement £8. 0s. 0d.

RALPH HUNTLEY

24 September 7 Car. The moytie of a messuage or tenement in Shaldforth.

For 21 years. Rent £2. 3s. 3d. Improvement £16. 0s. 0d.

WILLIAM HUNTLEY

29 October 7 Car. Moytie or one half of a messuage or tenement in Shaldforth.

For 21 years. Rent £1. 3s. 0½d. Improvement £8. 0s. 0d.

PHILLIP HADDOCK

6 July 9 Car. Moytie or one half part of a messuage or tenement in Shaldforth.

For 21 years. Rent £1. 3s. 1d. Improvement £8. 0s. 0d.

WILLIAM HALL

10 August 14 Car. Messuage or tenement in Shaldforth.

For 21 years. Rent £2. 5s. 3d. Improvement £16. 0s. 0d.

WILLIAM TAYLOR

28 August 10 Car. Moytie or one half of a tenement in Shaldforth as is now divided and enclosed That is to say All that west end of a certain ground commonly called the New Close And all that west end of ground there called the west corne field And all that west end of a certain ground there called the Hills And also all that west end of a certain ground there called the South Meadows all which said parcels of ground are bounded with and adjoining upon the ground belonging to the township of Cassop on the south The ground belonging to the township of Sherburne on the north and west And certain ground belonging to one William Huntley on the east.

For 21 years. Rent £1. 2s. 7d. Improvement £8. 0s. 0d.

ANTONYE HUNTLYE

6 September 6 Car. Messuage or tenement And all that garth thereunto belonging in Shaldforth and all pastureage and feeding for one sow and one horse and 8 sheep within and upon the common fields of Shaldforth.

For 21 years. Rent 6s. 8d. Improvement £1. 10s. 8d.

ANNE SWALWELL widdow

11 February 13 Car. Messuage or tenement in Shaldforth.
For 21 years. Rent £2. 5s. 2d. Improvement £16. 0s. 0d.

Easington Township Leaseholds

GEORGE PAXTON

5 October 16 Jac. Parcel of waste ground in Easington And also all
that cottage with a garth with common of pasture for one horse
and one cow and 5 sheep.
For the lives of George Paxton, Emma his wife and Edmund
Paxton. All in being.
Rent 9s. 6d. Improvement 13s. 4d.

WILLIAM PAXTON

4 November 10 Car. Messuage or tenement in Easington
For the lives of Christopher, Robert and Collin Paxton. All in
being.
Rent £1. 13s. 0d. Improvement £6. 8s. 0d.

ELLEN relict of Henrye Clarke

16 October 2 Car. Messuage or tenement with one main land containing 9 acres in Easington
For the lives of Henry, Ellin and Richard Clarke. Only 1 life
in being. Rent £1. 12s. 4½d. Improvement £6. 0s. 0d.

ELIANOR PAXTON

5 November 11 Car. Messuage or tenement with one land and one
maine and one half land in Easington.
For 21 years. Rent £2. 8s. 4½d. Improvement £8. 10s. 0d.

CHRISTOPHER BELL

5 May 11 Car. Messuage or tenement and also that messuage and
half a husband land commonly called the Pinders land in Easington.
For 21 years. Rent £2. 3s. 4½d. Improvement £7. 10s. 0d.

RICHARD HESTER

18 September 11 Car. Demesne lands containing 9 acres in Easington and also demesne lands containing 18 acres in Easington.

For 21 years. Rent £1. 10s. 0d. Improvement £6. 0s. 0d.

GEORGE PAXTON

5 November 11 Car. Messuage or tenement in Easington.
For 21 years. Rent £1. 15s. 4d. Improvement £6. 10s. 0d.

GEORGE ROBINSON

5 November 11 Car. Messuage or tenement in Easington.
For 21 years. Rent £1. 12s. 4½d. Improvement £6. 0s. 0d.

RICHARD JURDSON

5 November 11 Car. Messuage or tenement and one mayne land in Easington.
For 21 years. Rent £1. 12s. 4½d. Improvement £6. 0s. 0d.

THOMAS PAXTON

5 November 11 Car. Messuage or tenement and one half mayne of land containing 4½ acres in Easington.
For 21 years. Rent 13s. 0d. Improvement £3. 0s. 0d.

JOHN DRAWER

16 March 6 Car. 12 acres of demesne land in Easington.
For 21 years. Rent 12s. 0d. Improvement £2. 0s. 0d.

KATHERINE JOHNSON

5 May 11 Car. 9 acres of demesne lands in Easington.
For 21 years. Rent 10s. 0d. Improvement £2. 0s. 0d.

WILLIAM WARDELL

14 December 11 Car. Messuage or tenement together with 1 mayne land and ½ mayne containing 14 acres in Easington.
For 21 years. Rent £1. 9s. 4½d. Improvement £6. 0s. 0d.

ROBERT AIRE

10 October 7 Car. One messuage or tenement together with 1½ maynes of land containing 13 acres in Easington.
For 21 years. Rent 16s. 3d. Improvement £9. 0s. 0d.

THOMAS PAXTON

5 November 11 Car. Messuage or tenement together with 1½ maynes of land in Easington.

For 21 years. Rent £1. 18s. 3d. Improvement £7. os. od.

WILLIAM PAXTON

5 November 11 Car. Messuage or tenement and 1 mayne land in Easington.

For 21 years. Rent £2. 7s. 8½d. Improvement £8. os. od.

JOHN SIMPSON

20 Car. 6 November 18 acres of land in Easington.

For 21 years. Rent £1. os. od. Improvement £4. os. od.

WILLIAM INGLEBYE

29 March 20 Car. Piece or parcel of pasture ground commonly called Fleming Field and being near Ludworth

For the lives of Christopher, John and Robert Conyers. All in being.

Rent £1. os. od. Improvement £9. os. od.

Cassop Township Leaseholds

RALPH ROAD

17 October 2 Car. Messuage tenement or husbandryland in Cassop.

For the lives of George Road, Robert Taylor and William Burdon. Two lives in being.

Rent £2. 11s. 3d. Improvement £11. 10s. od.

WILLIAM BUSHBYE

10 August 14 Car. Messuage or tenement with 3 lands containing 30 acres of arable land in Cassop.

For the lives of William, Anthonye and Henrie Bushbye. All in being

Rent £5. os. od. Improvement £23. os. od.

ANTHONY WILSON

7 October 2 Car. Messuage tenement and husbandryland in Cassop.

For the lives of Anthony, John and Samuell Willson. Two lives in being

Rent £2. 10s. od. Improvement £11. 10s. od.

HENRY BISHOP

26 September 6 Car. Messuage or tenement in Cassop.

For the lives of Henrie Busby, Anthony Trollop and William Trollop
Rent £2. 11s. 3d. Improvement £11. 10s. 0d.

JOHN DAVISON

16 June 13 Car. Moytie and one half of a messuage in Cassop.
For the lives of John and Elizabeth Davison and Henry Busby. All in being. Rent £2. 10s. 0d. Improvement £11. 10s. 0d.

WILLIAM DAVISON

27 September 6 Car. One messuage and tenement in Cassop.
For the lives of William, John and Robert Davison. Two lives in being. Rent £2. 11s. 3d. Improvement £11. 10s. 0d.

HENRYE BUSBYE

2 June 16 Car. Moytie and one half part of a messuage in Cassop.
For 21 years. Rent £2. 10s. 0d. Improvement £11. 10s. 0d.

Quarrington Township Leaseholds

THOMAS GIFFORD

24 October 24 Elz. Closes and parcels of meadow ground at Quarrington commonly known as Armestrong Close Alehouse Close and Russetts Close, Knottyebutts Ethlestons Close Calfe Close and the Awards and all that parcel of ground called Snayley Lees And all those 2 closes called Highfield and Sumer Croft also the long rigg and all that piece of certain ground there called the Barne Flatt containing one rood lying in the backside of Lionell Curds house in Quarrington.
For 80 years. Rent £4. 8s. 8d. Improvement £27. 15s. 4d.

RALPH ALLANSON

Lands and tenements part of the Graunge of Quarrington
No lease produced, the premises are to be sold as in possession.
Rent £22. 4s. 8d. Improvement £138. 18s. 0d.

Sherburn Township Leaseholds

ROBERT DIXON

27 July 9 Car. Messuage or tenement and 3 acres of land within the

3 several fields of Sherburn one beastgate in the Moor 5 sheep gates in the infield and 2½ sheep gates in the moor.

For the lives of Robert, Thomas and Jane Dixon. Two lives in being. Rent £2. 3s. 1½d. Improvement £16. 0s. 0d.

WILLIAM WHITFIELD

13 July 9 Car. One messuage or tenement in Sherburne.

For the lives of William and Robert Whitfield and Jane Sparrow All in being. Rent £2. 9s. 0d. Improvement £16. 0s. 0d.

WILLIAM HALL

20 April 16 Car. One messuage in Sherburne.

For the lives of George Road, William Davison and Anthony Haddock. Two lives in being. Rent £2. 3s. 1½d. Improvement £16. 0s. 0d.

JOHN ROWELE

6 May 11 Car. One messuage in Sherburn

For the lives of John Rowle, Mary his wife and Henry Rowele. All in being. Rent £2. 10s. 8d. Improvement £16. 0s. 0d.

HENRY COOKE

7 October 6 Jac. One messuage in Sherburne.

For the lives of Henry, Anne and Margarett Cooke. All in being. Rent £2. 10s. 8d. Improvement £16. 0s. 0d.

JOHN RAWLING

20 September 9 Car. One messuage in Sherburne.

For the lives of John the father, John and Anne Rawling. Two lives in being. Rent £2. 4s. 0d. Improvement £16. 0s. 0d.

WILLIAM BROWNE

10 October 16 Jac. One messuage in Sherburne and 3 acres of arable land in the 3 several fields there and also one cowgate in Greene pasture and one beast gate in the moor 5 sheep gates in the Inge Field and 2½ sheep gates in the moor.

For the lives of William, Thomas and Margarett Brown. All in being. Rent £2. 10s. 0d. Improvement £16. 0s. 0d.

JOHN WHITFIELD

2 November 17 Car. One cottage with one horsegate one cowgate

5 sheepgates and one calfgate in Sherburn.
    For 21 years. Rent 5s. 0d. Improvement £1. 10s. 0d.

MICHAEL PATTISON

1 November 17 Car. One cottage with one horsegate one oxegate one calfgate and 5 sheepgates.
    For 21 years. Rent 6s. 0d. Improvement £1. 10s. 0d.

WILLIAM HALE

14 August 13 Car. One cottage or cotehouse in Sherburne.
    For 21 years. Rent 6s. 0d. Improvement £1. 10s. 0d.

WILLIAM NICHOLSON

1 November 17 Car. One cottage with one horsegate one cowgate or calfgate and 5 sheepgates.
    For 21 years. Rent 7s. 0d. Improvement £1. 10s. 0d.

BRIAN BIOLSTON

8 November 8 Car. One messuage or tenement in Sherburn
    For the lives of Henry, John and Richard Pearson. All in being.
Rent £3. 4s. 8d. Improvement £24. 0s. 0d.

Shotton Township Leaseholds

JOHN IMPSON

18 April 11 Car. One messuage or tenement in Shotton and one cottage in Shotton with 1½ lands and 1½ maynes
    For the lives of John, Nicholas and Richard Thompson. Two lives in being Rent £1. 19s. 0d. Improvement £9. 0s. 0d.

RICHARD ROAD

7 November 7 Car. One messuage or tenement in Shotton with 2 lands and 2 maynes and ½ land and all that cottage in Shotton.
    For the lives of Richard, Thomas and Richard Road. All in being. Rent £3. 3s. 4d. Improvement £13. 0s. 0d.

WILLIAM HILL

20 June 9 Car. One messuage in Shotton.
    For 21 years. Rent £2. 9s. 4d. Improvement £12. 0s. 0d.

JOHN RICHARDSON

20 June 7 Car. One messuage or tenement in Shotton with 1½ lands and ½ mayne of lands and one cottage in Shotton.

For 21 years. Rent £1. 8s. od. Improvement £6. 15s. od.

GEORGE SHALDFORTH

19 June 13 Car. One messuage and one mayne of land in Shotton.

For 21 years. Rent 12s. od. Improvement £2. 5s. od.

ELIZABETH HEDDRINGTON

27 June 9 Car. One cottage in Shotton.

For 21 years. Rent 3s. 6d. Improvement 10s. od.

JOHN TOMPSON

10 September 7 Car. One messuage with 1½ lands and one mayne and one coathouse and a Pander land in Shotton.

For 21 years. Rent 14s. 10d. Improvement £9. os. od.

RICHARD JARDSON

One messuage with one mayne of land in Shotton.

For 21 years. Rent 10s. od. Improvement £2. 5s. od.

MICHAEL BRYAN

20 June 7 Car. One messuage or tenement and one cottage in Shotton with 1¾ lands and also 1 mayne of land in Shotton.

For 21 years. Rent £1. 16s. od. Improvement £9. os. od.

THOMAS LIGHTON

25 September 6 Car. One messuage or tenement in Shotton with 1½ lands and 1½ maynes and one cottage.

For 21 years. Rent £1. 18s. 8d. Improvement £9. os. od.

JAMES BYARS

6 September 1 Car. One moytie or half part a messuage or tenement in Shotton together with the moytie of a cotehouse the moytie of 1½ lands the moytie of 1½ maynes and also the moytie of a parcel of ground called Pander land

For the lives of John, William and Richard Readhead. All in being. Rent £1. 1s. od. Improvement £4. 10s. od.

JAMES BYARS

29 August 11 Car. Fourth part of a messuage or tenement and cottage and also that full 4th part of 1¾ lands with the 4th part of one mayne in Shotton.

For the lives of Francis, Robert and Richard Byars. All in being. Rent 9s. 1d. Improvement £2. 5s. od.

GEORGE PAXTON and WILLIAM STODDART

6 September 1 Car. Moytie or one half part of one messuage or tenement with a moytie of one cotehouse the moytie of 1½ lands the moytie of 1½ maynes and also the moytie of one parcel of ground called Pounders land in Shotton

For the lives of John, Richard and William Readhead. All in being. Rent £1. 10s. od. Fine £4. 10s. od.

JOHN RICHARDSON

5 November 10 Car. One messuage or tenement with one cottage 1¾ lands one mayne of land in Shotton

For the lives of Anne, George and Phillip Richardson. Two lives in being. Rent £1. 7s. 3d. Improvement £6. 15s. od.

THOMAS BURDON

20 November 6 Car. One messuage in Shotton.

For 21 years. Rent £1. 18s. od. Improvement £9. os. od.

And all singular messuages crofts tofts mills houses edifices buildings burns stables gardens orchards curtilages lands tenements arable meadow and pasture ground feedings commons and common pasture wastes and waste ground turbage heaths moors marshes marsh grounds fells woods underwoods timber trees and other trees waters watercourses rivers streams pools mill dams site of mill multure sersuite sucken mines opened and not opened quarries and all courts leets views of frankpledge and whatsoever to view of frankpledge appertaining Courts Baron Halimott Courts and other courts whatsoever services fines issues amerciaments perquisites and profitts of the said Courts and leets reliefs herriots escheats forfeitures lesses goods and chattles of felons and of fugatives and of felons of themselves of outlawed persons and of persons put in erigent waifes estrayes feodands wrecks of the sea treasure trove fishings huntering hawking and all other the royalties juridissons franchisers liberties priviledges immunities profitts commodities ways passages easements advantages enrolments rents services possessions and heriditaments whatsoever with their and every of their appurtenances to the said mannor messuage cottages mynes lands and premisses for or any of them or any part or parcel of them on any of them belonging insident or in any wise appertaining or which the late Bishop of Durham or by his predecessors in right of the said Bishoprick at any time within 10 years next before the beginning of this present Parliament or anyone had held or enjoyed or ought to have held or enjoyed as part parcel or *(torn)* ... belonging to the said mannor and premisses or any of them

Memorandum
That the said sum of £6. 13s. 4d. is the value that is set upon the perquisites of Courts And that the sum of £12. 19s. 5½. first above mentioned arises out of the free and copyhold rents of the said mannor.
Reprises: The Steward of the Halimott Courts £2. 0s. 0d. per annum.

Memorandum
That the copyholders are copyholders of inheritance
This particular is grounded upon a Survey taken by John Duncalfe and others as also 3 several additional surveys thereof being by them severaly returned into the Registers Office the 30th July the 22nd November 1648 the 24th January And the 12th July A.D. 1648* And is made forth examined and signed by an Order of the Contractors of the 22nd February 1649

> H. Elsynge
> Registrar

Contractor for
27th September 1650.
The mannor and premisses above mentioned with their rights members and appurtenances are contracted for and agreed to be sold unto Walter Boothbye of London Merchant (except hereafter excepted)

This particular is rated in fee simple for the said Walter Boothby

* These are not surviving to the Editor's knowledge.

at fifteen years purchase for the present yearly value and the rents of the said mannor

Easington with the leasehold lands of the said mannor withall and singular the rights incumbrances and appurtenances being £201. 18s. 4½d. in possession And at 6 years purchase for the improved yearly value of several of the premisses in lease for one life respectively being alltogether £24. 0s. 0d. in revercon And at 4 years purchase for the improved yearly value of other of the premisses in lease for 2 lives in being respectively being alltogether £115. 5s. 9d. in revercon And of 3 years purchases for the improved yearly value of several other of the premisses in lease for 3 lives respectively being together £225. 16s. 4d. in revercon And of 14 years purchase for the improved yearly values of several others of the premisses respectively in lease some for one year and others for 2 years or thereabouts in being being together £85. 10s. 8d. in revercon.

SURVEY OF THE MANOR OF
BISHOP MIDDLEHAM

Survey of the   George   Lilburn   Edward   Colson
Mannor of   George Dalles Frederick Faber
Bishop Midleham

Noia Juratore   Thomas Middlehope
John Farrowe   Henry Greenwell
Ralph Lambert   Thomas Hutchinson
Clement Widdifield   Thomas Smith
Lancellot Ellis   Thomas Midleton
Thomas Hutchinson   Richard Wrighte

1. Imprimis we present that their is a mannor house in form of a mansion house built of stone with a dove house but the same is totally demolished the stones thereof not worth the pulling down, there is one barn and one granary in good repair all which is walled about with stone the sight thereof and altogether by estimation 8 acres worth per acre per annum 13s. 4d. improvement £5. 6s. 8d. we find no garden orchard yard cartellage nor standing timber upon the same, All which are now in the possession of Nicholas Swaile Esq. ut patet per lease produced to the Surveyors. The situation of which is at Sedgefield 6 miles from the City of Durham 10 miles from the main road 6 miles from Bishop Auckland from Darlington 7 miles most of the land lieth upon a lime stone quarry in a champion country.

2. Item we present that there is certain demesne lands belonging to the foresaid mannor all inclosed the several names of every field arable pasture or meadow with the several acres of each (vzt) pasture are as followeth vzt Thinford all plotts of arable lands containing by estimation 80 acres worth per annum 4s. each acre the annual rent £16. os. od. prior to improvement

3. One pasture close called High Farnacres with 14 ridges containing by estimation 48 acres with two low meadows containing 12 acres and one parcel of ground called the Moll Also now in the occupation of Christopher Silby at farme for this present year at the rent of £32. 5s. od. One parcel of meadow ground called 9 acres now in the possession of John Hutchinson at farm for this present year the rent of £20. 5s. od. The said rent payable by the foresaid tennant is by two and equal proportions to be paid at the feasts of St. Martyn the Bishop in Winter and St. Cuthbert or within 14 days after the nature and condition of the soil is part of it sands and other of it low bogg ground lying in an inclosed country

Item we present that there is another part walled about and containing by estimation 70 acres worth per annum at every acre 7s. £24. 10s. od. We find no deer either roe or fallow conyes or other game the same being dispersed many years former it is good for pasture. Nicholas Swailes Esq. is tennant in lieu of rutting The timber standing and growing upon the premisses being all Eshe is worth to be felled £15. os. od. It doth appear unto us by Mr. Swailes lease that he is to have liberty to take in and upon the premisses sufficient house boote hedge boote fire boote plow boote cartboote and timber for the upkeep of the premisses and houses there All the demesnes and premisses are worth to be sold above the rent ... £88. 15s. 8d. per annum

4th, 5th and 6th we return to be negative answers

7th Item we present that there is two water corn mills belonging to the Lord of the mannor the one in Sedgefielde in the possession of Richard Wright with a cow house and stable house with 3 oxgange of land there unto belonging worth upon improvement above the rent ... £15. 10s. od. per annum
(vzt)
The mill and one oxgang per annum £6. 10s. od.
the other two oxgang per annum   £9. os. od.
We present that the said mill is in great decay and that the copyhold and leaseholders of Sedgefield township ought to repair the same And that the several copyholders and leaseholders of Sedgefield are required to grind at the foresaid mill
The other mill is a water corn mill and lyeth within the Township

of Cornforth with one acre of ground or thereabout belonging unto the same the value of which is worth per annum on improvement above the rent £10. os. od. The same is in good and reasonable repair and the tennant thereof Robert Willisforde holdeth the same for 3 lives ut patet per lease returned by the surveyors

8th. Item we present that all copyhold and leaseholders are bound to Grind at the Lord's mill being within the township of Midleham and Cornforth

9th. Item we present that there is a limestone quarry within the township of Cornforth the improvement thereof is small worth and the tennants by lease their held the same for which they are to carry such quantities of lime as shall maintain the several man-nors of Durham, Bishop Auckland and Shildon they having allowed them for every wayne load of lime so carried 2s. 2d. and for the lime itself 1s. 4d. per load and had wood for burning and low game out of Auckland Park for which they payed 1s. 8d. for every wayne load

10th, 11th and 12th we refer ourselves to the Surveyors by which will appear the several tenures that all the lands within this mannor are holden and how many tennants there be

13th. Item we present that the fine upon death or alieanation of copyhold are fixed as we do verily believe and not arbitrarily for that time beyond the memory of man to the contrary the several copyholders upon death or alieanation have payed a certain fine to the Lord of this mannor impressed upon them by the name or title of a St. Mar. which hath been always the same upon every tennant although upon some less than the annual rent reserved upon others the full rent reserved upon others more than the rent and all those certain as appeareth by the several copyholds of one and the same thing for many resiants together as appeareth by the presentment of the Surveyors herewith returned.

14th. Item we present that the Copyhold tenements are in good repair for anything we know to the contrary timber there is none growing upon any of them that we know of or any quarries but what is before mentioned in the 9th Article

15th. That the works custom and services of the copyholders are little worth

16th. That we know of no cottages within this mannor

17th and 18th. We answer the negative

19th. Item we present and say that we do not know what the profitts of the courts waifes strayes fellons goods fines amerciaments or other the like are usually worth per annum unto the Lord

20th. Item we present that Warrens or Coneys the Bishop hath none within this mannor

21st. Item we present that the Lord of this mannor hath the right of presentation full gift nomination disposition and advowson of the Rectory or parsonage of Sedgefield We do find that the mansion house thereto belonging is a spacious building of a large pattern but much in decay and ruin by the default of Mrs. Sarah Vincent wife to the late incumbent Mr. Vincent
There is also 14 other houses called Coate houses belonging to this parsonage indifferently repaired. As also one mill belonging to the Glebe land being a wind mill All which we value to be worth per annum ... £190. 0s. 0d. It is not expropriate. And Mr. Anthony Laxthorne is now parson there by Order from the Committee of Plundered Ministers

22nd. We present that the tithes belonging to this parsonage is Communibus Annis ... £130. 0s. 0d. both glebe and tithe ... £500. 0s. 0d.

23rd. Item we present that the chancel belonging to the rectory is much out of repair and the windows thereof by the default of Mr. Vincent also

24th. We answer that we know not of no wood or coppinds with this mannor

25th. We reserve ourselves to the Survey returned herewith annexed And this is all that we can lay unto these Articles

John Farrar	Thomas M
his mark	his mark
Clement Widdifield	Henry Grimwell
his mark	his mark
Lambutt Ellis	Thomas Hutchinson
Thomas	Robert Johnsone
Richard Wright	his mark
Ralphe Lambert	Thomas Smyth
	Thomas Midlton
	Peter Hodgshon

Item hereat there hath been some late differences between Henry Sotter and Anne his wife of Sedgefield on the one part and Richard Rotherby of the same on the other part considering the tenant right of an oxgang of land holden of the Bishop by lease to Gilbert Rotherby late of Sedgefield that brother of the said Richard Rotherby and husband of the foresaid Anne now wife to the said Henry Sotter We the Jury do present considering the same as followeth That the said Richard Rotherby shall enter as tennant of the premisses for this present year provided that Henry Sotter and Anne his wife shall continue in the same house he now dwelleth in and also to reap lead and carry away all that 2 acres of oats be it more or less now standing upon the ground and that the said Richard Rotherby shall from henceforth during this year discharge the Lord's rent with all other taxes and S^t M^{rs} value for the said lands

Bishop Midleham
An exact and perfect Rentrole of the foresaid township

Athery Cuthbert	£1. 5s. 0d.	Bill Richard	13s. 0d.
Bedford Thomas	10s. 0d.	Batcherby Elizabeth	10s. 0d.

Bishop Midleham Township

for Lamberts Land	£3. 12s. 6d.	Hutchinson William	£1. 9s. 6d.
Frevell Nicholas Esq.		Hutchinson John	£1. 13s. 0d.
	£1. 13s. 4d.	Hutchinson Thomas	10s. 10d.
Idem	£2. 8s. 9d.	Hutton Raphe	£1. 7s. 8d.
Several parcels	£18. 1s. 0d.	Hindmars William	19s. 0d.
Grinewell Margaret	2s. 0d.	*Idem*	1s. 2d.
Hutchinson Henry	£2. 0s. 4d.	Hutchinson Margaret	8s. 10d.

Hutchinson Peter	2s. 4d.	Myers Jane	11s. 1d.
Idem	1s. 2d.	Myers Jane	6s. 4d.
Hutchinson Robert	10s. 0d.	Midleton Thomas	4s. 0d.
Halliday Rugard	1s. 2d.	Richardson Michael	4s. 0d.
Hindmars William	10s. 2d.	Selby Christopher	8s. 9d.
Idem	2s. 4d.	Widifield Clement	3s. 4d.
Hutchinson Henry	13s. 6d.	*Idem*	3s. 4d.
Hutchingson John	2s. 6d.		
Midleton Thomas	£1. 14s. 0d.	sum total	£43. 8s. 3d.
Idem	10s. 0d.		

Bishop Midleham Demesnes

Our sovereign Lady Queen Elizabeth of blessed memory by indenture dat 15.October.23. of her Majesty's said reign granted by Richard the Bishop of Durham holdeth all those lands meadows pastures and feedings called or known by the name or names of Bishops Close in situate lying and being within Byersgreen in the County Pallatine of Durham: And also all that Park and appurtenance in Bishop Middleham and in the said County Pallatine of Durham all lands or tenements called or known by the name or names of the Park in Middleham and appurtenances And also all and singular Close Messuage Lands pasture and arable lands whatsoever called or known by the name of the Demesne lands of the mannor of Bishop Midleham in the foresaid County Pallatine of Durham and appurtenances: And one acre of land called Deepewell lying and being in the fields of Middleham and appurtenances; To hold from the feast of the Annunciation of our Blessed Lady then last past unto the end and term of Fourscore years paying per annum at the Exchequor in Durham to the Bishop and his successors

Vzt.

For the Bishops closes per annum	£8.	0s.	0d.
For the Park per annum	£3.	6s.	8d.
For the Demesne Lands	£6.	13s.	4d.
For the Deepewell close per annum		1s.	10d.
	£18.	1s.	0d.

The lease to be void for non payment of the rent within 30 days after the feast: The leasor is to bear the charge of all the repairs of foresaid premisses And is to have liberty to take in and upon the premisses sufficient houseboote Hedgeboote fireboote plowboote and cartboote and timber for the repairs of the premisses and houses there

This lease is confirmed by the Dean and Chapter of Durham under their seals of office bearing date the first day of December A.D. 1585. 28. Elizabeth Regina

George Frevile Esq. by indenture of Assignment dated 1st.June.28. Elizabeth Regina granted by her said majesty holdeth the said Bishops Close Middleham Park the Demeasne Lands belonging to the said mannor of Bishops Middleham: and the acre in Middleham fields called Deepewell: with all and singular perquisites appurtenances, contained and comprised in the grant or lease thereof made to the said Majesty by Richard then Bishop of Durham for the whole term therin contained: without making attempt or doing service or paying buyrent for the said to her Majesty But paying to the Bishop and his successors the yearly rent in the said lease reserved being per annum ... £18. 1s. 0d.

Nicholas Frevile Esq. is the immediate tennant to the foresaid premisses worth upon improvement above the rent £88. 15s. 8d. per annum.

Memorandum
Bishops Close is valued likewise and returned in the Survey of Bishop Auckland

Bishop Middleham Copyholds

THOMAS MIDLESON

26 April 22 Jac. One cottage with a garden, pasture for one cow in Fourmards, pasture for 12 sheep upon the moor two ridges in the west field two acres in the middlefield upon Todd's flatt one acre called Newton Landedge in the eastfield 2½ ridges at Grimewell Hole also two ridges and one half an acre at North Closegate in the eastfield two ridges at Smethhorne and one half an acre, one acre in Myre Knolls called 8 butts two ridges in Nor Closes one dale of meadow lying in Stinkinglees.

By surrender of Robert Hutchinson. Fine 2s. 6d.

Idem

7 May 23 Car. One cottage, one house sometimes of waste containing in length 10 yards in breadth 6 yards.
  As heir to his father. Fine 1s. 6d.

Idem

8 May 19 Car. One cottage with a garden
  By surrender of Ralph Water. Fine 4d.

Idem

18 November 12 Car. One cottage with one acre of lands and a half.
  By surrender of George Wilkinson. Fine 4d.
  Rent for these four copyholds 4s. 0d.

CLEMENT WIDDIFIELD
17 May 1 Jac. One cottage and 6 acres of land and one other cottage in Middleham 4 acres of land pasture for 10 sheep upon the moor and his parcel of meadow called Grangebrigg Crooke.
  By surrender of Raphe Hutton *et al.* Rent 6s. 8d. Fine 7s. 10d.

MARGARET HUTCHINSON
7 May 13 Car. One cottage.
  In widdowright.

Eadem

dat ut supra. One cottage and 2 acres of Chequor lands and 6 acres of husbandlands.
  In widdowright. Rent 8s. 10d. Fine 10d.

CHRISTOPHER SELBY
5 May 18 Jac. One house with a gardin and 1½ acres of land.
  By surrender of William Mowbray. Rent 1d. Fine 6d.

JANE wife of Richard Halliday
30 April 22 Elz. One cottage.
  In widdowright of Richard Widdifield her former husband. Rent 1s. 2d. Fine 1s. 4d.

JANE MYRES relict of John Myers
20 May 13 Car. One messuage and garden.
   In widdowright. Rent 1s. 2d. Fine 6d.

Eadem and **MARY MYERS** her daughter
dat ut supra. One cottage and 5 acres of land.
   By surrender of John Hutchinson. Fine 2d.

JANE MYERS and **KATHERINE, ANNE** and **ELIZEBETH**
her daughters
24 September 14 Car. 6 acres of lands, 6 acres belonging to a cottage
called Neshes Hall.
   By surrender of Henry Hutchinson. Fine 3s. 4d.

Eadem
dat ut supra. One parcel of land called Towngate, one tenement
called Coxelands, 6 acres belonging to a cottage called Eastwell.
   By surrender of Henry Hutchinson. Fine 1s. 8d.
   Rent for these three copyholds 6s. 4d.

Memorandum
That these fines are paid with Lambutts lands in the last pages of
this township

ELIZABETH BOTCHERBY
7 October 1 Car. One cottage and two acres of Chequor land.
   As heir to John Groomhill. Fine 1s. 8d.

Eadem
dat ut supra. One tenement and 6 acres of lands.
   As heir to John Groomhill. Fine 2s. 0d.
   Rent for these two copyholds 10s. 2d.

HENRY HUTCHINSON
22 November 8 Car. One messuage called Hynderlands.
   By surrender of Thomas Bullock. Fine 13s. 4d.

Idem
15 October 38 Elz. One cottage and a half.
   By surrender of Ralphe Mayson. Fine 1s. 9d.

Rent for these two copyholds 13s. 6d.

WILLIAM HINDMARS and Jane his wife
20 January 13 Car. One cottage and 7 acres of land and a half.
    By surrender of William Allanson. Rent 10s. 2d. Fine 5s. 0d.

Idem
26 April 9 Car. One cottage with a garth adjoining.
    By surrender of John Farow. Rent 2s. 4d. Fine 2s. 4d.

MARIE WARD and Nicholas her son
7 August 19 Car. One cottage and one croft now or late in the
tenure of Peter Warde, and another cottage with a garth sometime
in the tenure of Richard Wright.
    By surrender of Peter Ward. Fine 1d.

Memorandum
That this rent is also included in Lambutts Lands

ROBERT HUTCHINSON
3 April 4 Car. One cottage and a garden.
    By surrender of Raphe Hutton. Rent 5s. 0d. Fine 1s. 4d.

PETER HUTCHINSON
7 March 21 Car. One cottage and 6 acres of land in Bishop Middleham.
    By surrender of Robert Hutchinson. Rent 2s. 4d. Fine 2s. 0d.

Idem
3 April 14 Car. One croft called Nether Croft and one cottage with
a garth.
    By surrender of Raphe Hutton. Rent 1s. 2d. Fine 2s. 0d.

ROBERT HUTCHINSON
25 April 14 Jac. One cottage and six acres of land.
    By surrender of George Warde. Rent 7s. 0d. Fine 2s. 0d.

MARGARET GRIMEWELL
12 October 14 Car. One cottage and one acre of land.
    In widdowright. Rent 2s. 0d. Fine 2s. 0d.

RICHARD BELL
25 November 7 Car. One cottage together with 12 acres of husband lands in a certain field called Mardison's as it is now inclosed.
By surrender of Raphe Hutton. Rent 13s. od. Fine 5s. od.

JOHN HUTCHINSON
7 May 23 Car. One cottage and one acre of land in Midleham.
As heir to his father. Rent 2s. 6d. Fine 2s. 6d.

Memorandum
That there is a certain Copyhold Lands called Clement Lamberts Lands in this township possessed by several of the inhabitants and is expressed in former fines amongst other lands All which payeth per annum £3. 12s. 6d.

Nicholas Richardson is a copyholder and payeth 4s. rent per annum but there is no fine or coppies

Bishop Middleham Leaseholds

GEORGE FREVILE THOMAS BELL JOHN HUTCHINSON
20 July 9 Car. Pasture ground called Sprusley and Nore Close in the townfields of Bishop Middleham with all pastures, feedings whatsoever.
For the natural lives of George Frevile and Thomas Bell, then 13 years and John Hutchinson then 14 years.
Rent £2. 8s. 9d. Improvement £22. os. od.

DAME ELZ. FREVILE late of Walworth deceased
13 October 3 Car. Messuage or tenement in Bishop Middleham.
For the natural lives of John Calverley, Tymothie Calverley sons of Sir John Calverley and Francis Jennison. Rent £1. 13s. od. Improvement £7. os. od.

THOMAS HUTCHINSON
13 October 3 Car. Tenement and garth and certain lands arable meadow and pasture called Hallands within the territories and townfields of Bishop Middleham.
For 21 years. Rent 10s. 10d. Improvement £2. 13s. 4d.

THOMAS MIDDLETON

1 October 6 Car. Messuage or tenement in Bishop Middleham.

For 21 years. Rent £1. 14s. od. and 2 fat lambs at Pent. or 10s. od. Improvement £7. os. od.

JANE MYERS

22 September 12 Car. Cottage situate in Bishop Midleham 9 acres of arable and all garths, gardens, meadows etc.

For 21 years. Rent 11s. 1d. Improvement £1. 15s. od.

HENRIE HUTCHINSON

22 October 7 Car. One messuage or tenement 30 acres of Chequor lands 6 acres of arable land meadows and pasture.

For 21 years. Rent £2. os. 4d. Improvement £6. os. od.

WILLIAM FRIZELL

20 June 7 Jac. 15 acres of arable land and all meadows commons etc. in the townfields of Bishop Midleham.

For 21 years. Rent 13s. od. Improvement £2. os. od.

William Frizell proved by asignation dat.29.September.10.Car. assigns his interest in the premisses to Margarett Hutchinson and Richard her son. Margarett Hutchinson and Richard proved by their assignment dat.6.December.10.Car. they assigned their interest in the premisses to John Hutchinson who is now the immediate tennant.

WILLIAM HINDMARS

18 October 9 Car. Certain lands meadows and pastures called Hallands within the townfields of Bishop Middleham.

For 21 years. Rent 19s. od. and a fat lamb at Pent or 5s. od. Improvement £4. 10s. od.

THOMAS BEDFORD

26 September 14 Car. One garth and 9 acres of arable land in the townfields of Middleham (vzt) 3 acres in the Crosseflatt, 4 acres the Cotta Plots 2 acres in Panders acres in the Newfield.

For 21 years. Rent 10s. od. Improvement £1. 10s. od.

JOHN HUTCHINSON

27 April 13 Car. Tenement and garth and certain lands arables, meadows, pastures called Hallands.

For 21 years. Rent 18s. od. and 2 hens yearly or 2s. od. Improvement £3. os. od.

RAPHE HUTTON

10 April 14 Car. Tenement and 30 acres of arable land, one acre of meadow and six pasture gates in Bishop Middleham.

For 21 years. Rent £1. 7s. 8d. Improvement £5. os. od.

Thomas Bayles by assignment made from the said Raphe dat. 19.May.14.Car. holdeth one moytie of the premises expressed in the foresaid lease

RAPHE HUTTON

25 September 1 Car. Messuage or tenement in Bishop Middleham with all houses, buildings, lands, meadows, commons, moors, pastures, feedings etc.

For 21 years. Rent £1. 19s. 6d. Improvement £5. os. od.

Raphe granted by assignment dat. 16 January 7 Car. assigned the last mentioned premises to William Hutchinson of Bishop Midleham

Mainsforth Township—Leaseholders for Lives

CUTHBERT ASHEY, CHRISTOPHER BYERLEY

6 October 18 Jac. One messuage or tenement in Mainsforth with all houses, buildings, lands or meadows and pastures and commodities.

For the natural lives of Cuthbert Harrison then 3, Jannett Ashy then 30. John Adamson then 8. All in being. Rent £1. os. od. and 2 fat capons or 5s. od. Improvement £15. os. od.

Thomas Holmes by patent dat. 3 April 12 Car. Re. granted by Thomas late Bishop of Durham holdeth the office of Bayliffe of the mannor lordship of Bishop Midleham for the term of his natural life And is to collect and gather the rents within the said mannor and to a Acompt List the Exchequor at Durham, And is to have for his fee per annum ... £1. os. od.

The said was confirmed by the Dean and Chapter and William Laborne executed the place by deputation from the said Holmes

Memorandum

This patent is valued at ten pounds per annum with the fee: for that here hath full term as you may see by the Lease

Corneforth

An exact and perfect Rentrole of the foresaid town

Attis Lancelot	£2.	6s.	0d.
Attis William			4d.
Buckhouse		6s.	8d.
Colledge Thomas	£2.	6s.	0d.
Eden William	£1.	7s.	4d.
Frizell William	£1.	3s.	0d.
Frezell William		6s.	8d.
Haswell William	£2.	6s.	0d.
Hutchinson Thomas	£1.	14s.	0d.
Jackson Henry	£2.	4s.	8d.
Joblin John	£1.	14s.	0d.
Laborne William	£1.	14s.	0d.
Middleton John	£1.	3s.	0d.
Wright Thomas	£1.	3s.	0d.
Wheatley Thomas	£2.	6s.	0d.
Woodhouse John	£2.	15s.	10d.
Widdifield Robert	£5.	6s.	8d.
Woodhouse John		10s.	0d.
	£30.	13s.	2d.

Cornforth Township Freehold

WILLIAM EDEN Gentleman and Elizabeth his wife, Mrs. Margarett Howard Mathew Smith and Anne his wife
15 August 9 Elz. Messuage or tenement and 10 acres of land in Cornforth.

Rent £1. 7s. 4d.

Cornforth Township Copyholds

WILLIAM ETTIS
27 April 19 Car. The north side of a cottage in Cornforth called Blackhall.

By surrender of John Ettis. Rent 4d.

WILLIAM FRIZELL

12 August 6 Car. One messuage called the Peale and 18 acres of lands.

As heir to William Frizell. Rent 6s. 8d. Fine 6s. 8d.

Memorandum

That these persons hereafter named are leaseholders for lives within the foresaid town and pay the several rents hereafter mentioned but what lives are in being we cannot make you a particular return they not appearing before us though often summoned yet to the end we might know the value thereof we procured to go along with us the foresaid Jury who upon their oathes have returned there rents improvements thereafter expressed
vzt.

Henrie Jackson payeth rent per annum	£2. 4s. 8d.
Worth upon improvement above the rent	£17. 15s. 4d.
John Woodhouse gentleman payeth rent per annum	£2. 15s. 10d.
Worth upon improvement above the rent	£31. 4s. 2d.
John Woodhouse junior payeth rent per annum	10s. 0d.
Worth upon improvement above the rent	£7. 10s. 0d.
The whole township payeth per annum for the common bakehouse	6s. 8d.

but they produced no evidence or have any they say

Cornforth Township Leaseholds

RAIPHE TATAM

7 June 2 Jac. Water corn mill called Cornforth Mill

For the natural lives of Thomas Tatam, Robert Tatam, sons of the said Raiph and Robert Laxe.

Thomas Tatam dead. Rent £5. 6s. 8d. Improvement £10. 0s. 0d.

Raiphe Tatam by assignment dat. 14 May 20 Jac. assigned his interest in the said mill to Robert Widdifield And Widdifield now attesteth the same.

MARTIN WATTER and WILLIAM WATTER

17 September 21 Jac. House and farmholds within the territories and townfields of Cornforth.

For the natural lives of the said Martin Watter, William Watter then aged 30 years and Elizabeth Watter. Martin Watter dead. Rent £1. 14s. od. Improvement £15. os. od.

The lease is assigned to John Jopling who is the immediate tennant.

THOMAS COLLIDGE

30 June 10 Car. Messuage or tenement set lying and being in Corneforth as it is now divided.

For the natural lives of the said Thomas then aged 19 years, William Collidge his brother then aged 8 years and Dorothie Collidge his sister then aged 14. All in being. Rent £2. 6s. 8d. Improvement £18. os. od.

THOMAS WRIGHT

17 April 14 Car. Messuage or tenement in Cornforth.

For the natural lives of Thomas and Anne his wife then aged 32 years and Thomas his son Thomas Wright junior still living the others dead. Rent £1. 3s. od. Improvement £9. os. od.

JOHN ETTIS

27 September 21 Jac. Tenement or farmhold in Cornforth.

For the natural lives of Lancelott Ettis then 20 years, William Ettis then 14 years and John Ettis then 12 years. John Ettis dead. Rent £2. 6s. od. Improvement £17. os. od.

THOMAS HUTCHINSON

27 September 21 Jac. Messuage, tenement or farmhold in the townfields of Corneforth.

For the natural lives of the said Thomas then 38 years, Elizabeth his wife then 38 years and Thomas Hutchinson junior then 7 years. All in being. Rent £1. 14s. od. Improvement £13. 10s. od.

WILLIAM LABORNE

27 September 21 Jac. Messuage or tenement in Cornforth.

For the natural lives of said William Laborne, then 20 years, Margarett his wife and William his son Margarett dead. Rent £1. 14s. od. Improvement £13. 10s. od.

WILLIAM FRIZELL

20 June 7 Car. Messuage or tenement and two oxgangs of land in Cornforth.

For the natural lives of William Frizell then 26, Margarett his wife then 23 and William Frizell son of the said William and Margarett. William Frizell, son, dead. Rent £1. 3s. od. Improvement £7. 17s. od.

ROBERT HASWELL

27 September 21 Jac. Messuage or tenement containing 2 lands in Corneforth.

For the natural lives of said Robert Haswell, William Haswell and John Haswell. All in being. Rent £2. 6s. od. Improvement £18. os. od.

WILLIAM WHEATLEY

12 November 15 Car. One messuage or tenement in Corneforth within the precincts and fields thereof.

For the natural lives of said William Wheatley then 25, John Crathorne then 3 and Thomas Crathorne then 7. All in being. Rent £1. 6s. od. Improvement £18. os. od.

JOAN MIDLETON relict of Thomas Midleton

4 September 15 Car. Messuage or tenement in Corneforth.

For the lives of Joan Middleton then 31, Thomas Midleton then 11, and Margarett her daughter then 4. Margarett Midleton living. Rent £1. 3s. od. Improvement £8. 17s. od.

Sedgefield Township

A perfect rentrole of the foresaid township

Batcherby Gilbert	10s. 7d.	Christopher John	5s. 2d.
Birkely Robert	£1. 1s. 2d.	Elstobb William	18s. 6d.
Blaxton Henry	£1. 1s. 2d.	Emerson John	2d.
Browne Robert	£1. 1s. 2d.	Ffrevile Nicholas	12s. 8d.
Bradley Robert	1s. od.	Idem for Bollerby Esq.	1s. od.
Blaxton Henry	6s. 1d.	Idem for Freerent	2d.
Bland Richard	1d.	Flather Raiphe	2d.
Browne Robert	18s. 10d.	Grayson Raiphe	4d.
Blaxton Thomas	2d.	Hodgshon Peter	£1. 1s. 2d.
Christopher John	£2. os. 8d.	Hyndmars Robert	£1. 1s. 2d.
Edward James	4d.	Hixon John	18s. od.

Haggerston Thomas		8d.	Roger Richards	9s. 6d.
Harrison John	£2. 0s.	4d.	Road John	4d.
Hixon Rowland	8s.	4d.	Roadshaw Christopher	13s. 0d.
Johnson John	£1. 1s.	2d.	Richardson Raiphe	1s. 6d.
Idem	15s.	0d.	Smyth Thomas	£2. 2s. 4d.
Johnson Robert	£1. 1s.	2d.	Idem	18s. 11d.
Idem	£1. 10s.	0d.	Shambles rent	2s. 0d.
Lambe Roger	4s.	1d.	Smyth Raiph	6d.
Idem		4d.	Shacklock Richard	4d.
Milne	£2. 0s.	0d.	Wright Thomas	£1. 11s. 9d.
Margison Raiphe	£2. 2s.	0d.	Idem	16s. 0d.
Midleton Thomas	18s.	9d.	Walker John	11s. 2d.
Middleton Elz.	1s.	4d.	Watkin Robert	10s. 7d.
Margison Robert	15s.	11d.	Idem	4s. 1d.
Neisham widdow		4d.	Wright Abraham	9s. 9d.
Nicholson Raiph		2d.	Wright Richard	9s. 9d.
Ourd Raiph	4s.	1d.	Younger John	£1. 1s. 2d.
Ourd Thomas	2s.	1d.	Idem	1s. 7d.
Ourd Lionell		6d.	Younger Robert	2d.
Parkinson Hugh	2s.	5d.		
Robinson Geoffry		4d.	Sum total	£38. 5s. 8d.
Richardson Lancelott		6d.		
Robinson John	11s.	0d.		
Richardson				
Edwarde	£2. 13s.	2d.		

Sedgefield Township Copyholds

RAIPHE RICHARDSON
16 March 14 Car. One cottage and a garden in the middle of Sedgefield.
    By surrender of Thomas Roth. Rent 1s. 6d. Fine 6d.

RAIPHE FLETCHER
12 October 15 Car. One parcel of land late the Lord's waste.
    By surrender of William Dawson. Rent 2d. Fine 1d.

LIONELL OURD
6 May 14 Car. One house near the Lord's field.

By surrender of George Robinson and Francis his wife. Rent 6d. Fine 1d.

GEORGE ROBINSON
18 October 15 Car. One house with a garden.
By surrender of Humphrey Mayson. Rent 4d. Fine 4d.

ROBERT YOUNG
1 April 14 Car. By special warrant from the Lord, his waste And house built at a new improvement.
Rent 2d. Fine 2d.

LANCELLOT RICHARDSON
19 May 9 Car. The north half of a messuage and a garth in Sedgefield.
By surrender of Christopher Dodds. Rent 6d. Fine 6d.

RICHARD HIXON
18 June 13 Car. 38 acres of land 1 rood and six perches in the southfield, 41 acres and 14 perches in the southfield moor 15 acres in Hauxley Field and one messuage and 8 acres in the westfield close.
By surrender of Robert High. Rent 8s. 4d. Fine 14s. 6d.

RICHARD WRIGHTE
15 June 13 Car. 2 acres and a half and 60 acres in Hauxley field.
By surrender of Robert High. Fine 6s. 8d.

Idem
dat ut supra. One messuage and one garth, 62 acres of land 3 rood 22 perches in Hauxley Field and one close called Emmers Flatt.
By surrender of Robert High. Fine 2s. 0d.
Rent for these two copyholds 9s. 0d.

JARRARD SALVIN, Esq., TOBY EWBANK, HENRY SMYTH, RAIPH ALLENSON, gentleman.
8 December 18 Car. One close called the North Garth containing 2 acres of land in the northfield of Sedgefield also one acre in westfield and one cottage sometimes in the tenure of Robert Bellberby

2 oxgang of land, 40 acres of land in the Dead Flatt in the north-field and 43 acres as it is divided.

By surrender of Nicholas Frevile. Fine £1. 8s. 6d.

ibidem

dat ut supra. One house and a messuage besides the Mannor of Bishop Middleham there together with one garden and one ox stall belonging to the same house also one cottage with a garden called the Nether Hall in Middleham aforesaid, sometime Richard Heighington's, and also one meadow called the fourtie acres sometimes called New Meadowe and Edmond Meadowes in Middleham And 8 acres of meadow called Wellheads and the reversion of the same and one close called the Iland besides the Mannor of Midleham and one meadow or parcel of land called Willy Carr.

Fine £1. 8s. 0d.

Rent for these two copyholds 12s. 8d.

Memorandum

That these three former surrenders was made upon trust and shall be charged and got, and that the said Jarrard Salvin, Toby Ewbanke, Henry Smyth and Raphe Allenson and the survival and surviands of them his and their sequells in time shall grant, surrender, assigne and dispose of the said messuages, lands, tenements, hereditants and premisses and every or any part or parcel thereof and of the rents issues or presentments As there was to the said Nicholas Frevile himself or to such other person or persons and to such other interests and purposes as the said Nicholas Frevile shall by any writing or writings to be by him signed sealed and delivered in the presance of two or more credible witnesses, or by his last will and testament in writing to be published in the presence of two or more credible witnesses shall limit and appoint And for want of such limitation and appointment then to the only use and behoofe of the said Nicholas Frevile and of his heirs and assigns

THOMAS HAGGESTON

25 March 12 Jac. One garth called Westgarth.

As heir to John his brother. Rent 8d. Fine 4d.

JOHN ROBINSON

8 October 14 Car. One messuage and one garden in Sedgefield.

By surrender of Richard Reath. Rent 10d. Fine 11d.

THOMAS SMYTH
30 June 12 Car. One close of meadow called Rods Flatt.
 By surrender of Leonard Middleton. Fine 6d.

Idem

16 June 13 Car. One messuage, 49 acres in the south moor and one close called north close.
 By surrender of Robert High. Fine 6s. 8d.

Idem

dat ut supra. 36 acres in the north field and 9 acres in Westerton.
 By surrender of Robert High. Fine 6s. 8d.

Idem

19 November 7 Car. One close called East Close.
 By surrender of Marmaduke Mayson. Fine 2s. 0d.

Idem

4 July 6 Car. One close of meadow called Howleforth also North Close containing 6 acres of land.
 By surrender of Marmaduke Mayson. Fine 3s. 0d.
 Rent for these five copyholds 17s. 11d.

THOMAS BLAKSTON
4 April 22 Car. One Mansion House with a kilne and one garth called Kilnegarth with all stable and orchards.
 By surrender of Gilbert Marshall. Rent 2d. Fine 2d.

JOHN JOHNSON
9 October 13 Car. 13 acres of land in the west field.
 By surrender of Robert High. Fine 1d.

Idem

24 June 14 Car. 41 acres in the south moor and 3 closes one called Watkin Field, another called Watts Bank, the third called Comos Close, 3 messuages and 15 acres of land in the westfield and 52 acres in the Ryall Field

By surrender of Robert High. Fine £1. 0s. 0d.

Idem

1 November 17 Car. One close called Ryall Close containing 1 acre.
By surrender of Robert High. Fine 2s. 0d.
Rent for these three copyholds 15s. 0d.

ROBERT JOHNSON

15 June 13 Car. 40 acres of land in the North end of the Brack 4
messuages and 2 closes called Howleforth.
By surrender of Robert High. Fine 1s. 4d.

Idem

dat ut supra. 2 cottages, one parcel of land containing 80 acres in
Winterton, 15 acres in Westfield.
By surrender of Robert High. Fine 2d.
Rent for these two copyholds £1. 10s. 0d.

EMETT HIXON

9 October 12 Car. One house and a garth lying behind the same.
By surrender of Thomas Wrighte. Fine 6d.

Memorandum

That Richard Wrighte's land payeth the rent of this land

CHRISTOPHER READSHAW

19 May 18 Car. 58 acres of land and 19 perches in Hauxley Field
as it is now divided.
By surrender of Thomas Parnell *et al*. Fine 5s. 8d.

Idem

dat ut supra. 22 acres of land in the Easte Moore as it is now divided.
By surrender of Thomas Parnell *et al*. Fine 13s. 4d.

Idem

dat ut supra. One messuage and a little close adjoining upon the
same 40 acres of land and 29 perches in the east moor called the
Greene Hill as it is now divided.
By surrender of Sir Raiphe Conyers. Fine 2d.

Idem

dat ut supra. One parcel of land containing in length 60 yards and in breadth 26 yards late of the Lord's waste.

By surrender of Sir Raiphe Conyers. Fine 2d.

Idem

dat ut supra. One cottage in the north side of the town of Sedgefield.

By surrender of Sir Raiphe Conyers. Fine 6d.

Rent for these five copyholds 13s. 0d.

CHRISTOPHER DODD and Anne his wife

28 April 13 Car. One house and one garden.

By surrender of Robert Johnson. Fine 2d.

Memorandum

That Robert Johnson payeth the rent for this copy

ABRAHAM WRIGHT

2 December 22 Car. One messuage 30 acres and 2 roods of land in the east moor.

By surrender of Thomas Wrighte. Rent 9s. 9d. Fine 2d.

HUGH PARKINSON

3 May 18 Car. One cottage and a croft lying at the west end of Sedgefield.

By surrender of Sir Raiphe Conyers. Rent 2s. 5d. Fine 2s. 8d.

RICHARD REAY

15 June 13 Car. 16 acres of land 2 roods and 18 perches in Hauxley Field.

By surrender of Robert High. Fine 2d.

Idem

dat ut supra. One cottage and 21 acres of land 2 roods and 20 perches in the east moor

By surrender of Robert High. Fine 3s. 2d.

Rent for these two copyholds 9s. 6d.

THOMAS OURD

1 September 14 Car. One messuage 16 acres 3 roods and 2 perches in Ryall Field 10 acres and a rood and 10 perches in east moor.
By surrender of Raiphe Ourd. Rent 4s. 2d. Fine 3s. 4d.

RAIPHE NICHOLSON

1 November 17 Car. One messuage and a garth joining upon the same sometimes belonging 2 oxgangs of land.
By surrender of John Eale. Rent 2d. Fine 1s. 0d.

RAIPHE SMYTH

9 January 9 Car. One cottage late of the Lord's waste with a garden lying behind the same.
By surrender of Cuthbert Smyth. Rent 6d. Fine 1s. 0d.

JOHN CHIPCHASE

21 July 11 Car. One messuage and two oxgangs of land forty years from the date of these presentments paying per annum to the School of Riveington 10s. and payeth rent to the Bishop.
Rent £2. 0s. 8d. Fine 3s. 4d.

JOHN READE

2 February 22 Car. One house and a garden lying behind the same for his natural life.
Fine 2d.

Idem

5 July 6 Car. One house and a garth lying behind the same.
By surrender of Marmaduke Mayson. Fine 2d.

Idem

2 February 22 Car. One close called Milnegate Close.
By surrender of Richard Wright. Fine 2d.
Rent for these three copyholds 4d.

JOHN HARRISON

15 June 13 Car. 41 acres of lands and 14 perches in the south moor.
By surrender of Robert High. Fine 6s. 8d.

Idem

2 May 14 Car. The half of one messuage and 53 acres of land one rood and one perch in Ryall Field.

By surrender of John Harrison his father. Fine 3s. 4d.

Rent for these two copyholds £2. os. 4d.

ROBERT MAYSON

8 April 13 Car. 61 acres and 2 roods of land in Ryall Field and east moor.

By surrender of Robert Mayson. Fine 9s. od.

Idem

dat ut supra. One messuage and one close called Hauxley Close.

By surrender of Robert Mayson. Fine 1s. od.

Rent for these two copyholds 15s. 11d.

ROBERT WATKIN

17 June 13 Car. Demiseth to Isabell Blaike one messuage one garden 32 acres of land one rood and one perch in Ryall Field.

Rent 4s. 2d. Fine 3s. 4d.

THOMAS MIDLETON

6 November 17 Car. 57 acres of land one rood and 14 perches.

By surrender of Jane Midleton. Fine 3s. od.

Idem

dat ut supra. 58 acres of land and 5 perches lying in Crowmyres Field.

As heir to Leonard Midleton his father. Fine 4s. od.

Idem

dat ut supra. One close called Swinburne close.

As heir to Leonard Midleton his father. Fine 1s. od.

Rent for these three copyholds 18s. 7d.

JOHN HIXON

4 December 22 Car. One cottage, one house, 5 acres of land lying in east moor.

As heir to Anthony Hixon his father. Fine 1s. od.

Idem

dat ut supra. One close called Ryall Close containing 3 acres of land (vzt) one acre in every field.

As heir to Anthony his father.

Rent for these two copyholds 18s. od.

ROBERT MAYSON

1 November 14 Car. 62 acres and 26 perches in the south moor.
As heir to Humphrey Mayson his father. Fine 5s. od.

Idem

dat ut supra. One messuage, 8 acres of land in Hauxley Field and 4 closes called the East Field Closes.

As heir to Humphrey Mayson his father. Fine 3s. 4d.

Idem

dat ut supra. 66 acres of land 3 rood and 25 perches in the south field And the bakehouse in Sedgefield.

As heir to Humphrey Mayson his father. Fine 5s. od.

Rent for these three copyholds £2. 2s. od.

JOHN EMERSON

7 November 14 Car. One little house in Sedgefield in the north street.

By surrender of Marmaduke Mayson. Rent 2d. Fine 2d.

Sedgefield Township Freehold

JAMES COWARD

4 May 9 Jac. Little house on the north of the Quire in free and common Socage By the grant and surrender of Anthony Gregson.
Rent 4d.

Memorandum

That these presentments hereunder written pay the several rents hereafter mentioned but have produced no writing copy deeds or other evidence unto or how they hold the same although they have been often summoned thereat

Bradley	1s. 0d.	Neisham widdow		4d.
Blaxton Henry	6s. 1d.	Ourd Thomas	2s.	1d.
Brown Robert	18s. 10d.	Richardson		
Elstobb William	18s. 6d.	Edward	£2. 13s.	2d.
Frevile Nicholas	1s. 2d.	Shambles rent	2s.	0d.
Gregson John	4d.	Shacklock Richard		4d.
Lambe Roger	4s. 5d.	Young John	1s.	7d.
Midleton Elizabeth	1s. 4d.			

Sedgefield Township Leaseholds

THOMAS WRIGHT

30 June 10 Car. Water corn mill in Sedgefield and also two messuages or tenements in Sedgefield together with 3 oxgang of lands and one close lying in the eastfield

For the natural lives of said Thomas Wright, Abraham Wright aged 12, and Richard Wright then aged 12. All in being. Rent £3. 11s. 9d.

(For the mill Rent £2. 0s. 0d. Improvement £6. 10s. 0d. 2 messuages and 3 oxgang Rent £1. 11s. 9d. Improvement £9. 0s. 0d.)

Item: 2 bushells of good wheat yearly, Durham measures or in lieu thereof 16s. 0d.

ROBERT WATKIN

24 August 14 Car. One coat house, one close lying on the east moor and also 3 acres of ground in Sedgefield.

For 21 years. Rent 10s. 7d. Improvement £4. 0s. 0d.

ROBERT BROWNE

23 October 14 Car. Messuage or tenement situate in the townfields of Sedgefield, and also one close lying in the east moor, one other close then in the occupation of Robert Browne and William Browne and one meadow close containing 3 acres.

For 21 years. Rent £1. 1s. 2d. Improvement £8. 0s. 0d.

Item: paying per annum 20½d. and 6 sheaves of wheat formerly payed to the Bailiff of Bishop Middleham And one bushell of oats usually paid to the coroner of Stockton Ward at Michaelmas Day

JOHN CHIPCHASE

19 December 9 Car. Beast gates on the south moors at Sedgefield

One horsegate one beastgate, 7 sheepgates and one half on the east moor there, one horse gate upon fallowfield together with all meadows, pastures etc.

For 21 years. Rent £5. 2s. 3d. Improvement £3. 0s. 0d.

JOHN JOHNSON

16 June 13 Car. Messuage or tenement and one parcel of pasture ground containing 20 acres one rood and 20 perches or thereabout lying in the south moor, and also one meadow close lying upon Ryall's Fielde Burne commonly called Potter's Close, and one parcel of ground lying in Ryall Field containing 26 acres and 2 roods.

For 21 years. Rent £1. 1s. 2d. Improvement £8. 0s. 0d.

Item: paying per annum 22½d. and 6 sheaves of wheat heretofore paid to the Bailiff of Bishop Midleham And one bushell of oats usually paid to the Coroner of Stockton Ward at Michaelmas only.

GILES BOTCHERBY

15 September 22 Jac. One messuage or tenement and one oxgang of land within the fields of Sedgefield.

For 21 years. Rent 10s. 9d. Improvement £4. 10s. 0d.

Item: paying 11d. and 3 sheaves of wheat formerly paid to the Baliffe of Bishop Middleham and 2 pecks of oats usually paid to the Coroner of Stockton Ward at Michaelmas.

RAIPHE BUCKLEY

27 August 14 Car. Tenement and one close in Ryall Field and also one close boundering on the west of John Johnson's lane, on the east of Mr. Henry Blaxton's on the north of Peter Hodgshon's being within the territories of Sedgefield.

For 21 years. Rent £1. 1s. 2d. Improvement £9. 0s. 0d.

Item: paying 22½d. and 6 sheaves of wheat heretofore paid to the Bayliffe And one bushell of oats heretofore paid to the Coroner of Stockton Ward at Michaelmas

ROBERT JOHNSON

29 August 14 Car. Two messuages or tenements and one close lying in the Brack, boundering on the west side of Thomas Smythe's

ground, Foxton Moor on the south and Mordon Ground on the west, within the townfields of Sedgefield.

For 21 years. Rent £1. 1s. 2d. Improvement £8. 0s. 0d.

Item: paying 22½d. and 6 sheaves of wheat heretofore paid to the Bayliff of Bishop Middleham And one bushell of oats heretofore paid to the Coroner of Stockton Ward at Michaelmas

JOHN YOUNGE

24 September 14 Car. Messuage and one close in Ryall Field and also one close lying in the east moor at Sedgefield (woods, mines and quarries excepted).

For 21 years. Rent £1. 1s. 2d. Improvement £9. 0s. 0d.

Item: paying 22½d. and 6 sheaves of corn to the Baliff and one bushell of oats to the Coroner of Stockton Ward at Michaelmas

PETER HODGSHON

28 August 14 Car. One messuage or tenement, one close lying in Crow Myre. One other close on the east moor one close called Ryal Close.

For 21 years. Rent £1. 1s. 2d. Improvement £9. 0s. 0d.

THOMAS SMYTH

9 May 11 Car. Two messuages or tenements and 4 oxgangs of land within the townfields of Sedgefield.

For 21 years. Rent £2. 2s. 4d. Improvement £18. 0s. 0d.

Item: paying 3s. 9d. and 12 sheaves of wheat to the Bailiff of Bishop Midleham and also two bushells of oats heretofore payed to the Coroner of Stockton Ward at Michaelmas

JOHN WALKER

9 December 9 Car. One cottage on Front Street with one oxgang of land in the townfield of Sedgefield.

For 21 years. Rent 11s. 2d. Improvement £4. 10s. 0d.

ROBERT HINDMARS

21 August 14 Car. Tenement and close called Jolliopp also one close lying in the east moor.

For 21 years. Rent £1. 1s. 2d. Improvement £9. 0s. 0d.

Item: paying 20½d. and 6 sheaves of wheat heretofore paid to the Baliffe and one bushell of oats usually paid to the Coroner.

HENRY BLAXTON
A farm.

For 21 years as we are informed. Rent £1. 1s. 2d. Improvement £8. 0s. 0d.

Memorandum

That Mr. Blaxton cannot produce his lease unto us so that we cannot return what tenure is in the same

Mr. Hilton The Coroner of Stockton Ward his Rentrole

Butler	£1. 2s. 0d.	Lambe Thomas	2s. 0d.
Davison Robert	10s. 8d.	Lambert	£1. 1s. 4d.
Donkin James	5s. 4d.	Orde Raphe	6s. 11d.
Eam William	8d.	Place Christopher	5s. 0d.
Frevile Nicholas	£1. 19s. 8d.	Pottis Nicholas	5s. 0d.
Idem	19s. 8d.	Stelling Anthony	5s. 0d.
Farowe John	16s. 2d.	Sayer	£2. 1s. 1d.
Halliman William	16s. 8d.	Salvin Garard	£5. 13s. 4d.
Hudson John	11s. 6d.	Trotter	14s. 6d.
Hart William	6s. 8d.	Watson Thomas	12s. 0d.
Hutton	£1. 0s. 4d.	Ward Peter	8s. 0d.
Johnson Robert	13s. 4d.	Watson William	4d.
Hitchin Francis	18s. 6d.		
Lackenby Symon	10s. 6d.	Sum total	£22. 12s. 7d.
Lawson Thomas	6s. 8d.		

Here follows the full and perfect account of the rents charged and entered in this Survey of the Mannor of Bishop Midleham and the several Townships vzt. Bishop Midleham, Cornforth and Sedgefield as well of the money or rent paid into the Exchequor at Durham As to the Coroner of Stockton Ward, Bayliffe of the whole mannor and Collector of the foresaid several townships

Bishop Midleham whole year's rent amounting to £43. 9s. 1d.
Whereof paid to the Collector of the said township per annum £23. 19s. 0d.
Corneforth township: whole year's rent amounting to £30. 13s. 2d.
This whole year's rent is and for many years past has been gathered by the Collector of the said town

Sedgefield township: whole year's rent amounted to	£38. 8s. 0d.
Whereof paid to the Collector of the said township per annum	£36. 14s. 9d.

The residue of the rents with the foresaid townships not collected by the Collector of the said several townships are gathered by the Bayliff of the said Mannor of Bishop Midleham per annum — £21. 3s. 4d.

Sum total of the whole year's rent within the several townships in this Survey mentioned is per annum — £112. 10s. 3d.

The improvements in this whole Mannor are above the rent reserved valued at by us and the Jurors per annum — £493. 17s. 6d.

Defalcacons out of the foresaid rent (vzt) to the Bayliff of the said Mannor of Bishop Midleham and Coroner of Stockton Ward are per annum — £3. 6s. 8d.

So there remains de claro per annum — £109. 3s. 7d.

The Coroner is charged with	£22. 12s. 7d.
which makes the whole per annum	£131. 16s. 2d.

Memorandum
That the fee of £2. 6s. 8d. is allowed to the Coroner of Stockton Ward, whose patent we returned in the Survey of Stockton for gathering the rent mentioned in the rental by him brought unto us, and returned in this Survey with rents as here affirmed (and we have as yet seen nothing to the contrary and free rents If otherwise we find them we shall make a particular return thereof)

Frederick Faber
George Dailes
George Lilburne
Edward Colston

INDEX OF PLACES

INDEX OF PERSONS